HITLER'S
WAR DIRECTIVES
1939 – 1945

Edited by

H. R. TREVOR-ROPER

PAN BOOKS LTD : LONDON

First published in UK 1964 by Sidgwick & Jackson Ltd.

This edition published 1966 by Pan Books Ltd.,
8 Headfort Place, London, S.W.1

The text of these directives was originally published
in Germany under the title of *Hitlers Weisungen für
die Kriegführung 1939–45, Dokumente des Oberkom-
mandos der Wehrmacht* edited by Walther Hubatsch
and published by Bernard and Graefe Verlag, of
Frankfurt on Main

Printed in Great Britain
by Cox & Wyman Ltd
London, Reading and Fakenham

CONTENTS

Part II. THE DEFENSIVE WAR

LIST OF MAPS

INTRODUCTION

THE Second World War was Hitler's personal war in many senses. He intended it, he prepared for it, he chose the moment for launching it; and for three years, in the main, he planned its course. On several occasions, between 1939 and 1942, he claimed to have won it. It was – or would have been – a personal victory; for although the aims which he sought to realize were old nationalist aspirations, the policy and the strategy for their realization had been imposed by him. Consequently, when he failed, the failure too was his: so obviously his that the old national aspirations which he represented have too often been quietly forgotten.

Of course there are reservations to be made. The war, even in its earliest, most successful phases, did not exactly correspond with Hitler's preconceived plans. It could not, for his plans, though fixed in their ultimate purpose, were always elastic in detail. Always, up to the last moment, Hitler nursed alternative projects, and his final choice of method would depend on circumstances. And as these circumstances varied, so his plans varied too. They varied particularly in relation to Germany's immediate neighbours, the lesser powers of Eastern Europe who might be either his satellites or his victims.

For instance, in certain circumstances, Hitler might have made war on Russia in alliance with Poland. There were forces in Poland, the Poland of Pilsudski and 'the Colonels', which might willingly join in the anti-Bolshevik crusade, just as Rumania, the Rumania of Marshal Antonescu, would afterwards do. On the other hand, he might as easily have made war on Rumania as he did on Poland: there was also the Rumania of Titulescu. Again, in 1941, Hitler did not at first intend to conquer Yugoslavia: he assumed that Yugoslavia would co-operate in the *Blitzkrieg* against Greece; he only had to change his plans when Yugoslavia changed and he found himself faced not by the compliant Regent, Prince Paul, but by the Serbian nationalists led by General Simović. All these were changes of circumstances to which he responded. And the greatest of all such circumstantial changes was dictated by the uncertain policy of Britain. It is not true, as has often been said, that Hitler was convinced by his asinine Foreign Minister, Joachim von Ribbentrop, that Britain would not make war against him. Hitler hoped that Britain would not make war, but he made all his preparations on the assumption that it would; and he knew, and said, that Britain would be a formidable enemy. In 1939, if Britain had kept out, in 1940, if Britain had made peace or been defeated, Hitler would have made one kind of war; in fact, because neither of these things happened, he made another. He took account of circumstances and was ready for change.

This must be said because it has been argued that Hitler did not pursue a consistent policy: he merely followed events. Of course he followed events. No man, whatever his power or his genius, can control all events. Every politician makes use of them. But if Hitler's policy was elastic, if he always, up to the last moment of decision, had two strings (or even three) to his bow, these were always alternative means to the same end; and that end was constant. Hitler was determined, one way or another, *so oder so* (in his own favourite phrase), first to break the Versailles Treaty which gave to the frontiers of Eastern Europe the guarantees of the Western Powers, the victors of 1918, and, secondly, having thus secured his own rear, to hurl his armies, the German armies which had to be re-created after the débâcle of 1918, against Russia. He thus hoped to restore, in the East, not the frontiers of 1914 – that 'traditional', 'monarchist' programme was to him, as he said, a contemptible ambition – but, at the very least, the frontiers of 1917, the frontiers achieved by the victorious armies of the Second Reich and secured, alas too briefly, by the Treaty of Brest-Litovsk. It was because the German armies, in 1917, had conquered Russia that Hitler was so sure they could conquer it again; and it was because those conquests had been lost not in the East but in the West, by the victory of the Western Allies in 1918, that he was resolved, this time, to separate the East from its Western guarantors, if necessary by a preliminary war against those guarantors, and so avoid the fatal consequences of a war on two fronts, a *Zweifrontenkrieg*.

So oder so, one way or another – the phrase had many applications. One of them was, by peace or by war. As a disciple of Clausewitz, Hitler regarded war as the continuation of policy by other means. If he could have achieved his aims by peace, or by mere threat of war, doubtless he would have tried to do so. Whatever his taste for war, whatever his convictions, or illusions, about his own strategical genius, he did not necessarily prefer the method of war. He counted himself a political genius first, and his earliest triumphs, which were bloodless, might well confirm him in that estimate. Moreover, the first stage in his programme, the neutralization of the West, might well be achieved by purely political means. Hitler did not expect war over the re-occupation of the Rhineland, Germany's re-entry into its own 'back-garden' in 1936. He did not expect war over the annexation of Austria, the *Anschluss*, in 1938. He did not even – though he felt the temperature rising – expect war over the annexation of the Sudetenland and the neutralization of Czechoslovakia in 1938–9; 'Britain and France,' he declared in 1937, 'have most probably already written off Czechoslovakia.' If all went well he might hope, though he could not reckon, to complete the first stage of the operation in peace; by mere threats, blackmail, diplomatic pressure to detach Britain and France altogether from the *cordon sanitaire* of small states which they had set up between defeated Germany and defeated Russia after 1918. In that case there would have been no need for a war against Poland or against the West. Abandoned by the West, Poland and Rumania would have had to choose between Germany and Russia in the second stage of Hitler's programme, now about to be opened; and they would probably have chosen Germany.

But if the first stage of the programme could, theoretically, be completed without war, what about the second stage? It may be possible to persuade a man to stand by while a third party is murdered, but the indifference of the victim himself is less easily purchased. In order to realize his ultimate aim, the restoration and extension of the lost German empire in the East, Hitler had always recognized that diplomacy could not be enough. Ultimately there must be war: war against Russia. And this war would not be a traditional, old-fashioned war, a war to end in a treaty and in the adjustment of legalities to confirm a new balance of international power. It would be – necessarily – a war of ideologies, of conquest, even of extermination.

Such a war would be a very serious matter. It could not, Hitler believed, be left to his successors to carry out. Hitler distrusted his successors, as he distrusted his predecessors, who had been too soft. Only he, he believed, 'the hardest man in centuries', had the qualities for such a 'Cyclopean task': the vision, the will-power, the combination of military and political, political and 'world-historical' insight. Therefore the whole programme of conquest, from beginning to end, must be carried through by him, personally. Nor could it be left to his subordinates, his generals. He distrusted his generals too. Like all professional soldiers, they disliked the prospect of great wars. Military parades, quick victories in limited campaigns – these were part of their business; but a major war of revenge against the West, or a major war of conquest against the East, was a prospect that alarmed them. It alarmed them as soldiers; it also alarmed them as conservatives. The former would be, like the war of 1914–18, another European civil war in which the basis of their class might crumble. The latter, even if successful, would entail, for its conduct and realization, an internal revolution in the German Army; if unsuccessful, it would lead to the Bolshevization of Europe. To envisage such a war with confidence one had to be, not a conservative Prussian staff-general, but a revolutionary nationalist, able to command obedient, if reluctant, generals: in fact, a Hitler.

Hitler knew exactly when he wanted his war. Time, he believed, was on the side of the Russians, with their vast continent and its resources which they were now mobilizing. Therefore, if he was to strike, he must strike now. He must reverse the course of history before it had become irreversible. On the other hand, he must not strike too soon: he must give himself time to get ready. There were military preparations, economic preparations, diplomatic preparations. From the beginning he had in his mind a clear time-table – clear, that is, in its general lines, variable in details according to circumstances. He must launch his war on Russia, he believed, in '1943 at latest'. That meant that he must have detached Eastern Europe from the West, have neutralized or defeated the West, by 1943, if not earlier; and since that process in itself might entail war, it meant that he must have created the military instrument for waging major war earlier still. In fact, in 1937, Hitler envisaged the possibility of making war on the West as early as 1938; and in his last months, looking back on his ultimate failure, he would regret that he had not launched it then.

Such a programme left no time to spare, and from the moment of securing power in Germany Hitler was preparing his instruments. Rearmament began almost at once. The effective replacement of Schacht and the inauguration of the Four Year Plan, which prepared the German economy for a war, took place in 1936. At the same time Hitler established his control over the Armed Forces. By the end of 1937 he was able to initiate his generals into his programme. By 1938 the diplomatic preparation had begun. After Munich, in September 1938, it looked as if Hitler had achieved the first part of his programme without war. All he had to do now was to build up his position in the East and prepare for the great Titanomachia with that Asiatic genius, whom he both hated and admired, 'half giant, half beast', Stalin.

In fact, of course, it did not work out thus. In fact the West, though diplomatically defeated, refused, at the last minute, to disengage itself from the East. The British guarantee to Poland and Rumania showed Hitler that, in order to have a free hand in the East, he must first break the West. Perhaps, if he threatened enough, or if he destroyed its eastern client, Poland, in a quick campaign, the West would surrender

without war. If so, so much the better. But if not, he must be
prepared to fight and defeat the West, in order finally to clear
the way for the eastern crusade.

In the summer and autumn of 1939 Hitler tried every kind
of threat. His policy might vary, but its aim was constant:
Poland, whether by political surrender or by military conquest, must be transformed from a Western into a German
satellite. At the last minute, by the Russo-German pact, Hitler
supposed that he had achieved his aim. He had shut out the
West. How could the West now implement its guarantees?
Surely it would now back out of an impossible position. But
when the West did not back out, Hitler went ahead. He made
war on Poland. Still he hoped that the West would back out.
If it had not yielded to threats, might it not yield to facts? In
the hope that it would yield Hitler would give it a chance. He
would do nothing against the West till Poland had been
destroyed. Then the West would surely see the futility of perseverance. If not, a direct attack would have to be launched
and the West taught a sharper lesson, at its own expense. The
essential thing was that, by politics or war, the victors of 1918
be driven out of eastern Europe, and the way made clear for
Hitler's main task, 'the be-all and end-all of Nazism', as he
would call it: the war against Russia in '1943 at latest'.

Such was Hitler's programme, as he planned it, and as he
carried it out, in the years leading up to the war of 1939. He
did not, like the men of 1914, 'blunder into war': he went into
it with his eyes wide open. And since his eyes were open, and
others half-shut, or smarting from the dust which he himself
had thrown in them, he was determined that he alone should
control his war. He alone understood his whole policy; he alone
could vary its details to meet circumstances and yet keep its
ultimate aims and essential course constant; and war, which
was but policy continued by other means, was far too serious
a business to be left to generals, or indeed to anyone else.
Others might see – it is plain that they did see – the war of
October 1939 as a local war for the recovery of Danzig and
the Polish Corridor, for the restoration of the 'contemptible'

frontiers of Bismarckian Germany. Others might be deceived by the Russo-German Pact, which also had Bismarckian echoes. They might think it permanent. How fatal it would be to let such men prescribe strategy! To Hitler, though he publicly professed these limited aims, the war (as he privately admitted) was 'not for Danzig at all', and the Russo-German Pact was a temporary expedient, fundamentally hateful to him. It was thus as essential for him to control strategy as it had been to control policy: to fit the various campaigns into their place in the programme which he consistently pursued, but did not always choose to reveal.

Fortunately, for this purpose, he had the machinery. In the years between 1934 and 1938, between the death of Hindenburg and the first threat of world war, Hitler had fastened his grip on the German Armed Forces and had effectively converted the General Staff of the Army from an independent political force, capable of making and unmaking governments, into a docile instrument of his will. The means whereby he had achieved this change – the exploitation of the President's senility, of personal rivalries, and of private scandal – are well known and need not be recapitulated. English-speaking readers can follow them in detail in Sir John Wheeler-Bennett's fascinating book *The Nemesis of Power*. What is immediately important for our purpose is the result. By establishing himself, with the consent of the Army leaders, as Hindenburg's successor, by assuming to himself the position of War Minister and Supreme Commander of the Armed Forces, by imposing on all soldiers of the Reich a new oath of personal loyalty to himself, and by setting up, instead of the old ministry of Defence, the new machinery of the *Oberkommando der Wehrmacht* (*OKW*) or High Command of the Armed Forces, staffed by carefully chosen supporters, Hitler created a new chain of command and made it possible for his own orders, whether military or political, to be transmitted through the whole war-machine of the Reich without the possibility of legal opposition; and it was through this machinery that he applied and controlled his strategy throughout the war. For this reason a short description of the machinery is necessary.

The *OKW* was set up on 4 February 1938 to replace the old War Ministry (*Reichskriegsministerium*). By June 1938 it consisted of four departments: the *Wehrmachtführungsamt* for operational orders; the *Amt Ausland/Abwehr* for foreign intelligence; the *Wirtschaftsund Rüstungsamt* for supply; and the *Amtsgruppe Allgemeine Wehrmachtangelegenheiten* for general purposes.* Of these by far the most important, for our purpose, is the *Wehrmachtführungsamt* (*WFA*). It replaced the *Wehrmachtamt*, which in turn had replaced the old *Ministeramt* of the Ministry of Defence. The head of the *Wehrmachtamt*, from its foundation in 1935 until its dissolution in 1938, had been Wilhelm Keitel, an officer who had shown considerable ability in the field of military administration and supply but who was completely without force of character. In 1938, when the new organization was set up, Hitler saw in Keitel the ideal instrument, and he promoted him to be the head of it with the title *Chef OKW*, Chief of the High Command of the Armed Forces. As head of the *Wehrmachtführungsamt* Keitel appointed Max von Viebahn, who, however, proved unequal to the task and was relieved after two months. Thereafter, as long as the Reich was at peace, this post was left vacant. Its functions were performed by a man whose name is always associated with that of Keitel in the history of the war: Alfred Jodl. Jodl was an able and ambitious man, of sharp intellect and great military knowledge, especially in operational matters. His official position in 1938–9 was head of the *Abteilung Landesverteidigung*, or Home Defence Department, of the *Wehrmachtführungsamt* (*WFA/L*). This was its most important department, in which all the details of operational planning were worked out, and from which operational orders were sent to the High Commands of the Army, Navy, and Air Force for the

---

* I have given the names by which the departments were known by the beginning of the war. In the early stages of the *OKW*, nomenclature was variable. The *Amt Ausland/Abwehr* had begun as *Amtsgruppe Auslandsnachrichten und Abwehr*, the *Wirtschafts- und Rustungsamt* as the *Wehrwirtschaftsstab;* etc.

conduct of the war. On the approach of war, Jodl became official head of the *Wehrmachtführungsamt* and his place as head of the *Abt. Landesverteidigung* was taken by his deputy, Walter Warlimont. In August 1940 the *Wehrmachführungs-amt* was changed into the *Wehrmachführungsstab* (*Wfst*), but its functions remained the same and Jodl remained as its head, with the title *Chef Wehrmachtführungsstab*. In December 1941 the *Abt. Landesverteidigung* lost its separate identity, being merged in the *Wehrmachtführungsstab* instead of subordinate to it; but equally here the essential continuity remained. Warlimont continued to fill his role as planning assistant to Jodl, though his title was now changed to *Stellvertretende Chef Wehrmachtführungsstab*, deputy head of the Armed Forces Operations Staff.

OKW, *Wehrmachtführungsstab*, *Abt. Landesverteidigung* – or, as they will always be rendered in this translation, 'High Command of the Armed Forces', 'Armed Forces Operations Staff', 'Defence Department' – these are the indispensable instruments through which Hitler, all through the war, formulated his strategy and imposed it on his generals, even on the once solid, independent German General Staff, the *OKH* or High Command of the Army. And the agents were even more consistent. Names of offices might change but the officers in command remained constant. While chiefs of the Army General Staff and commanding generals in the field came and went, Keitel and Jodl remained steadily at their posts until the day of final surrender; after which they appeared together before the International Military Tribunal at Nuremberg and, by its judgement, were hanged for their complicity in Hitler's crimes. Warlimont remained at his post till September 1944, when he was relieved on account of illness and replaced, in November, by General August Winter. He survives and has contributed to history his own account of Hitler's war machine and war strategy.*

---

* W. Warlimont, *Im Hauptquartier der deutschen Wehrmacht* (Frankfurt a/M, 1962). An English translation of this book, by General Richard Barry, was published in 1964.

Such was the machinery whereby Hitler directed his military operations. In order to exploit it, he needed to have it always at hand, and in fact the *OKW*, which began the war as a reconstituted War Office, became in the course of it more and more a dependent part of the court. That court, the 'Führer Headquarters', migrated from place to place. Sometimes – as during the Polish campaign – it was in the Führer's special train. Sometimes it was in Berlin. And when the great campaigns were in process, it would be in a special citadel, furiously requisitioned, built, or fortified, behind the active front: in the German Palatinate, in Northern France, in the Ukraine, in East Prussia. But wherever the Führer Headquarters went, the *OKW* went with it; and going with it, it became more and more detached from the Armed Forces to which it gave orders, or rather, to which it transmitted the orders given by Hitler on the basis of the reports daily supplied by the *Wehrmacht-führungsstab*.

Theoretically, the *Wehrmacht*, like other public departments, was represented at the Führer Headquarters by a liaison officer. Hitler's *Wehrmacht* adjutant was Colonel Rudolf Schmundt who, from 1942, was also head of the Army Personnel Office. In this capacity Schmundt exercised enormous power in placing and promoting those officers who, like himself, regarded Hitler as 'the greatest statesman and strategist of all time'. But in fact Keitel and Jodl were constantly in attendance themselves. Every day, at noon, Hitler held his *Lagevortrag* or 'situation conference' at which Jodl – for the first two years it was always Jodl – submitted a report which had been prepared for him by Warlimont. Hitler would listen, discuss the situation, and then, after it had been fully debated, issue his orders. These orders, together with a full account of the discussion, were then passed by Jodl to Warlimont to be converted into formal documents and issued to the appropriate authorities. In Warlimont's office, which grew constantly in size as Hitler intervened more and more in the details of strategy, the official war diary was kept. This diary was destroyed at the end of the war, on the orders of General

Winter, Warlimont's successor; but it has since been very largely reconstituted from fragments and copies by the labours of the two men who were responsible for writing it, the late Helmut Greiner and Dr Percy Schramm.*

Of course, other officers, and in particular the commanders-in-chief of the Armed Forces, had access to Hitler. They were periodically summoned to the Führer Headquarters. But their visits were not regular and they could not compete with the constant presence of the regular courtiers. Besides, Hitler preferred to deal with them through Keitel and Jodl. He disliked new faces. He liked Keitel and Jodl, who gradually sank into the position of mere orderlies, like the rest of the court. And Keitel and Jodl liked the monopoly of power which their industry and subservience ensured to them. Consequently both Keitel and Jodl, while they became increasingly indispensable to Hitler, became increasingly odious to the generals in the High Command of the Army and in the field. Keitel in particular was despised for his spinelessness. This carpet Field Marshal was to them the rubber stamp which converted Hitler's strategy into military orders. They referred to him as Lakaitel, 'lackey'.

Out of this system, and by this method, Hitler's strategic orders emerged. They were based on the work of the *OKW Wehrmachtführungsstab*, which in its turn drew on other authorities, and their technical form, when they had such form, was given to them by that staff. But they were signed, in general, by or for Hitler, the *Oberster Befehlshaber der Wehrmacht*, 'Supreme Commander of the Armed Forces', or Keitel, *Chef OKW*, 'Chief of the High Command of the Armed Forces'. Among these orders, which are numerous and various, a special, slender category was dignified by the name *Führerweisungen* or 'Führer Directives'.

What is the distinctive quality of the 'Führer Directives'? It would be difficult to answer this question merely from their content or character, for their character wavered radically and,

---

* Helmut Greiner, *die Oberste Wehrmachtführung 1939-1943* (Wiesbaden 1951); *Kriegstagebuch des OKW 1940-1945*, ed. P. E. Schramm (4 vols., Frankfurt am Main, 1961-   ).

we may think, arbitrarily in the course of war. But it seems clear that, in the beginning, Hitler intended them to be orders of a general, expository, long-term nature. A *Weisung*, a 'directive', says Dr Hubatsch, quoting Grimm's *Deutsches Wörterbuch*, is distinguished from a *Befehl*, an order, by the fact that whereas both give binding instructions, a *Weisung* leaves the method of execution to the decision of subordinate authorities; and General Warlimont adds that, whereas an 'order' is summary, imperative and immediate, a 'directive' is, to a larger extent, explanatory and prophetic: it looks forward and its instructions are reasoned general instructions which remain valid for a considerable time. This distinction, though loose, is real; and it is a distinction that was particularly congenial to the character of Hitler.

For Hitler, with his strong sense of his own historic mission, and his conviction that he alone knew how to guide and use historic forces, liked to lay down general programmes, to expound future events, and to dictate 'political testaments'. Such utterances, he felt, even if his successors did not follow them, would at least ensure that history would judge him aright. Already before 1939 documents of this kind were described by him as *Weisungen*, 'directives'; for the word, or at least the usage, came in with the régime: it was part of the new Nazi vocabulary. For instance, in the autumn of 1933 there was a 'Directive for the Armed Forces in the event of Sanctions'. There were 'Directives for the unified preparation of a possible war' on 26th June 1936, and a 'Directive for the unified preparation of the Armed Forces for War' on 24th June 1937. On 11th March 1938, on the eve of the *Anschluss* with Austria, a numbered series of directives was begun. There was 'Directive No. 1' for the occupation of Austria, and, on the same day, 'Directive No. 2' for the bloodless invasion of Austria. If the *Anschluss* had led to war, no doubt the series would have been continued; but it did not, so that series stopped. Only a week afterwards, a new 'Directive No. 1' was issued for the occupation of Memel should the Poles invade Lithuania. Two months later, when Hitler turned his attention to Czechoslovakia, another unnumbered 'directive' outlined 'Case Green' (*Fall Grün*) for the occupation of Czechoslovakia. This was dated 30th May 1938. It is possible that other directives followed in this series: two unnumbered drafts have been found, and a 'Directive No. 4' of 18th October seems to wind up 'Case Green'. Meanwhile the Munich agreement, which closed one line of strategy, opened another. On 30th September 1938, the very day of the agreement, yet another numbered series began – only, once again, to die out. Thus by the end of 1938 three numbered series had begun, only to fade away as the crisis which engendered them was settled and bloodless victory had been won.

In 1939 the pattern was repeated. On 11th April, when Hitler turned his attention away from Czechoslovakia, now digested, he issued a new 'Directive for the Armed Forces' envisaging the invasion of Poland. It was not numbered. But in the autumn, when he resolved to launch his attack on Poland, he felt that the historic moment had come and he began a new numbered series. This time the crisis was not resolved and the series was not cut short. It ran for four years and reached No. 51. It is the series that is printed in this book.

If the false starts in 1938 shed one beam of light on the character of Hitler's numbered War Directives from 1939 to 1943, the cessation of the numbered series in 1943 sheds another. For Hitler's numbered Directives, which only began when he was about to launch an aggressive war, only continued as long as that war was effectively controlled by him. In the first two years, the war, in spite of disappointments in detail, had gone well in general. It is true, the West had not given Hitler a free hand against Poland; but Poland had nevertheless been conquered. It is true, the West had not recognized the conquest of Poland as final, and so had forced a major campaign in the West; but that campaign had been completely victorious. It is true, Britain had not surrendered; but British power to prevent the realization of Hitler's eastern policy had been destroyed. Up to the winter of 1941, therefore, Hitler could feel that he had controlled the course of his war and could be proud of his grand strategy. Even after the first Russian winter his confidence remained high: the early part of 1942 was a period of continued advance in the East, of victory in Africa, of security in the West. Only with the winter of 1942–3 did the tide clearly begin to turn. Only in 1943 did Hitler clearly lose the initiative. And it was at that time that he decided no longer to issue numbered directives. By that decision he emphasized the prophetic quality of the directives. They had begun as manifestos of political and strategic purpose, successive revelations of the future which he was determining. When that future was uncertain, as in 1938, he had paused; and then begun a new series. When it became suddenly black, and could no longer be determined by him, the series lost its purpose and he stopped.

Of course there was always another side to the directives. With his passion for detail, his insistence on his own military expertise, Hitler was incapable of reserving his interventions for great occasions or general utterances. If the earliest directives are genuine 'directives' – long-term general expositions, half political, half strategical, addressed to the Chiefs of Staff of the three services – this limitation was soon forgotten. Before long Hitler was involving himself in tactical *minutiae*, interfering in administrative detail, arguing with his subordinate commanders. This undercurrent of military pedantry is never far from the surface in his directives and confirms the remark of General Halder, the *Chef OKH* or Chief of the Army General Staff (whom Hitler ultimately dismissed), that the Führer's military interest was confined to grand strategy and petty detail, while all the major decisions in war lie in the area between. Reading these directives, we can well understand the irritation of the professional soldiers when they received 'Führer directives' reminding them of elementary principles of war or adjusting the movement of battalions.

As Hitler lost the initiative and could no longer confidently and imaginatively expound the future course of his war, this petty interference became more pronounced, and finally, after November 1943, with the cessation of numbered directives, it is all that is left. For the last eighteen months of the war he continued to issue commands through the same channels as the old directives, and the most important of them are printed here; but the old assurance has now gone. We see the Führer turning desperately from one theatre to another, uncertain where his overstretched front will break, where the Russians, whom he had so often defeated, will counter-attack, where the Western allies, whom he had so triumphantly driven out of Europe, will return, where the 'bandits' – i.e. the resistance-forces of occupied Europe – will strike. The only unity of these later orders is the unity imposed by general fear. At the end, as all the advancing enemy forces converge on the Reich, this unity once again begins to dominate the detail. The war once again becomes one war, a war not now for universal empire, directed by historical necessity and prophetic human genius, but for survival against all odds, inspired by unthinking fanaticism, hysterical fear, and the hope of unpredictable flukes. And yet even at the end the call for heroic resistance is interrupted by the old nagging interference in detail. 'I must point out,' Hitler would inform his commanders-in-chief on all fronts during the Allied advance in Western Europe, 'that the maintenance of signals communications, particularly in heavy fighting and critical situations, is a prerequisite for the conduct of the battle'; and he insisted that his harassed generals report to him all their orders, 'so that I have time to intervene in this decision if I think fit, and that my counter-orders can reach the front-line troops in time.'

Thus Hitler's directives, supplemented by these later orders, provide an outline documentary history of Hitler's war: the war as he conceived it and as he controlled it; for even at the end, even when the initiative had passed to the Allies, it was still Hitler, through the *OKW*, who controlled the strategy of disaster. Historians of the war can add a mass of detail to this outline. They have the captured records, the reconstructed war-diary, the recollections of the survivors. But they can never dispense with these central documents which show, in crude but emphatic form, the war which Hitler envisaged, which he launched, and which he directed, in all its stages, past the intoxicating vision of universal victory to universal defeat.

The original texts of Hitler's directives are at present scattered among various archives. Many of them have been used in historical works and the texts of some of them have appeared in print; but the only systematic collections are an English version included in the official American work *Führer Directives and Other Top-level Directives of the German Army 1939–45* (2 vols, 1948), and the German compilation *Hitlers Weisungen für die Kriegführung 1939–45* (Frankfurt am Main, 1962) edited by Dr Walther Hubatsch. The former of these two works is a cyclostyled document produced in 1948 by the US Department of the Navy for official use only. It contains documents only, without any commentary. The latter is a scholarly work, by a distinguished historian who has traced the original text of each document and printed them all, in full, with some other matter, but again without commentary. For this English version I have used Dr Hubatsch's text, but in the interest of English readers I have taken certain liberties both of omission and of addition, which require explanation.

Dr Hubatsch has printed every document in full, with complete letterhead, including file-references, and with the distribution list at the end. I have decided that this somewhat deterrent apparatus is unnecessary for English readers. Apart from giving the complete letterhead of Directive No. 1, as a sample, I have thought it enough to place, at the head of each document, the address and date of dispatch, the authority by which it was sent, and, as some evidence of distribution, the number of copies made. I thought at one time of including the distribution list at the end of each document; but in the end I decided against this policy, since it would mean covering a great deal of paper with repetitious abbreviations of obscure departments or specialist officers. It seems to me enough to say, here and in general, that all directives were sent to the High Commands of the three branches of the Armed Forces and, of course, to the *OKW Wehrmachtführungsstab* (and its department *Abt. Landesvertidigung*, for so long as that had a separate existence) in which they had generally been produced; that others were occasionally sent to other departments of the *OKW* (e.g. Foreign Intelligence and Signals) or to German representatives at Italian or other allied headquarters; that the more specialized directives – e.g. concerning Greece or Lapland – were sent to the theatre high command; and that the distribution-lists tend to increase with time and the proliferation of departments of the *OKW*. In making these and other decisions to omit the technical apparatus of the directives, I have been influenced by the knowledge that those who need such details will be scholars who can easily turn to Dr Hubatsch's German edition.

Dr Hubatsch has also printed, together with the directives, a number of related documents. Some of these are corrections, some are additions to the 'Führer Directives'. Many of them are amplifications in detail – sometimes minute detail – of more general orders given in the directives. In deciding to omit a number of these secondary documents, I have been guided by one general principle. This collection is essentially a collection of Hitler's directives. It is not a history of German strategy. Therefore I have sought to make each directive as self-contained and as intelligible as possible, and I have excluded such documents as were not issued by Hitler himself and whose function is merely to add detail, not significance, to his directives. Thus, when Hitler issued a 'supplement' to any of his directives, I have printed that supplement; but if the *OKW* merely issued a more elaborate document applying in detail some part of Hitler's general instructions, I have not thought it necessary to print such a document. Similarly, when a directive has been followed by a correction, I have not imitated the documentary purism of Dr Hubatsch, who prints first the original text, even if erroneous, and then the correction, with its inevitable apparatus of references. I have corrected the text myself: silently, if it is a mere textual error that has been corrected; with a footnote reference, if it is a correction of substance.

I must also admit that I have taken certain other liberties. As Hitler numbered his own directives, I have thought it right to preserve his numbers; and as he began the series with the directive of 31 August 1939, which he headed 'Directive No. 1', I have begun there too. I have not followed Dr Hubatsch who, in order to include Annex II of the unnumbered directive of 3 April 1939 concerning Poland, has given it the number 'ıa' and numbered Hitler's 'Directive No. 1' as 'ıb'. Again, when dealing with the unnumbered orders issued after 3 November 1943, I have sought, in general, to keep in line with Dr Hubatsch; but I have not felt able to include his No. 67, which is not a document at all but a series of references to unprinted documents concerning defence-measures in the West in the last three months of 1944. Consequently my No. 67 is a translation of his No. 68, and we remain out of step to the end. This explains why his collection shows 75 'Directives' and mine only 74.

I have felt freer to take these liberties, and to make these omissions, for two reasons. First, the principle of selection adopted by Dr Hubatsch in respect of the unnumbered directives is not always clear. Until November 1943 any editor has the life-line of the numbered directives; but after that date – until such time as a complete collection of Hitler's different orders is available – he is obliged to choose among miscellaneous *Weisungen*, *Führerbefehle*, *Operationsbefehle*, and other documents. Dr Hubatsch has made his choice and I certainly would not criticize it; but as he has not stated any limiting principle, I have not felt obliged always to abide by it. Secondly, there is the structural difference between his German and my English text. Unlike Dr Hubatsch, I have allowed myself the luxury of a commentary. The brief introductory passages which I have inserted before most of the directives are designed to make each document readily intelligible by the reader by placing it in its context. But they have also given me certain liberty of action. In them I have been able to make use of those 'secondary' documents which have been printed or referred to by Dr Hubatsch, but which I have omitted; in them I have also made use of the documents printed in the two-volume collection of the US Department of the Navy, and of other documents known to me, which Dr Hubatsch has omitted. But my main purpose has been, in the briefest space and with the minimum of comment, to enable the 'Führer Directives' to speak for themselves, and to speak intelligibly, to English readers.

It remains for me to thank two friends whose help has been essential to me: Mr Brian Melland of the Cabinet Historical Office, who has given me valuable advice whenever I have needed it, and Mr Anthony Rhodes, for his part in the translation of these documents.

H. R. TREVOR-ROPER

9TH
APRIL
1940

OSLO
INVADED
9TH APRIL
1940

BERLIN

LONDON

DUNKIRK
EVACUATED
JUNE 4
1940

PARIS

VIENNA

PARIS
OCCUPIED
JUNE 14
1940

MARSEILLES

R.PO

ROME

GIBRALTAR

ALGIERS

MALTA

GREECE
SURRENDERS
APRIL 24
1941

0   300
MILES

HITLER'S OFFENSIVE

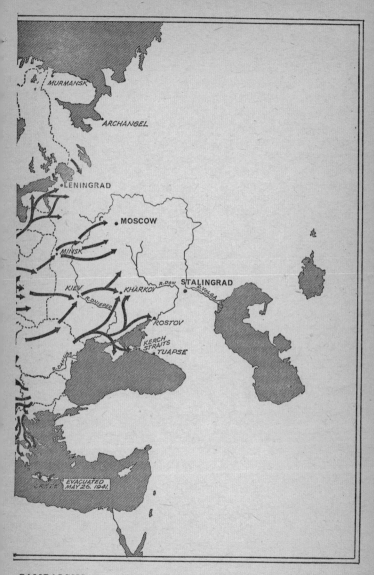

CAMPAIGNS

T—B

Part I

The Offensive War

1

On 3rd April 1939 Hitler, through Field Marshal Keitel, Chief of the High Command of the Armed Forces, issued a directive concerning war preparations. Annexed to it was a document containing details of '*Fall Weiss* (Case White)', the projected attack on Poland. In this document Hitler explained that, whereas he wished to maintain peaceful relations with Poland, Poland's attitude to Germany might change for the worse and 'then, in spite of the existing treaty' – the German-Polish treaty of non-aggression – 'it might be necessary to settle the account for good'. In such circumstances it was Hitler's resolve 'to smash the Polish armed forces and to create in the East a situation corresponding with the needs of Germany's defence'. The free city of Danzig would be proclaimed part of Germany 'at the start of the conflict, at the latest'. In preparation for such a conflict, the German government was seeking to isolate Poland diplomatically. Instructions were given to the three branches of the Armed Forces to ensure that, when orders were given, the attack would come as a surprise and the Polish armed forces could be 'annihilated'.

Throughout the following months – months of intense diplomatic activity and a 'war of nerves' against Poland – supplementary instructions were issued by the High Command of the Armed Forces. Finally, on 31st August, preparations were complete and Hitler issued his first 'war directive'.

The Supreme Commander of the Armed Forces.   Berlin, OKW/WFA Nr. 170/39 g. K. Chefs. L1. 31st August 1939.

Most Secret
Senior Commanders only   8 copies
By hand of Officer only*
                                                              Copy No. 2

* Footnote on page 38

Directive No. 1 for the Conduct of the War

1. Since the situation on Germany's Eastern frontier has become intolerable and all political possibilities of peaceful settlement have been exhausted, I have decided upon a *solution by force*.

2. *The attack on Poland* will be undertaken in accordance with the preparations made for 'Case White', with such variations as may be necessitated by the build-up of the Army which is now virtually complete.

The allocation of tanks and the purpose of the operation remain unchanged.

Date of attack 1st September 1939.

This time also applies to operations at Gdynia, in the Bay of Danzig, and at the Dirschau bridge.

3. In the *West* it is important to leave the responsibility for opening hostilities unmistakably to England and France. Minor violations of the frontier will be dealt with, for the time being, purely as local incidents.

The assurances of neutrality given by us to Holland, Belgium, Luxembourg, and Switzerland are to be meticulously observed.

The Western frontier of Germany will not be crossed *by land* at any point without my explicit orders.

This applies also to all acts of warfare *at sea* or to acts which might be regarded as such.

The defensive activity of the *Air Force* will be *restricted* for the time being to the firm repulse of enemy air attacks on the frontiers of the Reich. In taking action against individual aircraft or small formations, care will be taken to respect the frontiers of neutral countries as far as possible. Only if considerable forces of French or British bombers are employed

---

* This is the standard form of heading. In subsequent directives it will not be printed in full: only the authority, the place and date of issue, and the number of copies issued will be printed.

against German territory across neutral areas will the Air Force be permitted to go into defensive action over neutral soil.

It is particularly important that any infringement of the neutrality of other states by our Western enemies be immediately reported to the High Command of the Armed Forces.

4. *Should England and France open hostilities* against Germany, it will be the duty of the Armed Forces operating in the West, while conserving their strength as much as possible, to maintain conditions for the successful conclusion of operations against Poland. Within these limits enemy forces and war potential will be damaged as much as possible. The right to order *offensive* operations is reserved absolutely to me.

The *Army* will occupy the West Wall and will take steps to secure it from being outflanked in the north, through the violation by the Western powers of Belgian or Dutch territory. Should French forces invade Luxembourg the bridges on the frontier may be blown up.

The *Navy* will operate against merchant shipping, with England as the focal point. In order to increase the effect, the declaration of danger zones may be expected. The Naval High Command will report on the areas which it is desirable to classify as danger zones and on their extent. The text of a public declaration in this matter is to be drawn up in collaboration with the Foreign Office and to be submitted to me for approval through the High Command of the Armed Forces.

The Baltic Sea is to be secured against enemy intrusion. Commander-in-Chief Navy* will decide whether the entrances to the Baltic should be mined for this purpose.

The *Air Force* is, first of all, to prevent action by the French and English Air Forces against the German Army and German territory.

In operations against England the task of the Air Force is

---

* Grand Admiral Raeder.

to take measures to dislocate English imports, the armaments industry, and the transport of troops to France. Any favourable opportunity of an effective attack on concentrated units of the English Navy, particularly on battleships or aircraft carriers, will be exploited. The decision regarding attacks on London is reserved to me.

Attacks on the English homeland are to be prepared, bearing in mind that inconclusive results with insufficient forces are to be avoided in all circumstances.

signed: ADOLF HITLER

2

Poland was duly attacked at dawn on 1st September. The British government delivered an ultimatum to Germany that evening, and, after a day of intense diplomatic activity, a second ultimatum was followed by a declaration of war by Britain and France on 3rd September.

The Supreme Commander   Berlin,
of the Armed Forces   3rd September 1939.
                                                8 Copies

Directive No. 2 for the Conduct of the War

1. After the declaration of war by the *English Government*, the English Admiralty issued orders at 1117 hours on 3rd September 1939 to open hostilities.

France has announced that she will be in a state of war with Germany from 1700 hours on 3rd September 1939.

2. The immediate *aim of the German High Command* remains the rapid and victorious conclusion of operations against Poland.

The transfer of any considerable forces from the Eastern front to the West will not be made without my approval.

3. The basic principles for the conduct of the war *in the West* laid down in Directive No. 1 remain unchanged.

The declaration of war by England and France has the following consequences:

(a) *In respect of England.*
   Navy.
   Offensive action may now begin. In carrying out the war against merchant shipping, submarines also, for the time being, will observe prize regulations. Intensified measures leading to the declaration of danger zones will be prepared. I shall decide when these measures shall become effective.

   The entrances to the Baltic will be mined without infringing neutral territorial waters.

   In the North Sea the blockade measures envisaged for defensive purposes and for the attacks on England will be carried out.

   Air Force.
   Attacks upon English naval forces at naval bases or on the high seas (including the English Channel), and on definitely identified troop transports, will only be made in the event of English air attacks on similar targets and where there are particularly good prospects of success. This applies also to action by the Fleet Air Arm.*

   I reserve to myself the decision about attacks on the English homeland and on merchant shipping.

(b) *In respect of France.*
   Army.
   The opening hostilities in the West will be left to the enemy. Commander-in-Chief Army† will decide on the

---

   * An Appendix to this directive, issued on 6th September, adds, after the words 'Fleet Air Arm', the words: 'These limitations do not apply to operations in the *German Bight* [i.e. the area of the North Sea between Holland and Denmark], 'in the Western mined areas, or during actions directly supporting naval operations.'

   † Colonel General von Brauchitsch.

reinforcement of our forces in the West from such reserves as are still available.

Navy.

Offensive action against France will only be permitted if the enemy has first opened hostilities. In that case the same instructions apply to France as have been laid down for England.

Air Force.

Offensive action against France will only be undertaken after French attacks on German territory. The guiding principle must be not to provoke the initiation of aerial warfare by any action on the part of Germany.

In general the employment of the Air Force in the West will be governed by the need to preserve its fighting strength after the defeat of Poland for decisive action against the Western Powers.

4. '*Order X*' *issued on 25th August* 1939 *with OKW No. 2100/39 g. K.WFA/L. 11** is extended to all the Armed Forces with effect from 3rd September 1939.

The conversion of the entire German economy to a war basis is hereby decreed.

Further measures for mobilization in civil life will be introduced by the High Command of the Armed Forces on the request of the highest government authorities.

signed: ADOLF HITLER

3

The declaration of war by Britain and France was not followed by any immediate action in the West, and Hitler continued to concentrate on the quick destruction of Poland.

---

* This 'Order X' of 25th August had ordered partial mobilization, but without a declaration of war.

The Supreme Commander
of the Armed Forces

Berlin,
9th September 1939.
8 Copies

Directive No. 3 for the Conduct of the War

1. Operations against the Polish Army and Air Force will continue with the necessary forces until it is safe to assume that the Poles are no longer capable of establishing a continuous front which can tie down German forces.

2. Should it be clear that some part of the Eastern Army and of the Air Force are no longer necessary for the completion of this task and for the pacification of occupied territories, arrangements are to be made to transfer these forces to the West.

As the Polish Air Force becomes progressively weaker, further air defence units may be made available for use against our Western enemies.

3. Even after the half-hearted opening of hostilities by England, at sea and in the air, and by France, on the land and in the air, my personal approval must be obtained –

   (*a*) For any crossing of the German land frontier in the West.

   (*b*) For all flights beyond the Western frontier of Germany, unless they are necessary to meet heavy enemy air attacks.

   (*c*) For air attacks against England.
   The Air Force is, however, free to operate in the German Bight and in the Western mined areas, and in immediate support of naval action at sea.

   (*d*) For the Navy the instructions given in Directive No. 2 paragraphs 3*a* and *b* remain in force. No offensive action at sea is to be undertaken against France.

signed: ADOLF HITLER

4

By 17th September 1939 the Polish army had been completely broken. The Germans had reached the Vistula and encircled Warsaw. On the same day the Russian armies crossed the eastern frontier of Poland and began their advance up to the Demarcation Line which had been agreed in the secret Nazi-Soviet Pact of 23rd August. Next day they were in Vilna and Brest-Litovsk. By 23rd September only the towns of Warsaw and Modlin continued to resist the German advance.

The Supreme Commander   Führer Headquarters,
of the Armed Forces   25th September 1939.
                                         7 copies

Directive No. 4 for the Conduct of the War

1. The *final form of Government* of the former Polish territory in the area between the Demarcation Line and the German frontier has not yet been decided.

After the conclusion of hostilities around Warsaw and Modlin the Demarcation Line is to be adequately secured by formations of lower fighting power.

The forces of the Army and Air Force which are required for the *quick destruction of the continuing Polish resistance* behind the Demarcation Line (area San–Vistula–Narew–Pisia) will be retained in the East. I request a report on the strength of the forces which it is proposed to employ for both these purposes.

2. I shall myself decide whether *Modlin* and the part of *Warsaw* west of the Vistula are to be reduced by a general attack before 3rd October. This will depend upon the success of local attacks and the process of wearing down the enemy. Preparations will, however, be made for such an attack.

3. *The flow of refugees* westwards across the Demarcation Line will be halted at once, with the exception of refugees of German racial origin, and Ukrainian activists.

4. Decisions for the *further strategy of the war* will be made in the immediate future.

In the meanwhile no measures shall be taken by the Armed Forces, either in the matter of organization or of equipment, such as may limit freedom of decision. The possibility of going over to the offensive in the West at any moment must be kept open. Sufficient forces must be retained in East Prussia to occupy Lithuania with all speed, even if there should be armed resistance.

5. (*a*) *On land* the Directives given for the conduct of the war in the West remain in force for the present.

   (*b*) *At sea*, trade war according to International Prize Law is to be waged against both France and England, free from previous restrictions.

In addition, the following are now permitted: Attacks on French naval and air forces, French merchantmen in convoy, and all troopships; mining operations off the north French coast (embarkation points).

War on merchant shipping according to Prize Law by naval aircraft.

Attacks on 'passenger steamers', or large vessels which obviously carry passengers in considerable numbers in addition to cargo, will still be forbidden.

   (*c*) *For air warfare* in the West the existing limitations remain in force. Aircraft will cross the German frontier only for purposes of local reconnaissance or to attack hostile aircraft and observation balloons. The Air Force may also operate in the German Bight and in the Western declared mined areas and in direct support of naval operations against English and French ships.

A separate order will cover long range reconnaissance.

6. *With reference to submarine warfare*, from now on only the following terms will be used:

For submarine warfare in accordance with Prize Law – 'trade warfare' [*Handelskrieg*].

For unrestricted submarine warfare – 'the sea siege of England' [*Belagerung Englands zur See*].

7. *English merchantmen which are definitely known to be armed* may be attacked by submarines without previous warning.*

signed: ADOLF HITLER

5

On 28th September 1939 Germany and Russia regulated their partition of Poland by a 'Treaty of Frontier Regulation and Friendship'.

The Supreme Commander   Berlin,
of the Armed Forces   30th September 1939.
                                       8 copies

Directive No. 5

1. As a result of the conclusion with Russia on 28th September 1939 of a Treaty of Frontier Regulation and Friendship my intention is to regulate the political form of former Polish territories lying within the German sphere of interest according to the following principles:

(*a*) The new *political* frontiers of the Reich in the East will, generally speaking, comprise the former area of German settlement and in addition those areas which have special value for military purposes, or for war economy, or for communications.

---

* As noted in pencil on the original, this paragraph was superseded by Directive No. 5.

Details of the frontier line have not yet been decided. I request that proposals in this matter be made to me through the High Command of the Armed Forces.

(b) The present Demarcation Line (Pisia–Narew–Vistula–San) will be constantly strengthened and built up as *a line of military security* towards the East. The garrisons necessary for this purpose will eventually be moved forward beyond the political frontier of the Reich.

I likewise request that proposals for the details of the defence line be submitted to me through the High Command of the Armed Forces.

(c) The line laid down in our Treaty of Frontier Regulation and Friendship with Russia, which will be defined in detail in an additional protocol to the Treaty, is to be regarded as *the limit of the German sphere of influence in relation to* Russia.

(d) *The political organization* of the area between this line and the new political frontier of the German Reich will be decided by me.

2. For the time being, the whole area of the former Polish State up to the line established by our treaty of Frontier Regulation and Friendship including the Suwalki-salient, will be an *area of Military Government* under Commander-in-Chief Army.

I request *Commander-in-Chief Army* to submit to me, at an early date, proposals for dealing with the following problems:

(a) The pacification of territory to be occupied. The time will be settled within the framework of the agreements reached in Moscow.

(b) The occupation of the security line along the course of the former Demarcation Line.

(c) The occupation of the whole territory by occupation troops. In this connexion the smallest possible forces will be employed on pacification duties east of the Demarcation Line.

Commander-in-Chief Air Force will leave in the East the forces which Commander-in-Chief Army requires to carry out these duties.

(d) The division of the area of Military Government into Districts, or the extension of existing Military Districts to include newly acquired territories.

3. In consequence of the latest political developments, the forces intended for East Prussia, in accordance with Directive No. 4, paragraph 4, last sentence, no longer need to be held in readiness.

4. All limitations hitherto imposed on *naval warfare* against France are cancelled. The war at sea will be carried on against France just as against England.

'Trade War' will in general be waged in accordance with Prize Law with the following exceptions:

Merchant ships and troopships definitely established as being hostile may be attacked without warning.

This also applies to ships sailing without lights in waters round England.

Merchantmen which use their radio transmitters after being stopped will be fired upon.

Attacks on 'passenger ships', or large ships which obviously carry considerable numbers of passengers in addition to cargo, are still forbidden.

5. For *air warfare in the West* the restrictions hitherto in force remain valid. The frontier of the Reich will be crossed by aircraft only for purposes of local and combat reconnaissance, to attack artillery liaison planes and captive balloons, and, to a limited extent, for long-range reconnaissance on the orders of Commander-in-Chief Air Force. Requests for long range reconnaissance on behalf of the Army are to be handled by direct liaison between Army and Air Force.

The Air Force may also attack English and French warships in the North Sea, and prosecute 'Trade War' in accordance with International Prize Law.

6. The orders detailed in paragraphs 4 and 5 now become effective in place of those contained in paragraphs 5*b* and *c* and paragraph 7 of Directive No. 4.

signed: ADOLF HITLER

6

With the completion of the Polish campaign Hitler had acquired his immediate objective; but unless he could make peace in the West, either by persuading Britain and France to accept the conquest and partition of Poland as final, or by conquering them too, he could not count on keeping his eastern gains. Early in October he put out peace feelers to the West; but meeting no response, he prepared for a full-scale attack on Britain and France. On 9th October 1939 he issued to the Chief of Staff of the Armed Forces (General Keitel) and the Commanders-in-Chief of the Army, Navy, and Air Force (General Brauchitsch, Admiral Raeder, and Field Marshal Göring) a long memorandum justifying this policy and explaining how it should be implemented. Since 1648, he said, a Franco-British world-system had thriven by keeping Germany divided, and it was only by the destruction of that system that a united German Reich would be finally established. Thanks to superior population, human quality, and equipment, Germany could defeat Britain and France, but, for various reasons, 'time is more likely to be an ally of the Western powers than of us'; 'therefore attack, which can decide the war, is preferable under all circumstances to defence. This attack cannot begin soon enough.' If properly carried out, it could end the war, and therefore, 'if at all possible, the attack should be carried out this autumn'. On the same day Hitler issued Directive No. 6, giving provisional orders for such an attack – known by the code name '*Fall Gelb* (Case Yellow)'. Directives Nos. 7 and 8 added further interim instructions.

The Supreme Commander
of the Armed Forces

Berlin,
9th October 1939.
8 copies

Directive No. 6 for the Conduct of the War

1. Should it become evident in the near future that England, and, under her influence, France also, are not disposed to bring the war to an end, I have decided, without further loss of time, to go over to the offensive.

2. Any further delay will not only entail the end of Belgian and perhaps of Dutch neutrality, to the advantage of the allies; it will also increasingly strengthen the military power of the enemy, reduce the confidence of neutral nations in Germany's final victory, and make it more difficult to bring Italy into the war on our side as a full ally.

3. I therefore issue the following orders for the further conduct of military operations:

(a) An offensive will be planned on the northern flank of the Western front, through Luxembourg, Belgium, and Holland. This offensive must be launched at the earliest possible moment and in greatest possible strength.

(b) The purpose of this offensive will be to defeat as much as possible of the French Army and of the forces of the allies fighting on their side, and at the same time to win as much territory as possible in Holland, Belgium, and Northern France, to serve as a base for the successful prosecution of the air and sea war against England and as a wide protective area for the economically vital Ruhr.

(c) The time of the attack will depend upon the readiness for action of the armoured and motorized units involved. These units are to be made ready with all speed. It will depend also upon the weather conditions obtaining and foreseeable at the time.

4. The Air Force will prevent attacks by the Anglo-French Air Forces on our Army and will give all necessary

direct support to its advance. It is also important to prevent the establishment of Anglo-French air bases and the landing of British forces in Belgium and Holland.

5. The Navy will do everything possible, while this offensive is in progress, to afford direct or indirect support to the operations of the Army and the Air Force.

6. Apart from these preparations for the beginning of the offensive in the West according to plan, the Army and Air Force must be ready, at all times, in increasing strength, to meet an Anglo-French invasion of Belgium, immediately and as far forward as possible on Belgian soil, and to occupy the largest possible area of Holland in the direction of the West coast.

7. These preparations will be camouflaged in such a way that they appear merely to be precautionary measures made necessary by the threatening increase in the strength of the French and English forces on the frontiers between France and Luxembourg and Belgium.

8. I request Commanders-in-Chief* to submit to me their detailed plans based on this directive at the earliest moment and to keep me constantly informed of progress through the High Command of the Armed Forces.

signed: ADOLF HITLER

7

The Supreme Commander
of the Armed Forces

Berlin,
18th October, 1939.
8 copies

Directive No. 7 for the Conduct of the War
For the prosecution of the war against the Western Enemy,

---

* Detailed Instructions for the conduct of the war in the West were addressed to the Commanders-in-Chief of the three services (Brauchitsch, Raeder, and Göring) on the same day, 9th October 1939.

until the beginning of the attack as planned, existing directives are hereby amplified as follows:

1. The following are permitted *with immediate effect:*

The Army may cross the French frontier with patrols, but only in so far as this is necessary for reconnaissance, and to maintain contact with enemy forces in withdrawal.

The Air Force may send fighter escorts over French territory in so far as this is necessary to protect reconnaissance aircraft.

It may also attack English naval units in *naval bases.* (Verbal notice to be given.)

The Navy may attack passenger ships in convoy or proceeding without lights.

The Führer will decide on all further measures to intensify the Trade War against England as soon as their political and economic effects have been considered by the High Command of the Armed Forces.

The attacks on English naval units at sea and in naval bases are to be kept up whenever a suitable opportunity offers and in close liaison between Navy and Air Force.

2. Should it be necessary to *oppose an Anglo-French invasion of Belgium* (Directive No. 6 paragraph 6) the Army may also enter *Luxembourg* territory.

The *Air Force* will, in this event, give direct support to the Army and will prevent attacks on the Army by the Anglo-French Air Force and the advance of enemy forces. It will also prevent the establishment of Anglo-French Air Forces and the landing of English troops in Belgium and Holland. For this purpose flights may be made over any part of the Western frontier of Germany. Attacks on industrial targets, or such as might highly endanger the civilian population, are forbidden in Belgium, Holland, and Luxembourg.

For the *Navy*, the principles set forth in Directive No. 6 paragraph 5 apply in this case also.

3. In order to conceal *our own plans for attack*, authorities immediately subordinate to the High Command of the Armed Forces (and in particular the Inspector of Signals

and the Security and Propaganda Divisions) will work in close collaboration, as will the staffs of individual arms of the services.

Proposals and requests in this connexion will be made as soon as possible to the High Command of the Armed Forces, Operations Staff (Defence Department).*

signed: ADOLF HITLER

8

The Supreme Commander
of the Armed Forces

Berlin,
20th November 1939.
8 copies

Directive No. 8 for the Conduct of the War

1. For the time being, a high state of preparedness must be maintained in order to deliver, at a moment's notice, the offensive which is being mounted. Only thus will it be possible to take immediate advantage of favourable weather.

The Armed Forces will make their preparations in such a way that the offensive can still be delayed even if orders for this delay reach Commands as late as A-Day† – 1, 2300 hours. At this hour at the latest Commands will receive the code-word, which will be either

'Danzig' ('Proceed with offensive') or
'Augsburg' ('Delay offensive').‡

Commander-in-Chief Army and Commander-in-Chief Air Force are requested, immediately after the date of the offensive has been decided, to report to the High Command

---

* *OKW (WFA/L)*. See Introduction, p. 20.

† *A-Tag = Angriffstag*, the day of attack; A-Day–1 = the day before the attack.

‡ The-code words 'Danzig' and 'Augsburg' were previously 'Rhein' and 'Elbe'.

of the Armed Forces, Operations Staff (Defence Department), the time which they have agreed for the beginning of the attack.

2. Contrary to earlier directives, all measures planned against *Holland* may be taken without special orders when the general offensive opens.

The attitude of the Dutch forces cannot be foreseen. Where no resistance is offered the invasion will assume the character of a peaceful occupation.

3. *Land operations* will be conducted in accordance with the Operation Order of 29th October.

That order is supplemented as follows:

(a) All precautions will be taken to enable the main weight of attack to be switched from Army Group B to Army Group A should the disposition of enemy forces at any time suggest that Army Group A could achieve greater success.

(b) Holland, including the West Frisian Islands, but (for the time being) excluding Texel, will be occupied in the first instance up to the Grebbe–Meuse line.

4. The *Navy* will undertake the blockade of Belgian ports and sea lanes and, contrary to former directives, those of Holland also. For submarines this action is authorized on the night preceding the offensive; for surface craft and aircraft from the moment of attack by the Army. The interval between the initiation of blockading operations and the time of the attack by land must, however, be kept as brief as possible even where submarines are concerned.*

Operations against the Dutch Navy will be undertaken only if the latter displays a hostile attitude.

The Navy will assume responsibility for the defence by

---

* On 11th December a supplementary order modified this paragraph, authorizing surface vessels to go into action at the same time as submarines, provided that they did not compromise the secrecy of the land operations.

coastal artillery of occupied areas of the coast against attack from the sea. Preparations for this will be made.

5. The tasks of the *Air Force* are unchanged. They have been amplified by the special orders given verbally by the Führer for airborne landings and the support of the Army in capturing the bridges west of Maastricht.

7th Airborne Division will be used for parachute landings only after the bridges across the Albert Canal are in our hands. When this occurs, immediate communication between Commander-in-Chief Army and Commander-in-Chief Air Force must be ensured.

Neither in Holland nor in Belgium–Luxembourg are centres of population, and in particular large open cities and industrial installations, to be attacked without compelling military necessity.

6. *Frontier Control.*

(*a*) *Until the opening of the attack*, traffic and communication across the Dutch, Belgian, and Luxembourg frontiers will be maintained at a normal level in order to ensure surprise. Civil authorities will make no preparations to close these frontiers until the beginning of the attack.

(*b*) *Upon the opening of the attack* the frontiers with Holland, Belgium, and Luxembourg will be *closed* to all traffic and communications of a non-military character. Commander-in-Chief Army will issue the relative orders to the military and civil authorities concerned. At the beginning of the attack the High Command of the Armed Forces will inform the highest government authorities that Commander-in-Chief Army is issuing direct orders for the closing of the frontiers and that these will include the Dutch frontier outside the theatre of operations.

(*c*) *On the other frontiers between the Reich and neutral states*, no restrictions on frontier traffic or communications will be applied on the opening of the offensive.

Further measures for the control of the passage of persons and communications have already been prepared and will be enforced as necessary.

pp. Chief of the High Command of the Armed Forces

signed: KEITEL

9

While 'Case Yellow' was being prepared, Hitler turned to the problem of the economic strength of Britain, whose capacity to drag out the war, and gradually to gain a military and political ascendancy over Germany, had been one of his reasons for insisting on Germany's need for quick victory.

The Supreme Commander
of the Armed Forces

Berlin,
29th November 1939.
11 copies

Directive No. 9
Instructions for warfare against the economy of the enemy

1. In our fight against the Western Powers England has shown herself to be the animator of the fighting spirit of the enemy and the leading enemy power. The defeat of England is essential to final victory.

The most effective means of ensuring this is to cripple the English economy by attacking it at decisive points.

2. The development of the general situation and of our armaments should provide within the foreseeable future favourable conditions for extensive operations against the economic foundations upon which England rests. *Early preparations must therefore be made,* by concentrating the appropriate weapons upon the most important objectives, to deal an annihilating blow to the English economy.

Non-military weapons will be employed in conjunction with the measures taken by the Armed Forces and in accordance with special orders.

3. Should the Army succeed in defeating the Anglo-French Armies in the field and in seizing and holding a sector of the coast of the Continent opposite England, *the task of the Navy and Air Force* to carry the war to English industry becomes paramount. Efforts will be made to secure the cooperation of the Sabotage and Fifth Column [S- and K-] organizations.

4. The Navy and Air Force will then carry out the following tasks, given in the order of importance:

(*a*) Attacks on the principal English ports by mining and blocking the sea lanes leading to them, and by the destruction of important port installations and locks.

In this connexion aircraft are extremely valuable in mine-laying, particularly outside English west coast ports, in narrow waterways, and in river estuaries.

(*b*) Attacks on English merchant shipping and on enemy warships protecting it.

(*c*) Destruction of English depots, oil storage plants, food in cold storage, and grain stores.

(*d*) Interruption of the transport of English troops and supplies to the French mainland.

(*e*) The destruction of industrial plant whose loss would be of decisive significance for the military conduct of the war, in particular key points of the aircraft industry and factories producing heavy artillery, anti-aircraft guns, munitions, and explosives.

5. The most important English ports, which handle 95 per cent of foreign trade and which could not be adequately replaced by other harbours, are:

London
Liverpool } for the import of foodstuffs and timber, and
Manchester } the *import* and refining of oil.

These three ports, accounting as they do in peacetime for 58 per cent of total imports, are of decisive importance.

Newcastle	Swansea	
Blyth	Cardiff	for the *export* of coal.
Sunderland	Barry	
Hull		

Alternative ports, of limited capacity, and for certain types of cargo only are:

Grangemouth	Holyhead
Leith	Bristol
Middlesbrough	Belfast
Grimsby	Newport
Southampton	Goole
Glasgow	Dundee

It will be necessary to keep constant watch for any possible shift in the use of these ports. We must also seek constantly to compress and shift English foreign trade into channels which are open to effective attack by our own Navy and Air Force.

French ports need only be attacked in so far as they are involved, geographically or economically, in the siege of England, or are used as harbours for troopships.

6. In ports where effective minefields cannot be laid, shipping will be crippled by *blocking the approaches* to the ports with sunken ships and by *destroying vital harbour installations*. In this connexion it is particularly important, in the harbours of

Leith, Sunderland, Hull, Grimsby, London, Manchester (Ship Canal), Liverpool, Cardiff, Swansea, Bristol–Avonmouth,

to destroy the large sea-locks upon which, particularly on the west coast, the regulation of the water level, and thus the effectiveness of the ports, depends.

7. In preparing these operations it will be necessary –

(*a*) Constantly to check and bring up to date all facts known to us about English ports, their equipment and capacity, and about the English war industry and supply depots.

(b) To develop with high priority an effective means of employing aircraft as mine-layers for sunken* as well as floating mines.

(c) To provide a supply of mines sufficient to satisfy the very heavy demands and equal to the capacities of the Navy and Air Force.

(d) To ensure that the conduct of operations be the joint responsibility of Navy and Air Force, coordinated as to time and place by both services.

Preparations to this end will be undertaken as quickly as possible. I request Commanders-in-Chief Navy and Air Force to keep me constantly informed of their intentions.

I reserve to myself the right to decide the moment at which the restrictions imposed by my previous directives for Naval and Air Warfare shall be lifted.

This will probably coincide with the opening of the great offensive.

signed: ADOLF HITLER

10

In spite of continued readiness, and many supplementary orders, 'Case Yellow' was continually postponed. On 19th January 1940, as we know from General Jodl's diary, the draft of a new directive was submitted to Hitler. This was to be Directive No. 10. After being amended, it was evidently sent to the High Command of the Army, but the original has not survived. The first paragraph, however, is known from an order of the High Command of the Army. Once again, an offensive in the West is announced. 'All available forces' are to be thrown into battle with the object of occupying Holland

---

* *Ankertauminen*, anchored mines, which endanger shipping beyond a depth of 40 metres.

and Belgium, and inflicting a decisive defeat on the French and
Allied armies in North France and Belgium. It appears that,
under pressure from the Commander-in-Chief Army, and his
generals in command of Army Groups, this directive was
again amended. Then, on 18th February 1940, the plan of
operations was changed, and a new version of Directive No. 10
was evidently issued (a reference to it will be observed in
Directive No. 11 below). Once again, only part of the text (the
first section) survives again in the form of an order of the High
Command of the Army. It is as follows:

The objective of offensive 'Yellow' is to deny Holland and
Belgium to the English by swiftly occupying them; to defeat,
by an attack through Belgian and Luxembourg territory, the
largest possible forces of the Anglo-French army; and thereby to pave the way for the destruction of the military strength
of the enemy.

The main weight of the attack across Belgium and Luxembourg will be south of the line Liège–Charleroi.

Forces engaged north of this line will break through the
Belgian frontier defences. Continuing the attack westwards
they will parry any immediate threats to the Ruhr from NE
Belgium and will divert to themselves the strongest possible
Anglo-French forces.

Forces operating south of the line Liège–Charleroi will
force a passage of the Meuse between Dinant and Sedan
(both inclusive) and will advance through the French frontier defences towards the Somme estuary.

10a

Meanwhile, another offensive was being prepared. While the
land war in the West was in suspense, the sea war against
England was active. In his memorandum of 9th October,
Hitler had declared that, 'used ruthlessly, the submarine can
today be an extraordinary threat to Britain'; but he added that

Germany's submarine routes were long and exposed. The 'sole remaining approach and departure route for our submarines' lay between Norway and the Shetland Islands. The British had laid an extensive mine barrage across this route in the war of 1914 and it was inconceivable, he wrote, that, in a long war, they would not do so again. Therefore it was essential to forestall or circumvent such barriers by submarine bases on the Atlantic coast. The destruction of the surface-raiding pocket battleship *Graf Spee* after the battle of the River Plate of 13th December 1939 emphasized Germany's dependence on submarines, which in turn relied on the use of Norwegian territorial waters. Moreover, Germany was also dependent on Swedish iron ore which, in winter, had to be brought from the North Norwegian port of Narvik through the same waters. Control of Norwegian territorial waters, direct or indirect, thus became a major interest of both Britain and Germany, and during the preparations for an offensive in the West Hitler ordered plans to be made for the seizure and occupation of both Denmark and Norway, under the code name '*Fall Weserübung* (Case Weser-exercise)'. The first order was given on 14th December 1939 immediately after the battle of the River Plate, following a meeting between Hitler and his Norwegian puppet, Vidkun Quisling. On 1st March 1940 Hitler issued the formal directive which, not being concerned with the main theatre, was not numbered in the series. It is here numbered 10*a*.

The Führer and Supreme Commander   Berlin,
of the Armed Forces   1st March 1940.
9 copies

Directive for 'Case Weser-exercise'

1. The development of the situation in Scandinavia makes it necessary to prepare for the occupation of Denmark and Norway by formations of the Armed Forces ('Case Weser-exercise'). This would anticipate English action against Scandinavia and the Baltic, would secure our supplies of ore

from Sweden, and would provide the Navy and Air Force with expanded bases for operations against England.

The protection of the operation against action by English Naval and Air Forces will be carried out by the Navy and Air Force within the limits of existing possibilities.

The forces employed on 'Case Weser-exercise' will be as small as possible having regard to our military and political strength in relation to the Northern nations. Weakness in numbers will be made good by skilful action and surprise in execution.

The basic aim is to lend the operation the character of a *peaceful* occupation, designed to protect by force of arms the neutrality of the Northern countries. Demands in this sense will be made to the Governments concerned at the beginning of the occupation and the necessary emphasis will be given, if required, by naval and air demonstrations.

Any resistance which is nevertheless offered will be broken by all means available.

2. I order General of Infantry von Falkenhorst, Commanding General XXI Army Corps, to prepare and command the operation against Denmark and Norway, as Commander 'Group XXI'.

He will be immediately subordinate to me in all respects. His staff will be composed of officers of the three Services.

Forces detailed for 'Case Weser-exercise' will receive special orders.

Naval and Air Forces employed will remain under the command of Commander-in-Chief Navy and Commander-in-Chief Air Force, and will operate in close liaison with Commander Group XXI. Of the Air Force, one Reconnaissance Wing (F) and two Motorized Anti-Aircraft Regiments are not subject to this ruling, but will be under the immediate command of Group XXI until the occupation of Denmark is completed.

Forces detailed to Group XXI will receive supplies from branches of the Armed Forces concerned, in accordance with the requirements of the Commander.

3. The crossing of the Danish frontier and the landing in Norway will take place *simultaneously*. The operations will be prepared with the utmost possible speed. Should the enemy take the initiative against Norway, we must be able to take our own counter-measures at once.

It is of the utmost importance that our operations should come as a *surprise* to the Northern countries as well as to our enemies in the West. This must be kept in mind in making all preparations, especially in the choice of dumps and embarkation points, and in the briefing and embarkation of troops. Should it become impossible to conceal preparations for embarkation, officers and men will be given a false destination. Troops will be informed of the true objective only after putting to sea.

4. *Occupation of Denmark* ('Weser-exercise South').

Task of Group XXI: The surprise occupation of Jutland and Fünen and subsequent occupation of Zeeland.

For this purpose troops will push through to Skagen and to the east coast of Fünen as quickly as possible, securing the most important points. Bases in Zeeland will be occupied at the earliest moment to serve as springboards for the further occupation.

The *Navy* will provide forces to secure the Nyborg–Korsör route and to seize the bridge across the Little Belt with all speed. If necessary it will also assist in landing troops. It will also be responsible for coastal defence.

The *Air Force* will provide air units primarily for purposes of demonstration and for dropping leaflets. Danish ground installations and air defences will be secured.

5. *Occupation of Norway* ('Weser-exercise North').

Task of Group XXI: the surprise occupation of important places on the coast from the sea and by landing from the air.

The *Navy* is responsible for preparing and carrying out the sea transport of the invasion troops and of the troops to be transported to Oslo afterwards. It will ensure seaborne supplies. Norwegian coastal defences are to be prepared with all speed.

The *Air Force*, after the occupation, will ensure adequate air defence, as well as the exploitation of Norway as a base for the prosecution of the air war against England.

6. Group XXI will keep the High Command of the Armed Forces constantly informed of the state of preparations and will submit a time-table. This must indicate the minimum lapse of time necessary between the issue of orders for 'Case Weser-exercise' and their execution.

11

Early in April the British and German pressure on Norway converged. On 8th April the British mined Norwegian waters; on 9th April 'Operation Weser-exercise' was launched. Hitler had issued the orders a week before. A British force was sent to Norway but was unable to prevent the conquest of the country. The British failure in Norway caused the fall of the Chamberlain government. Meanwhile, Hitler launched his attack in the West. On 10th May Winston Churchill became Prime Minister of Britain while the Germans were invading Belgium and Holland. Directives 11–15 deal with the series of battles in the West which led to the evacuation of Paris on 14th June and the formation, two days later, of the government of Marshal Pétain, which surrendered to Germany.

The Führer and Supreme Commander   Headquarters,
of the Armed Forces   14th May 1940.
                                                               5 copies

Directive No. 11

1. The progress of the offensive to date shows that the enemy has failed to appreciate in time the basic idea of our operations. He continues to throw strong forces against the line Namur–Antwerp and appears to be neglecting the sector facing Army Group A.

2. This fact and the swift forcing of the Meuse crossing

in the sector of Army Group A have established the first essentials for a thrust in all possible strength north of the Aisne and in a north-westerly direction, as laid down in Directive No. 10. Such a thrust might produce a major success. It is the task of forces engaged north of the line Liège–Namur to deceive and hold down the greatest number of enemy forces by attacking them with their own resources.

3. On the northern flank the Dutch Army has shown itself capable of a stronger resistance than had been supposed. For political and military reasons, this resistance must be broken *quickly*. It is the task of the Army, by moving strong forces from the south in conjunction with an attack against the Eastern front, to bring about the speedy fall of Fortress Holland.

4. All available motorized divisions will be transferred to the operational area of Army Group A as soon as possible.

Armoured and motorized divisions of Army Group B will also be switched to the left flank as soon as there are no further prospects of effective operations in their own sector and as the situation allows.

5. The task of the *Air Force* is to concentrate strong offensive and defensive forces for action, with the focal point at Army Group A, in order to prevent the transfer of enemy reinforcements to the front and to give direct support to our own forces.

In addition the rapid reduction of Fortress Holland will be assisted by the deliberate weakening of forces hitherto operating ahead of 6th Army.

6. The *Navy* will operate against sea traffic in the Hoofden and in the Channel as opportunity offers.

signed: ADOLF HITLER

12

The text of Directive No. 12 is not available. It probably did not go beyond the High Command of the Army. Its character can be deduced from two entries in the diaries of Jodl and Halder for 18th May. According to Jodl:

> The High Command of the Army has failed to carry out the intention to build up a southern flank with the utmost speed. Infantry divisions have continued to move westward instead of switching to the south-west. Thus 10th Armoured Division and 2nd and 29th Motorized Divisions are still tied down to protecting the flank. Commander-in-Chief Army and General Halder* were immediately called in and were ordered in the sharpest manner to take the necessary steps at once ... I [Jodl] also issued an amending order to the directive. This order switches 1st Mountain Division and the rear elements of 4th Army to the attacks in the south and south-west.

Halder's account is fuller:

> The Führer has an incomprehensible anxiety about the southern flank. . . . He is absolutely opposed to the continuation of operations towards the west, let alone the south-west, and still clings to the north-western idea. This led to an extremely unpleasant difference of opinion in the Führer's Headquarters between the Führer on the one hand and the Commander-in-Chief and myself on the other. A directive was issued on this occasion which is a confirmation in writing of our conversation which took place at 1000 hrs. Conversations between the Commander-in-Chief [Col-Gen. von Brauchitsch] and Col-Gen. von Rundstedt, and my conversation with Salmuth, produced the effects which the Führer desired (sharp switch of forward divisions to the south-west, main body of motorized forces to be ready to move to the west).

---

* General Franz Halder was Chief of the Army General Staff (*Chef OKH*).

13

The Führer and Supreme Commander
of the Armed Forces

Headquarters,
24th May 1940.
7 copies

Directive No. 13

1. The next object of our operations is to annihilate the
French, English, and Belgian forces which are surrounded in
Artois and Flanders, by a concentric attack by our northern
flank and by the swift seizure of the Channel coast in this area.

The task of the Air Force will be to break all enemy
resistance on the part of the surrounded forces, to prevent
the escape of the English forces across the Channel, and to
protect the southern flank of Army Group A.

The enemy Air Force will be engaged whenever opportunity offers.

2. The Army will then prepare to destroy in the shortest
possible time the remaining enemy forces in France. This
operation will be undertaken in three phases:

Phase 1: A thrust between the sea and the Oise as far as
the lower Seine below Paris, with the intention of supporting
and securing with weak forces the later main operations on
the right flank.

Should the position and reserves available permit, every
effort will be made, even before the conclusion of hostilities
in Artois and Flanders, to occupy the area between the
Somme and the Oise by a concentric attack in the direction
of Montdidier, and thereby to prepare and facilitate the later
thrust against the lower Seine.

Phase 2: An attack by the main body of the Army, including strong armoured forces, south-eastwards on either side
of Reims, with the intention of defeating the main body of
the French Army in the Paris–Metz–Belfort triangle and of
bringing about the collapse of the Maginot Line.

Phase 3: In support of this main operation, a well-timed subsidiary attack on the Maginot Line with the aim of breaking through the Line with weaker forces at its most vulnerable point between St Avold and Sarreguemines in the direction of Nancy–Lunéville.

Should the situation allow, an attack on the upper Rhine may be envisaged, with the limitation that not more than eight to ten divisions are to be committed.

3. *Tasks of the Air Force.*

(*a*) Apart from operations in France, the Air Force is authorized to attack the English homeland in the fullest manner, as soon as sufficient forces are available. This attack will be opened by an annihilating reprisal for English attacks on the Ruhr.

Commander-in-Chief Air Force will designate targets in accordance with the principles laid down in Directive No. 9 and further orders to be issued by the High Command of the Armed Forces. The time and plan for this attack are to be reported to me.

The struggle against the English homeland will be continued after the commencement of land operations.

(*b*) *With the opening of the main operations of the Army* in the direction of Reims, it will be the task of the Air Force, apart from maintaining our air supremacy, to give direct support to the attack, to break up any enemy reinforcements which may appear, to hamper the re-grouping of enemy forces, and in particular to protect the western flank of the attack.

The breakthrough of the Maginot Line will also be supported as far as necessary.

(*c*) Commander-in-Chief Air Force will also consider how far the air defence of the areas upon which the enemy is now concentrating his attacks can be strengthened by the employment of forces from less threatened areas.

In so far as the Navy is involved in any changes of this kind, Commander-in-Chief Navy is to participate.

4. *Tasks of the Navy.*

All restrictions on naval action in English and French waters are hereby cancelled and commanders are free to employ their forces to the fullest extent.

Commander-in-Chief Navy will submit a proposal for the delimitation of the areas in which the measures authorized for the coming siege may be carried out.

I reserve to myself the decision whether, and if so in what form, the blockade will be made public.

5. I request the Commanders-in-Chief to inform me, in person or in writing, of their intentions based on this directive.

signed: ADOLF HITLER

14

The Führer and Supreme Commander
of the Armed Forces   Führer Headquarters,
                                        8th June 1940.
                                        5 copies

Directive No. 14

1. The enemy is offering stiff resistance on our right flank and in the centre of 6th Army.

2. Therefore, according to the proposal of Commander-in-Chief Army, I approve the orders given this morning by Army Group B, viz.:

(*a*) Merely to hold down the enemy on the 6th Army front.

(*b*) To transfer XIV Corps to the left flank of 4th Army.

(*c*) To strike a crushing blow at the strong enemy forces on the 6th Army front by increasing the pressure exerted by the bulk of 4th Army south-eastwards and by the left flank of 6th Army south-westwards.

3. I further order:

(*a*) The basic intention, as laid down in Directive No. 13, viz.: to destroy enemy forces in the Château-Thierry–Metz–Belfort triangle, and to bring about the collapse of the Maginot Line, remains valid.

However, since Phase 1 of the operation is not yet ended and extremely strong resistance is being offered north of Paris, stronger forces must be employed on the lower Seine and against Paris than had originally been contemplated.

(*b*) Army Group A will move to the attack on 9th June south-south-westwards as ordered in Directive No. 13.

(*c*) 9th Army will thrust southwards towards the Marne. It will be reinforced as soon as possible by XVI Army Corps (including attached SS units and the SS Death's Head Division). Strong reserve forces must back up the juncture of the two Army Groups.

(*d*) I reserve to myself the decision as to the direction of any further thrust by 9th Army or whether it is to be left with Army Group B or put under command of Army Group A.

4. *The task of the Air Force*, in addition to what has been laid down in Directive No. 13, is as follows:

(*a*) To support the concentric attack on the flanks of the main enemy forces facing Army Group B.

(*b*) To keep under observation and under strong fighter cover the coast on the right flank of Army Group B and the area south-west of the Bresle sector.

(*c*) To help the advance of Army Group A at the focal point.

signed: ADOLF HITLER

15

The Führer and Supreme   Führer Headquarters,
    Commander of the Armed Forces   14th June 1940.
                                                                     6 copies

Directive No. 15

1. The *enemy*, compelled by the collapse of his front, is evacuating the Paris area, and has also begun the evacuation of the fortified triangle Epinal–Metz–Verdun behind the Maginot Line.

Paris has been declared an open city by means of posters.

It is not inconceivable that the main body of the French Army may withdraw behind the Loire.

2. Our relative strength and the condition of the French Army now make it possible to pursue henceforward *two objectives at the same time:*

(a) To prevent enemy forces withdrawing from the Paris area, and those on the lower Seine from establishing a new front.

(b) To destroy enemy forces in the areas facing Army Groups A and C, and to bring about the collapse of the Maginot Line.

3. I therefore issue the following orders for the further conduct of the *operations of the Army:*

(a) Enemy forces on the lower Seine and in the Paris area will be vigorously pursued by the advance of the right flank of the Army along the coast towards the Loire estuary and by a turning movement from the Chateau-Thierry area towards the Loire above Orleans. Paris will be occupied in force as soon as possible. The naval bases of Cherbourg and Brest, and also Lorient and St Nazaire, will be occupied.

(b) Forces at the centre, up to approximately the area of Châlons, will continue, for the time being, in the general direction of Troyes; their armoured and motorized divisions will thrust forward in the direction of the plateau of Langres.

Infantry divisions will first reach the area north-east of Romilly–Troyes. Preparations will be made for their later use in the central Loire area.

(c) Orders for other formations of the Army remain un-changed. They will destroy the enemy in the enclosed area of north-eastern France, ensure the collapse of the Maginot Line, and prevent the withdrawal of forces there towards the south-west.

(d) The 'Saarbrucken Shock Group' will move to the attack across the Maginot Line on 14th June in the general direction of Lunéville. The timing for 'Attack Upper Rhine' will be decided as soon as possible.

4. The *Air Force* has the following tasks:

(a) To keep up the momentum of our advance towards the Loire by means of air attacks. At the same time the advancing troops are to be supported by anti-aircraft artillery and protected against air attack.

The enemy's retreat by sea is to be made impossible by smashing ports and shipping on the north coast of France.

(b) The withdrawal of the enemy facing Army Groups A and C is to be held up. The focal point in this respect is in front of the tanks on the right flank of Army Group A.

Enemy transport by rail running south-west towards and beyond the line Neuchâteau–Belfort is to be pre-vented.

At the same time the breach of the Maginot Line by Army Group C is to be supported.

Anti-Aircraft artillery is to facilitate the attack by the right flank of Army Group A and, in particular, the penetration of French fortifications.

signed: ADOLF HITLER

16

With the fall of France Hitler was left with only one enemy between himself and the permanent establishment of his domination in Europe. Britain had suffered serious losses, both political and military: its chief strength lay in its economic resources and insular position. Already, in Directive No. 9, Hitler had laid down the lines of his war on Britain's economy. On 26th May, with almost all Norway effectively occupied, and German troops in control of Holland and Belgium, a supplement to that directive was issued by Keitel. It ordered attacks on British food supplies whose destruction 'is of vital importance in breaking the will to resist', the interruption of public services (gas, water, and electricity), and, above all, the destruction of the aircraft industry 'in order to deprive the English Air Force, the last weapon which can be directly used against us, of the basis of its existence'. Now Hitler saw the prospect of a frontal attack on the island. On 2nd July 1940 he decided that a landing in England was possible, 'provided that air superiority can be attained and certain other necessary conditions fulfilled', and he asked for reports from the three Services. As yet, he made clear, 'the plan to invade England has not taken any definite shape': his preparations were only 'for a possible operation'; but a fortnight later he had reached more positive conclusions.

The Führer and Supreme   Führer Headquarters,
Commander of the Armed Forces   16th July 1940.
                                          7 copies

Directive No. 16
On preparations for a landing operation against England

Since England, in spite of her hopeless military situation, shows no signs of being ready to come to an understanding,

I have decided to prepare a landing operation against England, and, if necessary, to carry it out.

The aim of this operation will be to eliminate the English homeland as a base for the prosecution of the war against Germany and, if necessary, to occupy it completely.

I therefore order as follows:

1. The *landing* will be in the form of a surprise crossing on a wide front from about Ramsgate to the area west of the Isle of Wight. Units of the Air Force will act as artillery, and units of the Navy as engineers.

The possible advantages of *limited operations* before the general crossing (e.g. the occupation of the Isle of Wight or of the county of Cornwall) are to be considered from the point of view of each branch of the Armed Forces and the results reported to me. I reserve the decision to myself.

Preparations for the entire operation must be completed by the middle of *August*.

2. These preparations must also create such conditions as will make a landing in England possible, viz.:

(a) The English Air Force must be so reduced morally and physically that it is unable to deliver any significant attack against the German crossing.

(b) Mine-free channels must be cleared.

(c) The Straits of Dover must be closely sealed off with minefields on both *flanks*; also the Western entrance to the Channel approximately on the line Alderney–Portland.

(d) Strong forces of coastal artillery must command and protect the forward coastal area.

(e) It is desirable that the English Navy be tied down shortly before the crossing, both in the North Sea and in the Mediterranean (by the Italians)*. For this purpose we must attempt even now to damage English

---

* Mussolini had declared war on Britain and France on 10th June.

home-based naval forces by air and torpedo attack as far as possible.

3. *Command organization and preparations*

Under my overriding command and according to my general instructions, the Commanders-in-Chief will command the branches of the Armed Forces for which they are responsible.

From 1st August the operations staffs of Commander-in-Chief Army, Commander-in-Chief Navy, and Commander-in-Chief Air Force are to be located at a distance of not more than 50 kilometres from my Headquarters (Ziegenberg).

It seems to me useful that the inner operations staffs of Commander-in-Chief Army and Commander-in-Chief Navy should be placed together at Giessen.

Commander-in-Chief Army will detail one Army Group to carry out the invasion.

The invasion will bear the cover name '*Seelöwe* [Sea-Lion]'.

In the preparation and execution of this operation the following tasks are allotted to each Service:

(*a*) *Army:*

The Army will draw up the operational and crossing plans for all formations of the first wave of the invasion. The anti-aircraft artillery which is to cross with the first wave will remain subordinate to the Army (to individual crossing units) until it is possible to allocate its responsibilities between the support and protection of troops on the ground, the protection of disembarkation points, and the protection of the airfields which are to be occupied.

The Army will, moreover, lay down the methods by which the invasion is to be carried out and the individual forces to be employed, and will determine points of embarkation and disembarkation in conjunction with the Navy.

(b) *Navy:*

The Navy will procure the means for invasion and will take them, in accordance with the wishes of the Army, but with due regard to navigational considerations, to the various embarkation points. Use will be made, as far as possible, of the shipping of defeated enemy countries.

The Navy will furnish each embarkation point with the staff necessary to give nautical advice, with escort vessels and guards. In conjunction with air forces assigned for protection, it will defend the crossing of the Channel on both flanks. Further orders will lay down the chain of command during the crossing. It is also the task of the Navy to coordinate the setting up of coastal artillery – i.e. all artillery, both naval and military, intended to engage targets at sea – and generally to direct its fire. The largest possible number of *extra-heavy guns* will be brought into position as soon as possible in order to cover the crossing and to shield the flanks against enemy action at sea. For this purpose railway guns will also be used (reinforced by all available captured weapons) and will be sited on railway turntables. Those batteries intended only to deal with targets on the English mainland (K5 and K12) will not be included. Apart from this the existing extra-heavy platform-gun batteries are to be enclosed in concrete opposite the Straits of Dover in such a manner that they can withstand the heaviest air attacks and will permanently, in all conditions, command the Straits of Dover within the limits of their range. The technical work will be the responsibility of the Organization Todt.*

(c) *The task of the Air Force will be:*

To prevent interference by the enemy Air Force.

---

* The Organization Todt, commanded by Fritz Todt, was responsible for national engineering construction.

To destroy coastal fortresses which might operate against our disembarkation points, to break the first resistance of enemy land forces, and to disperse reserves on their way to the front. In carrying out this task the closest liaison is necessary between individual Air Force units and the Army invasion forces.

Also, to destroy important transport highways by which enemy reserves might be brought up, and to attack approaching enemy naval forces as far as possible from our disembarkation points. I request that suggestions be made to me regarding the employment of parachute and airborne troops. In this connexion it should be considered, in conjunction with the Army, whether it would be useful at the beginning to hold parachute and airborne troops in readiness as a *reserve*, to be thrown in quickly in case of need.

4. Preparations to ensure the necessary communications between France and the English mainland will be handled by the Chief, Armed Forces Signals.

The use of the remaining eighty kilometres of the East Prussia cable is to be examined in cooperation with the Navy.

5. I request Commanders-in-Chief to submit to me as soon as possible –

(a) The plans of the Navy and Air Force to establish the necessary conditions for crossing the Channel (see paragraph 2).

(b) Details of the building of coastal batteries (Navy).

(c) A general survey of the shipping required and the methods by which it is proposed to prepare and procure it. Should civil authorities be involved? (Navy).

(d) The organization of Air Defence in the assembly areas for invasion troops and ships (Air Force).

(e) The crossing and operation plan of the Army, the composition and equipment of the first wave of invasion.

(f) The organization and plans of the Navy and Air Force

for the execution of the actual crossing, for its protection, and for the support of the landing.

(g) Proposals for the use of parachute and airborne troops and also for the organization and command of anti-aircraft artillery as soon as sufficient English territory has been captured.

(h) Proposal for the location of Naval and Air Headquarters.

(i) Views of the Navy and Air Force whether limited operations are regarded as useful *before* a general landing and, if so, of what kind.

(k) Proposal from Army and Navy regarding command *during* the crossing.

signed: ADOLF HITLER

17

The Führer and Supreme Commander of the Armed Forces	Führer Headquarters, 1st August 1940. 10 copies

Directive No. 17
For the conduct of air and sea warfare against England

In order to establish the necessary conditions for the final conquest of England I intend to intensify air and sea warfare against the English homeland. I therefore order as follows:

1. The German Air Force is to overpower the English Air Force with all the forces at its command, in the shortest possible time. The attacks are to be directed primarily against flying units, their ground installations, and their supply organizations, but also against the aircraft industry, including that manufacturing anti-aircraft equipment.

2. After achieving temporary or local air superiority the air war is to be continued against ports, in particular against stores of food, and also against stores of provisions in the interior of the country.

Attacks on south coast ports will be made on the smallest possible scale, in view of our own forthcoming operations.

3. On the other hand, air attacks on enemy warships and merchant ships may be reduced except where some particularly favourable target happens to present itself, where such attacks would lend additional effectiveness to those mentioned in paragraph 2, or where such attacks are necessary for the training of air crews for further operations.

4. The intensified air warfare will be carried out in such a way that the Air Force can at any time be called upon to give adequate support to naval operations against suitable targets. It must also be ready to take part in full force in 'Undertaking Sea Lion'.

5. I reserve to myself the right to decide on terror attacks as measures of reprisal.

6. The intensification of the air war may begin on or after 5th August. The exact time is to be decided by the Air Force after the completion of preparations and in the light of the weather.

The Navy is authorized to begin the proposed intensified naval war at the same time.

signed: ADOLF HITLER

18

Plans for the invasion of England continued to be made throughout the summer of 1940. On 1st August Hitler ruled that all Services should be ready to launch the operation on 15th September; on 3rd September it was postponed till 21st September. But the essential pre-condition of air superiority was never obtained; the great air battles over Britain, culminating in the battle of 15th September, convinced Hitler that invasion was impossible; and on 17th September he gave orders that the operation be indefinitely but inconspicuously postponed. By the time that the second winter of war approached, Hitler had thus failed to secure his huge conquests;

nor did he feel that they would be secure till Britain had been crushed. This failure was particularly galling to him because he already felt the approach of Russian power in the East, from Finland to Rumania. The longer he found himself committed to war with Britain, the more he feared that his initial conquests in the East, which were to be the basis of a longer policy of conquest, would be undermined in his rear. It was therefore essential to him to find some means of bringing Britain to reason; and if that was impossible by direct attack, he must seek to achieve it by indirect means.

Fortunately such means, he thought, lay ready to hand. Italy had declared war on Britain and France in the hour of Hitler's victory, on 10th June. On 13th September Mussolini ordered the invasion of Egypt from Libya; on 15th October he also invaded Greece. Both invasions were unsuccessful. Meanwhile, General Franco, in Spain, was showing himself anxious to profit from Hitler's patronage, though reluctant to pay any price for it. Mussolini's necessities and Franco's appetite suggested new projects to Hitler. A winter campaign in the warm Mediterranean area might cut Britain off from other continents, just as the summer campaign in the North had cut it off from Europe. Thus Britain would be completely isolated and, in isolation, might be strangled, since it would not be beaten, into submission. Directive No. 18 reviews these possibilities.

The Führer and Supreme   Führer Headquarters,
Commander of the Armed Forces   12th November 1940.
                                            10 copies

Directive No. 18

The preparatory measures of the High Command for the conduct of the war in the near future will be made on the following lines:

1. *Relations with France.*

The aim of my policy towards France is to cooperate with

that country in the most effective manner possible for the future conduct of the war against England. For the present France will assume the role of a 'non-belligerent power' and will thus be required to allow German war measures on French territory and particularly in the African colonies. She will also be required to support these measures with her own forces as far as may be necessary. The most urgent duty of the French is to secure their African possessions (West and Equatorial Africa), offensively and defensively, against England and the de Gaulle movement. From this the full participation of France in the war against England may develop.

The conversations with France begun at my meeting with Marshal Pétain will, apart from the day-to-day work of the Armistice Commission, be carried out exclusively by the Foreign Office, in liaison with the High Command of the Armed Forces.

Further instructions will be issued when these conversations are concluded.

2. *Spain and Portugal.*

Political measures to bring about the entry into the war of Spain in the near future have already been initiated. The aim of *German* intervention in the Iberian peninsula (cover-name 'Felix') will be to drive the English from the Western Mediterranean. To this end –

(*a*) Gibraltar is to be captured and the Straits closed.
(*b*) The English are to be prevented from gaining a footing at any other point on the Iberian peninsula or in the Atlantic Islands.

The preparation and execution of this operation is planned as follows:

Phase I

(*a*) Reconnaissance parties (officers in plain clothes) will draw up the necessary plans for action against Gibraltar and for the capture of airfields. With regard to cover and collaboration with the Spaniards they will conform with the security measures of the Chief, Armed Forces Intelligence Division [*Ausland Abwehr*].*

(*b*) Special detachments of the Armed Forces Intelligence Division, in secret collaboration with the Spaniards, will undertake to secure the Gibraltar area against any attempts by the English to enlarge the area they control or to discover and interfere prematurely with our preparations.

(*c*) Formations detailed for the operation will be concentrated at a considerable distance from the Franco-Spanish frontier and without previous briefing of troops. Three weeks before troops are timed to cross the Spanish-French frontier (and after the conclusion of preparations for the occupation of the Atlantic Islands) a warning order will be issued.

In view of the low capacity of Spanish railways the Army will detail chiefly motorized formations for this operation, so that the railways are available for supplies.

Phase II

(*a*) Units of the Air Force, summoned through observation in the Algeciras area, will set out from French bases and make a well-timed air attack on English naval forces in Gibraltar harbour. After the attack they will land in Spanish airports.

(*b*) Shortly after this attack units detailed for operations in Spain will cross or fly over the Franco-Spanish frontier.

Phase III

(*a*) An attack will be made with German troops to seize Gibraltar.

---

* Admiral Canaris. (See also footnote on p. 190.)

(*b*) Forces will be made ready to invade Portugal should the English gain a footing there. Formations detailed for this purpose will enter Spain immediately behind the forces intended for Gibraltar.

PHASE IV

After the capture of the Rock, the Spaniards will be assisted to close the Straits; if necessary, from Spanish Morocco also.

The *strength* of the formations destined for 'Undertaking Felix' will be as follows:

Army.
Formations detailed for Gibraltar must be strong enough to capture the Rock even without Spanish support.

A smaller force must also be available to support the Spaniards in the improbable event of an attempted English landing on another part of the coast.

Motorized forces will be employed in the main for a possible invasion of Portugal.

Air Force.
The forces detailed for the attack on Gibraltar harbour must be sufficient to ensure a resounding success.

Dive-bomber units, in particular, are to be transferred to Spain to engage naval targets and to support the attack on the Rock.

Army formations will be allotted sufficient anti-aircraft artillery to allow them to engage targets on the ground also.

Navy.
Submarines will be used to engage the English Gibraltar squadron, particularly when it leaves harbour, as is likely after the attack.

To support the Spaniards in closing the Straits, preparations are to be made, in conjunction with the Army, to bring over *single* coastal batteries.

Italian participation in the operation is not expected.

The *Atlantic Islands* (especially the Canaries and Cape Verde Islands) will assume additional naval importance after the operations against Gibraltar, both for the English and for ourselves. Commanders-in-Chief Navy and Air Force are to consider the best means of supporting the defence of the Canaries by the Spaniards and the occupation of the Cape Verde Islands.

I also request that the problem of occupying Madeira and the Azores should be considered, together with the advantages and disadvantages which this would entail for our sea and air warfare. The results of these investigations are to be submitted to me as soon as possible.

3. *Italian Offensive against Egypt.*

The employment of German forces will be considered, if at all, only after the Italians have reached Mersa Matruh. But even then, the use of German air units will only be considered if the Italians will provide the necessary air bases.

The preparations of the Armed Services for operations in this theatre or in any other North African theatre of war will be made on the following basis:

Army: One Armoured Division (composition as already laid down) will stand by for service in North Africa.

Navy: German ships in Italian ports which are suitable as troopships will be converted to carry the largest possible forces either to Libya or to North-west Africa.

Air Force: Plans will be made for attacks on Alexandria and on the Suez Canal to close it to English warships.

4. *The Balkans.*

Commander-in-Chief Army will be prepared, if necessary, to occupy from Bulgaria the *Greek mainland* north of the Aegean Sea. This will enable the German Air Force to attack targets in the Eastern Mediterranean, and in particular those English air bases which threaten the Rumanian oilfields.

In order to be capable of fulfilling all tasks, and to keep Turkey in check, planning and march tables will assume the employment of an Army Group in a strength of about ten divisions. The use of the railway line running through Yugoslavia will not be assumed in planning the movement of these forces. In order to reduce the time required for the movement, the German Military Mission in Rumania will be shortly reinforced to an extent about which I require advice.

In conjunction with the proposed land operations, Commander-in-Chief Air Force will prepare to post air force units to the South-eastern Balkans and to set up an Air Force Signal Service on the southern frontier of Bulgaria.

The German Air Force Mission in Rumania will be reinforced to the extent proposed to me.

Requests by *Bulgaria* for equipment for its army (weapons and ammunition) will be met sympathetically.

5. *Russia.*

Political discussions for the purpose of clarifying Russia's attitude in the immediate future have already begun. Regardless of the outcome of these conversations, all preparations for the East for which verbal orders have already been given will be continued.

Further directives will follow on this subject as soon as the basic operational plan of the Army has been submitted to me and approved.

6. *Landing in England.*

Since changes in the general situation may make it possible, or necessary, to revert to 'Undertaking Sea-Lion' in the spring of 1941, the three branches of the Armed Forces will make every effort to improve in every way the conditions for such an operation.

7. I await *reports from Commanders-in-Chief* on the opera-

tions laid down in this directive. I will then issue orders on the manner of execution and the timing of individual operations.

In the interests of security, special measures are to be taken to limit the number of those working on these plans. This applies particularly to the undertaking in Spain and to the plans relating to the Atlantic Islands.

signed: ADOLF HITLER

19

'Undertaking Felix', the plan to capture Gibraltar and so exclude Britain from the Mediterranean, continued to occupy Hitler's mind in the last months of 1940, in spite of Franco's greed and obstinacy. Plans were drawn up, amplifying Directive No. 18, on 27th November 1940, and there is an undated draft of a further directive, headed 'Directive No. 19: Undertaking Felix', which gives detailed instructions for the operation. According to this directive, the entry of German troops into Spain would take place on 10th January 1941 and the attack on Gibraltar about 4th February. After Gibraltar had been seized, Spanish Morocco would be occupied in order to close the Straits, and an invasion of Portugal was envisaged. Commanders-in-Chief were to report their plans to Hitler on 16th December. However, on 10th December Keitel issued a brief order stating that Operation Felix, as defined in Directive No. 18, would not now be carried out 'as the necessary political situation no longer exists'. All measures planned were to be abandoned and preparations already begun to be halted. The draft of Directive No. 19 was buried, and a new directive, bearing that number, replaced it. The change in the 'political situation' was caused by the obstinate refusal of Franco to accept the German invasion; the new Directive No. 19 was occasioned by the deterioration of German relations with the government of Marshal Pétain in France.

Supreme Commander   Führer Headquarters,
of the Armed Forces   10th December 1940.
                                        12 copies

Directive No. 19*
'Undertaking Attila'

1. In case those parts of the French Colonial Empire now controlled by General Weygand should show signs of revolt, preparations will be made for the rapid *occupation of the still unoccupied territory* of continental France ('Undertaking Attila'). At the same time it will be necessary to lay hands on the *French home fleet* and on those parts of the French Air Force in home bases, or at least to prevent their going over to the enemy.

For military as well as political reasons, preparations for this operation will be camouflaged so as to avoid alarming the French.

2. The *occupation*, if necessary, will be carried out as follows:

(a) Strong motorized forces with adequate air cover will thrust rapidly along the valleys of the Garonne and Rhone to the Mediterranean, will occupy ports as quickly as possible (especially the important Toulon naval base), and will seal off France from the sea.

(b) Formations stationed on the demarcation line will move forward along the whole front.

The time which will elapse between the receipt of orders for the operation and the forward movement of troops will be kept as short as possible. Individual formations and units may be moved up now, so long as the purpose of this movement is not obvious.

Organized resistance by French forces is unlikely. Should resistance be offered locally it will be ruthlessly suppressed. Bomber formations of the Air Force, especially dive-

---

* The number 19 has been added later, by hand.

bombers, will be employed for this purpose and against possible centres of disturbance.

3. In order to take steps to prevent the *sailing of the French fleet* and its going over to the enemy, all possible information will be obtained of the position, state of readiness, possibility of capture, etc., of each ship. Commander-in-Chief Navy will issue the appropriate orders, in collaboration with the Armed Forces Intelligence Division, using the opportunities afforded by the Armistice Commission.

Commanders-in-Chief Navy and Air Force will consider, in conjunction with the occupying forces of the Army, how the French fleet can best be captured. Particular attention will be paid to –

Blocking exits of ports (especially Toulon).
Airborne landings.
Sabotage.
Submarine and air attacks on ships putting to sea.

Commander-in-Chief Navy will decide whether, and if so to what extent, units of the French fleet are to be excluded from the concessions granted to them under the Armistice Agreement.

I reserve to myself the right to decide how this operation will be carried out. *Offensive action* will be authorized only if French Armed Forces offer resistance or parts of the Fleet put to sea in spite of German orders.

4. Measures to seize French *airports* and the aircraft on them will be concerted direct between the Air Force and Army. Other possibilities (e.g. airborne operations) are to be exploited.

5. Commanders-in-Chief will inform me (in writing through the High Command of the Armed Forces) of their plans for 'Undertaking Attila'. In the case of the Army this has already been done. The time needed between the receipt of orders and the beginning of the operation is to be indicated.

6. Preparations for 'Undertaking Attila' must be kept the closest secret.

The Italians will be given no information about our preparations and intentions.

signed: ADOLF HITLER

20

In fact Hitler's thrust against Britain in the Mediterranean in the winter of 1940–1 did not take place in France any more than in Spain. It took place in the eastern end of the sea, where Mussolini's armies were suffering defeat in both Greece and North Africa. On 10th December 1940 Hitler undertook to send German air units to Southern Italy, for a limited period only, to attack British ships passing between Sicily and the North African coast, or even, if 'the critical situation in the Mediterranean' required, in the Ionian or Aegean seas. As Germany was not at war with Greece, no action was to be taken against Greece 'for the time being'. But three days later Directive No. 20 showed that this abstinence was to be very temporary. Britain was assisting the Greeks against Italy, and it was essential to Hitler, if he could not crush the British altogether, at least to deprive them of any foothold in Europe.

Supreme Commander
of the Armed Forces

Führer Headquarters,
13th December 1940.
12 copies

Directive No. 20
'Undertaking Marita'

1. The outcome of the battles in Albania is still uncertain. In the light of the threatening situation in Albania it is doubly important to frustrate English efforts to establish, behind the protection of a Balkan front, an air base which would threaten Italy in the first place and, incidentally, the Rumanian oilfields.

2. My *intention* is therefore –

(*a*) To establish in the coming months a constantly increasing force in Southern Rumania.

(*b*) On the arrival of favourable weather – probably in March – to move this force across Bulgaria to occupy the north coast of the Aegean and, should this be necessary, the entire mainland of Greece ('Undertaking Marita'). We can rely upon Bulgarian support.

3. The *build-up of the forces* in Rumania will be as follows:

(*a*) 16th Panzer Division, which arrives in December, will join the Military Mission, whose duties remain unchanged.

(*b*) Subsequently a force of about seven divisions will be moved to Southern Rumania. Engineer forces *in sufficient strength* to prepare the Danube crossings can be incorporated in the transports of 16th Panzer Division (as 'instruction forces'). Commander-in-Chief Army will apply for my orders for the employment of these troops on the Danube in due course.

(*c*) Preparations should be made to transport reinforcements until the total limit of twenty-four divisions intended for 'Undertaking Marita' has been reached.

(*d*) The Air Force must afford air defence for the concentration and will arrange for the necessary headquarters and supply dumps on Rumanian soil.

4. 'Undertaking Marita' itself will be prepared on the following basis:

(*a*) The first objective of the operation is the occupation of the Aegean coast and the Salonika basin. It may become necessary to pursue the attack via Larissa and the Isthmus of Corinth.

(*b*) The flank of the attack will be protected against Turkey by the Bulgarian Army; but German units will also be held in readiness to strengthen and support it.

(c) It is not yet certain whether Bulgarian formations will play any other role in the attack.

The attitude of Yugoslavia is also not yet clearly foreseeable.

(d) It will be the task of the *Air Force* to give effective support in all phases to the advance of the Army; to eliminate the enemy Air Force; and, as far as possible, to seize English bases in the Greek Islands with airborne troops.

(e) The question how far 'Undertaking Marita' is to be supported by the Italian forces, and how such operations are to be coordinated, is reserved for future decision.

5. The political effect of military preparations, which is especially felt in the Balkans, calls for the most precise regulation of all measures taken by the High Command.

The movement of troops through Hungary and their arrival in Rumania will be notified, *stage by stage*, by the High Command of the Armed Forces and will in the first instance be explained as reinforcements for the Military Mission in Rumania.

Conversations with Rumanians or Bulgarians which might reveal our intentions, as well as notification of the Italians, will depend in each case on my approval, as also will dispatch of reconnaissance parties and advanced headquarters.

6. At the conclusion of 'Undertaking Marita' the forces engaged will be withdrawn for *new employment*.

7. I expect Commanders-in-Chief to report to me on their plans. The Army has already done this. A precise timetable for the operations should be submitted to me, as well as proposals for the recall of men from the armaments industry where necessary (re-establishment of 'Leave Divisions').

signed: ADOLF HITLER

21

All this time, Hitler could not forget his ultimate aim: 'the winning of living-space in the East'. The original operations in Poland had been designed as preliminaries to this major conquest: Hitler would gladly have avoided the war in the West: he wished to be free to attack Russia by 1943 at latest. Once involved in war against the West, he had hoped to finish that war quickly, by decisive conquest, and then turn back to the East. In fact, he had found himself unable to conquer Britain, and while he struggled with this obstinate enemy, the Russians were exploiting his conquests to improve their own position in the East. In these circumstances Hitler felt that he could no longer wait for the final defeat of Britain. Provided Britain were excluded from the Continent, he would turn his back on it and strike, before it was too late, at Russia. Accordingly, on 18th December 1940 he issued his directive for 'Case Barbarossa'.

Führer and Supreme Commander Führer Headquarters,
of the Armed Forces 18th December 1940.
9 copies

Directive No. 21
'Case Barbarossa'

The German Armed Forces must be prepared, even before the conclusion of the war against England, *to crush Soviet Russia in a rapid campaign* ('Case Barbarossa').

The *Army* will have to employ all available formations to this end, with the reservation that occupied territories must be insured against surprise attacks.

The *Air Force* will have to make available for this Eastern campaign supporting forces of such strength that the Army will be able to bring land operations to a speedy conclusion and that Eastern Germany will be as little damaged as possible by enemy air attack. This build-up of a focal point in the East will be limited only by the need to protect from air attack the whole combat and arsenal area which we control, and to ensure that attacks on England, and especially upon her imports, are not allowed to lapse.

The main efforts of the *Navy* will continue to be directed against *England* even during the Eastern campaign.

In certain circumstances I shall issue orders for the *deployment* against Soviet Russia eight weeks before the operation is timed to begin.

Preparations which require more time than this will be put in hand now, in so far as this has not already been done, and will be concluded by 15th May 1941.

It is of decisive importance that our intention to attack should not be known.

The preparations of the High Commands will be made on the following basis:

I. *General Intention*

The bulk of the Russian Army stationed in Western Russia will be destroyed by daring operations led by deeply penetrating armoured spearheads. Russian forces still capable of giving battle will be prevented from withdrawing into the depths of Russia.

The enemy will then be energetically pursued and a line will be reached from which the Russian Air Force can no longer attack German territory. The final objective of the operation is to erect a barrier against Asiatic Russia on the general line Volga–Archangel. The last surviving industrial area of Russia in the Urals can then, if necessary, be eliminated by the Air Force.

In the course of these operations the Russian *Baltic Fleet* will quickly lose its bases and will then no longer be capable of action.

The effective operation of the Russian *Air Force* is to be prevented from the beginning of the attack by powerful blows.

II. *Probable Allies and their Tasks*

1. On the flanks of our operations we can count on the active support of *Rumania* and *Finland* in the war against Soviet Russia.

The High Command of the Armed Forces will decide and lay down in due time the manner in which the forces of these two countries will be brought under German command.

2. It will be the task of *Rumania* to support the attack of the German southern flank, at least at the outset, with its best troops; to hold down the enemy where German forces are not engaged; and to provide auxiliary services in the rear areas.

3. *Finland* will cover the advance of the *Northern Group* of German forces moving from Norway (detachments of Group XXI) and will operate in conjunction with them. Finland will also be responsible for eliminating Hangö.

4. It is possible that *Swedish* railways and roads may be available for the movement of the German Northern Group, by the beginning of the operation at the latest.

III. *Conduct of Operations*

A. *Army* (in accordance with plans submitted to me):

In the theatre of operations, which is divided by the Pripet Marshes into a Southern and a Northern sector, the main weight of attack will be delivered in the *Northern* area. Two Army Groups will be employed here.

The more southerly of these two Army Groups (in the centre of the whole front) will have the task of advancing with powerful armoured and motorized formations from the area about and north of Warsaw, and routing the enemy forces in White Russia. This will make it possible for strong mobile forces to advance northwards and, in conjunction with the Northern Army Group operating out of East Prussia in the general direction of Leningrad, to destroy the enemy forces operating in the Baltic area. Only after the fulfilment of this first essential task, which must include the occupation of Leningrad and Kronstadt, will the attack be continued with the intention of occupying Moscow, an important centre of communications and of the armaments industry.

Only a surprisingly rapid collapse of Russian resistance could justify the simultaneous pursuit of both objectives.

The most important task of Group XXI, even during these Eastern operations, remains the protection of Norway. Any forces available after carrying out this task will be employed in the North (Mountain Corps), at first to protect the Petsamo area and its iron ore mines and the Arctic highway, then to advance with Finnish forces against the Murmansk railway and thus prevent the passage of supplies to Murmansk by land.

The question whether an operation of this kind can be carried out with *stronger* German forces (two or three divisions) from the Rovaniemi area and south of it will depend on the willingness of Sweden to make its railways available for troop transport.

It will be the duty of the main body of the Finnish Army, in conjunction with the advance of the German North flank, to hold down the strongest possible Russian forces by an attack to the West, or on both sides of Lake Ladoga, and to occupy Hangö.

The Army Group operating *South* of the Pripet Marshes will also seek, in a concentric operation with strong forces on either flank, to destroy all Russian forces west of the Dnieper in the Ukraine. The *main attack* will be carried out from the Lublin area in the general direction of Kiev, while forces in Rumania will carry out a wide enclosing movement across the lower Pruth. It will be the task of the Rumanian Army to hold down Russian forces in the intervening area.

When the battles north and south of the Pripet Marshes are ended the pursuit of the enemy will have the following aims:

In the *South* the early capture of the Donets Basin, important for war industry.

In the *North* a quick advance to Moscow. The capture

of this city would represent a decisive political and economic success and would also bring about the capture of the most important railway junctions.

B. *Air Force*

It will be the duty of the Air Force to paralyse and eliminate the effectiveness of the Russian Air Force as far as possible. It will also support the main operations of the Army, i.e. those of the central Army Group and of the vital flank of the Southern Army Group. Russian railways will either be destroyed or, in accordance with operational requirements, captured at their most important points (river crossings) by the bold employment of parachute and airborne troops.

In order that we may concentrate all our strength against the enemy Air Force and for the immediate support of land operations, the Russian armaments industry will not be attacked during the main operations. Such attacks will be made only after the conclusion of mobile warfare, and they will be concentrated first on the Urals area.

C. *Navy.*

It will be the duty of the Navy during the attack on Soviet Russia to protect our own coasts and to prevent the breakout of enemy naval units from the Baltic. As the Russian Baltic fleet will, with the capture of Leningrad, lose its last base and will then be in a hopeless position, major naval action will be avoided until this occurs.

After the elimination of the Russian fleet the duty of the Navy will be to protect the entire maritime traffic in the Baltic and the transport of supplies by sea to the Northern flank (clearing of minefields!).

IV. All steps taken by Commanders-in-Chief on the basis of this directive must be phrased on the unambiguous assumption that they are *precautionary measures* undertaken in case Russia should alter its present attitude towards us. The number of officers employed on preliminary preparations will be kept as small as possible and

T—D

further staffs will be designated as late as possible and
only to the extent required for the duties of each individual. Otherwise there is a danger that premature knowledge of our preparations, whose execution cannot yet be
timed with any certainty, might entail the gravest political
and military disadvantages.

V. I await submission of the plans of Commanders-in-Chief
on the basis of this directive.

The preparations made by all branches of the Armed
Forces, together with time-tables, are to be reported to me
through the High Command of the Armed Forces.

signed: ADOLF HITLER

22

But, before launching the major war on Russia, Hitler had to
complete the exclusion of Britain from Europe. This meant, in
particular, the stopping of the gap opened by Mussolini's unsuccessful adventure in Greece. On 9th January 1941 Hitler
gave orders to discontinue preparations for undertakings
'Felix' and 'Sea-Lion', to keep undertaking 'Attila' on the
agenda – the Services must be ready to make a sudden swoop
on unoccupied France at short notice at any time – but to press
on with undertaking 'Marita'. Three days later he turned his
attention to the whole problem of the threat in the Eastern
Mediterranean, both in the Balkans, where the Italians were
being driven back to Albania by the Greeks, and in Africa,
where they were being driven back into Tripolitania by the
British, with huge losses.

The Führer and Supreme	Führer Headquarters,
Commander of the Armed Forces	11th January 1941.
	13 copies

Directive No. 22
German support for battles in the Mediterranean area
The situation in the Mediterranean area, where England

is employing superior forces against our allies, requires that Germany should assist for reasons of strategy, politics, and psychology.

Tripolitania must be held and the danger of a collapse on the Albanian front must be eliminated. Furthermore the Cavallero* Army Group must be enabled, in cooperation with the later operations of 12th Army, to go over to the offensive from Albania.

I therefore order as follows:

1. Commander-in-Chief Army will provide covering forces sufficient to render valuable service to our allies in the defence of Tripolitania, particularly against British armoured divisions. Special orders for the composition of this force will follow.

Measures will be so timed that this formation can be transported to Libya in conjunction with the movement now in progress of one Italian armoured and one motorized division to Tripoli (from about 20th February).

2. X Air Corps will continue to operate from Sicily. Its chief task will be to attack British naval forces and British sea communications between the Western and Eastern Mediterranean.

In addition, by use of intermediate airfields in Tripolitania conditions will be achieved for immediate support of the Graziani† Army Group by means of attack on British port facilities and bases on the coast of Western Egypt and in Cyrenaica.

The Italian Government will be requested to declare the area between Sicily and the North African coast a closed area, in order to facilitate the task of X Air Corps and to avoid incidents with neutral shipping.

3. German formations in the approximate strength of one

---

* Count Cavallero was Commander of Italian troops in Albania (21 Division) and since December 1940 Chief of the Italian Supreme Command.

† Marshal Graziani was Governor of Libya and Commander-in-Chief of Italian forces in North Africa.

Corps, including 1st Mountain Division and armoured units, will be detailed and made ready to move to Albania. The movement of 1st Mountain Division will begin as soon as the High Command of the Armed Forces has received Italian approval of this. Meanwhile, after discussion with the Italian Command in Albania, it will be decided what further forces in Albania can usefully be employed for an operational attack, and how they and the Italian Divisions would be supplied.

It will be the task of the German forces:

(*a*) To act as immediate stiffening in Albania in case further critical situations should arise.

(*b*) To enable the Italian Army Group to go over to the offensive at a later date with the purpose:

(1) of breaking through Greek defences at a decisive point for extensive operations;

(2) of opening the passes west of Salonika from the rear, thereby supporting a frontal attack by the List Army.*

4. Instructions for the chain of command of German forces engaged in North Africa and Albania and on the limitations which will be applied to the employment of these troops will be laid down by the High Command of the Armed Forces in cooperation with the Italian Armed Forces Staff.

5. German transports available in the Mediterranean and suitable for the purpose will be used, in so far as they are not already on convoy duties to Tripoli, for the passage of forces to Albania. The group of Ju 52 transport aircraft stationed in Foggia will also be employed in moving troops.

Every effort will be made to complete the movement of the main body of German forces to Albania before the movement of the covering force to Libya (see paragraph 1), which will require the bulk of German shipping.

signed: ADOLF HITLER

---

* i.e. the German army advancing from Bulgaria under Field Marshal List.

23

The rescue operations which Hitler planned in Tripoli and Albania were given the code name '*Sonnenblume* (Sunflower)' and '*Alpenveilchen* (Alpine Violet)' respectively. After a meeting with Mussolini on 19th and 20th January 1941 Hitler decided to modify his instructions. 'Undertaking Sunflower' was to be pressed forward: German forces were to be sent to Tripoli in mid-February and to 'go into action wherever British armour is expected or where final resistance must be offered'. This was the beginning of the famous *Afrika Korps*. But in Albania Mussolini was preparing, and wished to launch, his own offensive, and Hitler agreed to hold up 'Undertaking Alpine Violet': only one mountain division, without heavy vehicles, was to stand by for service in Albania if required (in fact, it was not required). Meanwhile, owing to 'possible changes in political conditions' – Mussolini still had hopes of converting Franco – preparedness for 'Undertaking Felix' was still to be maintained 'in so far as this is possible'. On 5th February Hitler issued general instructions on military co-operation with the Italians in these theatres. The German soldiers were to understand that they had been selected 'to render valuable assistance, both psychological and military, to our allies who, in every theatre, are struggling against an enemy greatly superior in numbers, and who, because of the limited productive capacity of Italian war industry, are insufficiently equipped with modern weapons'. While recognizing their own value, the Germans were to be 'free from any offensive arrogance' and to earn the respect of their allies 'solely through their actions, their exemplary discipline, their courage and military prowess.'

Next day Hitler returned to the question of the war against the British economy: a war which must now be carried out with more limited resources, owing to the imminence of 'Undertaking Barbarossa', but was no less important, owing to the British bombing raids which might jeopardize that operation.

Supreme Commander of the Armed Forces

Berlin, 6th February 1941.

10 copies

Directive No. 23

Directions for operations against the English war economy

1. *The effect of our operations against England to date:*

(*a*) Contrary to our former view the heaviest effect of our operations against the English war economy has lain in the high losses in merchant shipping inflicted by sea and air warfare. This effect has been increased by the destruction of port installations, the elimination of large quantities of supplies, and by the diminished use of ships when compelled to sail in convoy.

A further considerable increase is to be expected in the course of this year by the wider employment of submarines, and this can bring about the collapse of English resistance within the foreseeable future.

(*b*) The effect of direct air attacks against the English armaments industry is difficult to estimate. But the destruction of many factories and the consequent disorganization of the armaments industry must lead to a considerable fall in production.

(*c*) The least effect of all (as far as we can see) has been made upon the morale and will to resist of the English people.

2. *Consequences for our own future operations.*

In the *course of the next few months* the effectiveness of our *naval operations* against enemy merchant shipping may be expected to increase thanks to the wider use of submarines and surface ships. On the other hand, we are *unable to maintain the scope of our air attacks*, as the demands of other theatres of war compel us to withdraw increasingly large air forces from operations against the British Isles.

It will therefore be desirable in future to concentrate *air attacks* more closely and to deliver them chiefly against *targets* whose destruction supplements our *naval war*. Only by these means can we expect a decisive end to the war within the foreseeable future.

3. It must therefore be the *aim of our further operations* against the English homeland to concentrate all weapons of air and sea warfare against enemy imports, as well as to hold down the English aircraft industry and, where possible, to inflict still further damage on it.

For this purpose it will be necessary –

(*a*) To destroy the most important English harbours for imports, particularly port installations, and ships lying in them or building.

(*b*) To attack shipping, especially when homeward bound, by all methods.

(*c*) Systematically to destroy the key points of the aircraft industry, including factories producing anti-aircraft equipment and explosives.

These duties must still be carried out by such forces as remain available for operations against England even should a large proportion of the Air Force and a smaller proportion of naval forces be withdrawn in the course of the year for employment in other theatres.

4. For the *execution of these tasks*, it should be noted:

(*a*) The sinking of merchantmen is more important than attack on enemy warships.

The same is true of the use of aerial torpedoes.

By reducing the available enemy tonnage not only will the blockade, which is decisive to the war, be intensified, but enemy operations in Europe or Africa will be impeded.

(*b*) When attacks against ports or aircraft factories have

obviously been successful they will be repeated again
and again.

(c) By continuous laying of minefields the enemy's feel-
ings of uncertainty and losses will be increased.

(d) After attacking the large import-harbours, efforts will
be made, as far as the range of aircraft allows, to prevent the transfer of supplies to smaller ports.

Only when the weather or other conditions prevent attack
on the targets designated in paragraph 3 will attacks be made
on other armaments plants, towns of particular importance
to the war economy, and dumps in the interior of the country, and transport centres.

No decisive success can be expected from terror attacks on
residential areas or from attacks on coastal defences.

5. Until the *beginning of the regrouping* of forces for 'Barbarossa', efforts will be made to intensify the effect of air and
sea warfare, not only in order to inflict the heaviest possible
losses on England, but also in order to give the impression
that an attack on the British Isles is planned for this year.

6. Special orders will be issued for *cooperation between
naval and air forces* in reconnaissance over the sea.

7. Directive No. 9 of 29th November 1939, the amplifica-
tion of Directive No. 9 of 26th May 1940, and Directive No.
17 of 1st August 1940 are no longer valid.

signed: ADOLF HITLER

24

The imminence of 'Undertaking Barbarossa', and the risk of
leaving Britain undefeated in his rear, caused Hitler to take
various steps to strengthen the defences of Western Europe. He
also sought, by enlisting the Japanese, to create for Britain, too,
a two-front war.

High Command   Führer Headquarters,
of the Armed Forces   5th March 1941.
                                14 copies

Directive No. 24
Cooperation with Japan

The Führer has issued the following orders for co-operation with Japan:

1. The *purpose* of the cooperation based on the Three Power Pact must be to *induce Japan to take action in the Far East* as soon as possible. This will tie down strong English forces and will divert the main effort of the United States of America to the Pacific.

In view of the military unpreparedness of her enemies, the sooner Japan strikes, the greater her chances of success. 'Undertaking Barbarossa' establishes particularly promising political and military conditions for this.

2. In *preparing* for such cooperation it is important to strengthen *Japanese fighting power* by every means.

For this purpose Commanders-in-Chief of the branches of the Armed Forces will respond generously and comprehensively to Japanese requests for information about German experience in the war, and for economic and technical assistance. Reciprocity is desirable but should not impede negotiation. In this respect, priority will naturally be given to those Japanese requests which could have an early effect upon the conduct of the war.

The Führer reserves to himself the right to take decisions in special cases.

3. The *coordination of the operational plans of the two countries* will be the task of the Naval High Command.

The following principles will apply:

(*a*) The *common aim* of strategy must be represented as the swift conquest of England in order to keep America out of the war. Apart from this, Germany has no political, military, or economic interests in the Far East which need in any way inhibit Japanese intentions.

(*b*) The great success attained by Germany in *war on*

merchant shipping makes it appear particularly desirable that powerful Japanese forces should be devoted to the same end. Any possibility of support for the German war on merchant shipping is to be exploited.

(c) The position of the *Three Pact Powers* in respect of *raw materials* demands that Japan should secure for itself those territories which it needs for the prosecution of the war, particularly if the United States is engaged. Deliveries of rubber must continue even after Japan's entry into the war, since they are vital for Germany.

(d) The *seizure of Singapore*, England's key position in the Far East, would represent a decisive success in the combined strategy of the three powers.

Attacks on other English bases – on American naval bases only if the USA cannot be prevented from entering the war – are capable of destroying the system of enemy strongpoints in the area and thereby, like attacks on sea communications, of tying down significant forces of all kinds (Australia).

A deadline for the opening of operational discussions cannot yet be laid down.

4. The Military Commissions which will be constituted under the *Three Power Pact* will deal only with those matters which equally affect the three powers. This will apply in the first instance to war *against the enemy economy*.

Details will be arranged by the 'Chief Commission' in cooperation with the High Command of the Armed Forces.

5. No mention whatever of 'Undertaking Barbarossa' will be made to the Japanese.

The Chief of the High Command
of the Armed Forces.

signed in draft: KEITEL

'Undertaking Marita' will begin, with the temporarily limited objective of occupying the Salonika basin and gaining a foothold on the heights of Edessa. For this purpose, XVIII Army Corps can advance through Yugoslav territory.

Favourable opportunities will be seized to prevent the creation of an organized front between Olympus and the Edessa highlands.

(c) All forces still available in Bulgaria and Rumania will be committed to the attacks which will be carried out from the Sofia area to the North-west and from the Kyusten-dil-Gorna Dzhumaya area to the west, with the exception that a force of about one division, with air support, must remain to protect the Rumanian oilfields.

The protection of the Turkish frontier will, for the present, be left to the Bulgarians. A German formation consisting if possible of an armoured division will stand by in the rear in support.

(d) The thrust from the general direction of Graz towards the South-east will be made as soon as the necessary forces have been assembled. The Army is free to decide whether Hungarian territory should be crossed in breaching the frontier.

Security measures at the Yugoslav frontier are to be strengthened immediately.

As on the Bulgarian frontier, important objectives can be occupied even before the general offensive, simultaneously with the air attack on Belgrade.

(e) The Air Force will support with two Groups the operations of 12th Army and of the assault group now being formed in the Graz area, and will time the weight of its attack to coincide with the operations of the Army. The Hungarian ground organization can be used for assembly and in action.

The possibility of bringing X Air Corps into action from Italian bases will be considered. The protection of convoys to Africa must however continue to be ensured.

Preparations for the occupation of the island of Lemnos will be continued. I reserve the right to give orders for this operation.

Care must be taken to ensure adequate anti-aircraft protection for Graz, Klagenfurt, Villach, and Leoben, and also for Vienna.

4. Basic agreement with Italy will be reached, for the time being, by the High Command of the Armed Forces. The Army will detail liaison staffs with Italian 2nd Army and with the Hungarians.

The Air Force is authorized to begin immediate discussions with the Italian and Hungarian High Commands in order to delimit the area of the air operations of the three powers. The build-up of Hungarian ground installations can begin at once.

5. Commanders-in-Chief will inform me, through the High Command of the Armed Forces, of their plans for the operation, and of related problems.

signed: ADOLF HITLER

26

The operation orders for the *Blitzkrieg* against Yugoslavia were drafted in great haste, and 'Undertaking Marita' had to be modified to meet the new circumstances. Pressure was applied to Hungary to allow the passage of German troops and to take part itself in the invasion. On 2nd April the Hungarian Prime Minister, Count Teleki, shot himself rather than agree; but the Hungarian Chief of General Staff had already acceded to the German demand. Rumanian and Bulgarian participation was easily secured. Next day, in Directive No. 26, Hitler issued his plan of campaign.

The Führer and Supreme
Commander of the Armed Forces

Führer Headquarters,
3rd April 1941.
15 copies

Directive No. 26
Cooperation with our allies in the Balkans

1. The military tasks allotted to *countries in South-east Europe* in the campaign against Yugoslavia are based on the following political considerations:

Hungary, which will receive the Banat, will occupy this territory for preference, but has declared herself ready to take part in further operations for the destruction of the enemy.

Bulgaria will get back Macedonia and will therefore be chiefly interested in an attack in this direction, although no particular pressure will be exerted by Germany. The Bulgarians will also be responsible, with the support of a German armoured formation, for rear protection against Turkey. For this purpose Bulgaria will also employ the three divisions at present standing on her Greek frontier.

Rumania will limit her efforts, in her own interest as well as in that of Germany, to guarding the frontiers with Yugoslavia and Russia. The Head of the German Armed Forces Mission will take steps to ensure that Rumanian defensive precautions against Russia are increased [and that if possible the Rumanian forces in the Temesvar area (one infantry division and cavalry brigade) are moved further eastwards in order not to disturb contact between Hungarian 2nd Army and German XLI Army Corps].* At least the passage of

---

* The passage between square brackets was deleted by a subsequent order on 5th April.

Hungarian and German liaison units across the frontier between Rumania and Hungary must be allowed to proceed unhindered.

2. *Military cooperation* and chain of command in the forthcoming operation will be governed as follows:

The coordinated command of this campaign, in so far as the operational aims of the Italian and Hungarian forces within the framework of the whole operation are concerned, is reserved to me. It must be exercised in a manner which takes account of the sensibilities of our allies and enables the Heads of State of Italy and Hungary to appear to their peoples and to their armed forces as sovereign military leaders.

I shall therefore convey such military demands for the coordination of operations as are made to me by Commander-in-Chief Army and Commander-in-Chief Air Force, to the Duce and to Regent Horthy in the form of personal letters, as proposals and wishes.

The same attitude will be adopted by Commander-in-Chief 12th Army towards the Bulgarian civil and military authorities.

If individual Bulgarian divisions take part in operations against Yugoslavia they must come under command of the local German commanders.

3. A headquarters of 'The German General with the High Command of the Hungarian Forces' will be established in Hungary and its staff will include Air Force liaison staff.

This mission will ensure liaison between myself and the Regent and between the branches of the German Armed Forces and the Hungarian High Command.

All details of collaboration with Italian and Hungarian forces will be arranged by the branches of the Armed Forces concerned and by the liaison staffs to be set up between adjoining Armies and Air Fleets.

4. The *Air Defence Forces* of Rumania and Bulgaria will be incorporated in the German air defences of those

countries in so far as they are not employed in the operational areas of their own armies. Hungary will be independently responsible for the defence of its own territory on the understanding, of course, that the security of the German formations operating there, and the positions important to them, are secured by German forces.

5. Apart from the new agreement regarding coordinated command, our other understandings with Hungary remain in force. The Italian 2nd Army will only be free to move when the attack by the German 2nd Army and the mobile forces of XLVI Army Corps begins to be effective. It may be necessary that this attack be first directed in a southerly rather than south-easterly direction. The High Command of the Armed Forces will ensure that the Italian Air Force confine itself to the protection of the flanks and rear of the Albanian front, to the attack upon the Mostar airfield and on coastal airfields, and to cooperation on the front of the Italian 2nd Army as soon as that Army begins its attack.

6. I shall later lay down the *occupation duties* of the various countries after the campaign. From the beginning of operations collaboration with our allies will be so conducted as to emphasize our brotherhood of arms for the achievement of political aims common to all.

signed: ADOLF HITLER

27

On 6th April 1941 the attack on Yugoslavia began with a three-day aerial bombardment of the undefended city of Belgrade. At the same time the German forces invaded Greece, into which British troops had been arriving from Egypt. On 13th April Belgrade was occupied, and the German 12th Army, advancing from Bulgaria, had entered Macedonia and divided Yugoslavia from Greece.

On the same day Hitler issued Directive No. 27.

The Führer and Supreme   Führer Headquarters,
Commander of the Armed Forces   4th April 1941.
                                         17 copies

Directive No. 27

1. The Yugoslav forces are in process of disintegration. This, with the elimination of the Greek Army in Thrace, and the occupation of the Salonika Basin and of the area around Florina, creates conditions which, after sufficient forces have been concentrated, will permit an *attack on Greece* with the aim of annihilating the Anglo-Greek forces there, occupying Greece, and thus finally driving the British from the Balkans.

2. I therefore give the following orders for the prosecution of operations in the Balkans:

(a) *Yugoslavia*
The aim of the operation is to destroy the remaining Yugoslav forces and to clean up and occupy the country.

Formations of the German Army will be employed to occupy Old Serbia and the Banat. The protective area between the Morava and Danube, with its valuable copper mines, will be secured as swiftly as possible. The use for these purposes of formations not hitherto employed in Yugoslavia will be limited to the smallest possible extent.

The *Air Force* is to destroy what remains of the Yugoslav Air Force and will support ground operations so that any serious resistance which may still be encountered will be quickly overcome. If circumstances allow, air and anti-aircraft units not required for action in Greece may, with the agreement of the High Command of the Armed Forces, be withdrawn for employment elsewhere.

Any arrangements with the Italian Air Force which may be necessary as a result of the boundary between

2nd German Army and 2nd Italian Army are the responsibility of Commander-in-Chief Air Force.

The *Italian 2nd Army* is to clean up and occupy the area south-west of the road Karlovac–Bos Novi–Banja Luka–Sarajevo. It may, on occasion, be necessary for German mobile forces to thrust forward across this line in support of the Italian advance.

The *Hungarian 3rd Army* will clean up and occupy Yugoslav territory west of the Tisza as far as the Danube and the Drave. The participation of the two Hungarian motorized brigades in the further operations of the German 2nd Army has been requested and granted.

(b) Greece

As soon as adequate forces have been concentrated in the area of Florina and the Salonika Basin, the *decisive attack against Anglo-Greek forces in northern Greece* will be launched. The object of this operation will be, by a quick breakthrough in the direction of Larissa, to encircle and annihilate the enemy forces there, and to prevent the establishment of a new defensive front.

At the same time the *Italian* breakthrough on the Greek front in Albania will be supported by a thrust in a south-westerly direction.

Operations will continue with a quick advance of *mobile forces thrusting towards Athens* with the aim of occupying the rest of the Greek mainland including the Peloponnese. At the same time the Italian Army Group in Albania will advance west of the line from Lake Prespansko to the crest of the Pindus Mountains in the direction of the Gulf of Patras. If time and the state of the roads permit, any opportunity of blocking a withdrawal of the main Greek forces west of the Pindus must be exploited.

It will be the duty of the *Air Force*, apart from engaging the Greek and British Air Forces, to support the new ground operations in all possible strength and to carry the German troops constantly forward. Later operations aimed at the occupation of the Cyclades will also be supported.

Operational boundaries between the German and Italian Air Forces will be arranged through Commander-in-Chief Air Force.

The Army and Air Force will employ all means available to prevent a *possible evacuation of the British forces*. In particular an evacuation across the Mediterranean will be prevented, as far as possible, by constant air attack on Greek ports and particularly on concentrations of shipping, as also by mining approaches to ports.

3. Orders to carry out the proposed *parachute operation against Lemnos and to occupy Thasos and Samothrace* will be issued by me alone. They will be issued at the latest forty-eight hours before the beginning of operations.

For this purpose the *Army* will leave one division in Thrace, while the occupation of the rest of Thrace will be undertaken by the *Bulgarians* at a time which I shall determine.

4. *After the conclusion of operations* most of the *Army formations* engaged will be withdrawn *for new tasks*. It is planned to leave

> one or two divisions in Greece,
> one further division in Salonika,
> two to three divisions in Serbia.

For the *Air Force* (X Air Corps) the chief task at the conclusion of the operation will be to support the Africa Corps. In the immediate future the laying of mines in the Suez Canal is of great importance in order to prevent, or at least to impede, the arrival of enemy reinforcements from East Africa.

Arrangements will be made for the *air defence* of conquered territory.

Coastal defence will, for the present, be organized on the assumption that the north coast of the Aegean, including Salonika, will be taken over by the Bulgarians, the east coast of the Aegean, from there to the Gulf of Saros inclusive, will be taken over by us, and the remainder of the Greek coast will be in Italian hands.

Boundaries can only be finally laid down after the end of operations in the Balkans.

5. I expect Commanders-in-Chief to submit detailed reports of their *plans*.

Any *requests by branches of the Armed Forces* to our allies will be made in accordance with the principles laid down in Directive 26 of 3rd April 1941.

signed: ADOLF HITLER

28

On the 17th April Yugoslavia capitulated to the German Army. The whole force of the German armies now fell on Greece. On 20th April the Greek armies on the Albanian front surrendered. With their left flank exposed, the British had to retreat from their position at Thermopylae. On 24th April the Greek Government surrendered and the British evacuation of Greece began. The British still held the island of Crete with its important harbour of Suda Bay; but Hitler was determined to secure this essential forward base for the protection of the Balkans and for attack on Egypt (Directive 28). After that, he would be prepared to leave the task of occupying Greece largely to the Italians, who were still unaware of his plans for a far greater campaign in the East (Directive 29).

The Führer and Supreme　　　　Führer Headquarters,
Commander of the Armed Forces　　25th April 1941.
　　　　　　　　　　　　　　　　　10 copies

Directive No. 28
'*Undertaking Mercury [Merkur]*'

1. As a base for air warfare against Great Britain in the

Eastern Mediterranean we must prepare to *occupy the island of Crete* ('Undertaking Mercury'). For the purpose of planning, it will be assumed that the whole Greek mainland including the Peloponnese is in the hands of the Axis Powers.

2. *Command* of this operation is entrusted to *Commander-in-Chief Air Force* who will employ for the purpose, primarily, the airborne forces and the air forces stationed in the Mediterranean area.

The *Army*, in cooperation with Commander-in-Chief Air Force, will make available in Greece suitable reinforcements for the airborne troops, including a mixed armoured detachment, which can be moved to Crete by sea.

The *Navy* will take steps to ensure sea communications, which must be secured as soon as the occupation of the island begins. For protection of these communications and, as far as is necessary, for the provision of troopships, Commander-in-Chief Navy will make the necessary arrangements with the Italian Navy.

3. All means will be employed to move the airborne troops and 22nd Division, which is under the command of Commander-in-Chief Air Force, to the assembly area which he will designate. The necessary space for freight lorries will be put at the disposal of the Chief of Armed Forces Transport by the High Commands of the Army and Air Force. These *transport movements* must not entail any delay in the mounting of 'Undertaking Barbarossa'.

4. For *anti-aircraft protection* in Greece and Crete, Commander-in-Chief Air Force may bring up anti-aircraft units of 12th Army. Commander-in-Chief Air Force and Commander-in-Chief Army will make the necessary arrangements for their relief and replacement.

5. *After the occupation of the island*, all or part of the airborne forces must be made ready for new tasks. Arrangements will therefore be made for their replacement by Army units.

In preparing coastal defences Commander-in-Chief Navy

may if necessary draw upon guns captured by the Army.

6. I request Commanders-in-Chief to inform me of their plans and Commander-in-Chief Air Force to inform me when his preparations will be completed. The order for the execution of the operation will be given by me only.

signed: ADOLF HITLER

29

The Führer and Supreme
Commander of the Armed Forces

Führer Headquarters,
17th May 1941.
25 copies

Directive No. 29

1. *The aim of German operations* in the south-east, which was to drive the English from the Balkans and to widen the base for German air operations in the Eastern Mediterranean, has been achieved and will be further improved by completion of 'Undertaking Mercury'.

The *defence of Greek territory* will in future, with the exceptions mentioned below, be an Italian responsibility. Therefore German authorities must not intervene in general matters relating to the defence and administration of the country. They will, in particular, refuse any Greek requests for mediation.

For the *delivery of supplies*, an agreement is to be made with the Italian Armed Forces concerning supply routes and their protection.

2. The following apply to the *German Armed Forces:*

Army:

The only forces remaining in Greece will be those which are indispensable for the supply of 'Undertaking Mercury' (and which will be closely concentrated locally) and one division in Salonika (see paragraph 3) which will also be responsible for the security of Lemnos and for any other islands which may need to be occupied.

However, until the conclusion of 'Undertaking Mercury' areas required as jumping-off points for German troops, including the islands designated for this purpose, must remain in German hands. All forces not required according to these instructions will be withdrawn as soon as possible.

The Italian High Command will be notified that arrangements for a quick hand-over in Greece are to be made with *Commander-in-Chief 12th Army*. The latter will then transfer his headquarters to Salonika as *'Commander-in-Chief of German troops in the Balkans'* as soon as the situation ('Undertaking Mercury') allows.

Air Force:

X Air Corps, even after moving into Greece, will prosecute the war in the air independently under orders from Commander-in-Chief Air Force to whom it is directly subordinate. For the defence of the Balkan area it will cooperate with Commander-in-Chief 12th Army (Commander of German Troops in the Balkans) and for the war in North Africa with the Africa Corps. Orders concerning territorial matters which need coordinated ruling for the Balkan area will be given by Commander-in-Chief 12th Army to X Army Corps also.

Ground organizations in Greece and the islands will be at the disposal of Commander-in-Chief Air Force for the prosecution of the air war in the Eastern Mediterranean. Airfields and installations which are not required will be handed over to the Italian forces.

After the occupation of Crete the defence of the island will be the responsibility of Commander-in-Chief Air Force (Airborne Corps) who will decide upon the moment at which these forces can be relieved. I reserve to myself the right to issue orders in this respect and for the future occupation of the island.

Navy:

Apart from Salonika, the *port* of Athens and the coastal

strip between the two ports, in so far as this is necessary for traffic along the coast, will remain in the hands of the German Navy. Commander-in-Chief Navy will make the necessary arrangements for this with the Italians. The defence of the coast of Crete will also be the responsibility. of the Navy, if the island continues to be occupied by German troops.

In territorial questions the same rules apply as to X Air Corps.

On the North Aegean coast the Bulgarian coastal defences must continue to be under firm German influence.

Admiral South-east will be responsible for operations and the movement of shipping in the Aegean, under orders from Commander-in-Chief Navy, and employing the Italian naval forces placed at his disposal.

In other matters, Admiral South-east will cooperate with the Italian authorities as required.

3. For all military measures in the *Salonika area* the German Armed Forces have sole responsibility. The exact delimitation of this area will be a matter for proposals from the High Command of the Army (Commander-in-Chief of German troops in the Balkans).

4. The *administration* of Greek territory occupied by German troops will be carried out by the High Command of the Army in agreement with the Plenipotentiary of the German Reich in Greece. As far as possible use will be made of the Greek administration and German military authorities will refrain from interference.

5. In order that he may carry out the urgent economic duties assigned to him, the '*Military Commander Serbia*' will be provided by the High Command of the Army with all necessary facilities and with the troops which he requires for security purposes, so that he may accomplish his task independently.

6. I expect to be informed by Commanders-in-Chief

about the measures which they propose to take on the basis
of this directive and on agreements reached with the
Italians.

signed: ADOLF HITLER

30

'Undertaking Mercury' was launched on 20th May 1941, and
after six days of fierce fighting Crete fell into German hands.
While the battle was still raging, Hitler turned his attention to
the Middle East where a new opportunity had arisen. In
March 1941 there had been a palace revolution in Iraq, and
the pro-British Regent had been driven out by Rashid Ali,
who relied on German help and soon showed his hand by
attacking the British Air Force establishment at Habbaniya.
This attack was repulsed early in May, and Rashid Ali then
openly appealed to Germany. German aircraft arrived at Mosul
on 13th May. Meanwhile a British relief force was sent from
Palestine and arrived at Habbaniya on 18th May. By 23rd
May it had crossed the Euphrates and was preparing to advance on Baghdad. In these circumstances Hitler issued his
Directive No. 30.

The Führer and Supreme   Führer Headquarters,
Commander of the Armed Forces   23rd May 1941.
                                              22 copies

Directive No. 30
Middle East

1. The *Arab Freedom Movement* is our natural ally against
England in the Middle East. In this connexion the rising in
Iraq is particularly important. It strengthens the forces
hostile to England beyond the Iraqi frontier, disturbs
English communications, and ties up English troops and
shipping at the expense of other theatres of war.

I have therefore decided to hasten developments in the Middle East by supporting Iraq.

Whether, and if so how, it may be possible, in conjunction with an offensive against the Suez Canal, finally to break the British position between the Mediterranean and the Persian Gulf is a question which will be decided only after 'Barbarossa'.

2. Summarizing my detailed decisions I order that, for the *support of Iraq* –

> A Military Mission is to be dispatched.
> The Air Force is to afford support.
> Arms are to be delivered.

3. The *Military Mission* (cover name – 'Special Staff F') will be under the command of Air Marshal Felmy.
Its *duties* are:

(*a*) To advise and support the Iraqi forces.
(*b*) Where possible, to establish military contacts with forces hostile to England outside Iraq.
(*c*) To obtain experience and intelligence in this area for the German forces.

The *composition* of this organization will be regulated, in accordance with these duties, by the Chief of the High Command of the Armed Forces.
Chain of command will be as follows:

(*a*) All Armed Forces personnel sent to Iraq, including the liaison staff in Syria, will be under the command of the Head of the Military Mission.
(*b*) The Head of the Military Mission will be subordinate to the Chief of the High Command of the Armed Forces, with the limitation that orders to the Air Force will be issued exclusively by Commander-in-Chief Air Force.
(*c*) The Head of the Military Mission will deal only with the Iraqi military authorities. Negotiations with the

government of Iraq in matters affecting the Mission will be conducted by the representative of the Foreign Office in Iraq.

Where military matters with political implications are concerned the Head of the Military Mission will obtain the prior agreement of the Foreign Office representative.

(d) Members of the Military Mission are, for the time being, to be regarded as *volunteers* (as in the case of the Condor Legion).* They will wear tropical uniform with Iraqi badges. Iraqi markings will also be carried by German aircraft.

4. *Air Force.* The employment of the Air Force in limited numbers is intended, apart from its direct effects, to increase the self-confidence and fighting spirit of the Iraqi armed forces and people.

The form and extent of German intervention will be decided by Commander-in-Chief Air Force.

5. *Supply of Arms.* The Chief of the High Command of the Armed Forces will issue the necessary orders in this respect. (Deliveries to be made from Syria, in accordance with the agreement reached with the French in this matter, and from Germany.)

6. The *direction of propaganda* in the Middle East is the responsibility of the Foreign Office, which will cooperate with the High Command of the Armed Forces, Operations Staff, Propaganda Section.

The basic idea of our propaganda is as follows:

'The victory of the Axis will free the countries of the Middle East from the English yoke, and will give them the right to self-determination. All who love freedom will therefore join in the fight against England.'

---

* The Condor Legion was the German Air Force unit which took part, ostensibly as 'volunteers', in the Spanish Civil War.

No propaganda will be carried out against the French in *Syria*.

7. Should *members of the Italian Armed Forces* be employed on duties in Iraq, German personnel will cooperate with them on the lines laid down in this directive. Efforts will be made to ensure that they come under the command of the Head of the German Military Mission.

signed: ADOLF HITLER

31

Hitler's attempt to intervene in Iraq was a failure. On 30th May British forces reached Baghdad and Rashid Ali fled abroad. The Regent was restored and the British position in Iraq was strengthened. But meanwhile, with the capture of Crete, Hitler had established German control over the whole Balkan area. Directive No. 31 lays down the form of that control.

The Führer and Supreme   Führer Headquarters,
Commander of the Armed Forces   9th June 1941.
                                        20 copies

Directive No. 31

In order to establish a clear and unified system of command in the occupied areas of the Balkans I issue the following orders:

1. As '*Commander Armed Forces South-east*', with headquarters in Salonika, I appoint Field Marshal *List*.

Commander Armed Forces South-east is the highest representative of the Armed Forces in the Balkans and has full powers in all areas occupied by German forces.

Commander Armed Forces South-east is, as such, directly subordinate to me.

2. The following are *under the command* of the Commander Armed Forces South-east:

(*a*) Old Serbia area:
   '*Commanding General Serbia*' (General of Anti-Aircraft Artillery von Schröder).
(*b*) Salonika area and the islands of Lemnos, Mitylene, Chios, and Skyros:
   '*Commanding General Salonika–Aegean*' (appointment to be filled by the High Command of the Army).
(*c*) Athens, Crete, Cythera, Anticythera, and Melos areas:
   '*Commanding General Southern Greece*' (appointment to be filled by Commander-in-Chief Air Force).

3. The Commander Armed Forces South-east will exercise central control over military problems (apart from offensive air operations) arising from the occupation, security, supply, transport, and intelligence of all three branches of the Armed Forces in the occupied South-east area. He will decide them within the framework of the general task to be performed by our forces in the South-east. This will ensure a simpler system of command, and will relieve the High Command of the Armed Forces and the various branches of the Armed Forces from dealing with matters of detail and differences of opinion which are bound to arise between the staffs of the various Armed Forces working in the same area.

In particular Commander Armed Forces South-east will be responsible for:

(*a*) Ensuring the coordinated defence against enemy attack or civil disturbance of those parts of Serbia and Greece, including the Greek Islands, which are occupied by German troops.

   Apart from the above-mentioned commanders, who are responsible for the defence of their respective territories in accordance with his general instructions,

Admiral South-east and *Air Force Commander Balkans* are also subordinate to him. The staffs of both these officers will be incorporated in the staff of Commander Armed Forces South-east. He himself will decide to what extent the staffs of his subordinate commanders in the Salonika–Aegean area and in Southern Greece are to be incorporated in the staffs of other branches of the Armed Forces.

(b) Ensuring the unified command and protection of the extensive movements of sea-transport to and from Crete which will be necessary in the near future.

(c) Control of *cooperation with the Italian and, as far as necessary, with the Bulgarian forces* in the Balkans.

(d) *Arranging supplies* by land and sea to all forces stationed in the Balkans, in accordance with their requirements and with the transport available at any given time.

(e) Supervising the *military administration* of the commanders in all areas occupied by German troops.

4. The Commander Armed Forces South-east has all the *powers of a territorial commander* in those parts of Serbia and Greece occupied by German forces, including the Greek islands.

The areas exclusively occupied by *German* forces will be *operational areas*. Here Commander Armed Forces South-east will exercise full powers through his subordinate commanders.

Where German troops are stationed in territories occupied by the *Italians*, he will exercise military command over all branches of the Armed Forces in so far as the military duties of the German forces require.

5. For delimitation of the powers of Commander Armed Forces South-east in relation to those of the *Plenipotentiary of the Reich in Greece* see Appendix.*

---

* This appendix, signed by Keitel, is not here printed.

6. The *island of Crete* occupies a special position in the South-east area.

It is an operational area from which the air war in the Eastern Mediterranean is to be prosecuted in conjunction with operations in North Africa (see paragraph 7).

The organization and establishment of this base, its supply and protection, is at the moment the most urgent task confronting us in the south-east.

As a base of operations for the Air Force, Crete will be placed as a fortress under the command of a special Air Force Commander as Commandant. He will exercise executive powers in accordance with general instructions of Commander Armed Forces South-east as a deputy of Commanding General Southern Greece. He is responsible for the coordinated defence of the island with all forces stationed there and placed under his command for this purpose. He will also command the Army establishments necessary for Administration.

The *Italian area of occupation* is the eastern part of the island, up to a general line from the western edge of Merambelo Bay to the town of Hierapetra inclusive. In all tactical matters relating to the coordinated defence of the island, the Italians will be subordinate to the Commandant of the island.

7. The *air war* in the Eastern Mediterranean will be conducted according to the orders of Commander-in-Chief Air Force.

The necessary arrangements will be made by him direct with the Italian Air Force.

8. The transport of troops and the movement of supplies by sea and their protection by sea and air will be controlled by Commander Armed Forces South-east through Admiral South-east, in cooperation with the Italian Navy and X Air Corps.

Cooperation between Admiral South-east and the Rumanian and Bulgarian Navies, should they appear in the Eastern Mediterranean, will be regulated by Commander-in-Chief Navy direct with Admiral South-east.

9. *Directive 29* of 17th May 1941 is cancelled, in so far as
it is superseded by the above orders.

signed: ADOLF HITLER

32

With the Balkans securely held, the Continent seemed immune
against British intervention and 'Undertaking Barbarossa'
could be launched. The original directive, No. 21 of 18th
December 1940, had envisaged an attack on or soon after
15th May 1941, and had indicated that orders for deployment
would be issued eight weeks earlier – i.e. in mid-March. In
fact, on 13th March a 'supplement to directive 21' was issued,
over the signature of Keitel, laying down rules for the administration of occupied Russia, and outlining the 'special tasks'
assigned to the Reichsfuhrer SS – i.e. Himmler. These tasks, it
was stated, were entirely outside the jurisdiction of the Armed
Forces: they were 'determined by the necessity to settle the
conflict between two opposite political systems' and to lay the
basis for a political administration. A fortnight later the sudden
revolt in Yugoslavia had convulsed the Balkans and Hitler's
time-table. But the preparations continued. On 1st May, after
the military collapse of Yugoslavia and Greece, Hitler decided
to summon representatives of Finland, Hungary, and Rumania
and explain the massive build-up of forces on the Eastern
front, in which they too were to play a part. They were to be
told – but as late as possible – that 'the major offensive which
we plan in the West entails the establishment and maintenance
of a higher state of preparedness in the East'.

By 11th June Hitler was already looking ahead, beyond the
expected lightning victory in Russia. On that date Directive
No. 32 was drafted. The draft, which is unsigned, was sent to
the Commanders-in-Chief of the three Services as a provisional basis for work on 19th June. Three days later the
German armies advanced into Russia. On 30th June amendments to para B. 2 (a) and (b) were issued. The amendments

T—E

are not significant. The form printed below incorporates the final amendments.

The Führer and Supreme   Führer Headquarters,
Commander of the Armed Forces   11th June 1941.
                                            9 draft copies

Directive No. 32
Preparations for the period after 'Barbarossa'

A. *After the destruction of the Soviet Armed Forces*, Germany and Italy will be military masters of the European Continent – with the temporary exception of the Iberian Peninsula.* No serious threat to Europe by land will then remain. The defence of this area, and foreseeable future offensive action, will require considerably smaller military forces than have been needed hitherto.

The main efforts of the armaments industry can be diverted to the Navy and Air Force.

Closer cooperation between Germany and France should and will tie down additional English forces, will eliminate the threat from the rear in the North African theatre of war, will further restrict the movements of the British Fleet in the Western Mediterranean and will protect the south-western flank of the European theatre, including the Atlantic seaboard of North and West Africa, from Anglo-Saxon attack.

In the near future Spain will have to face the question

---

* As will be seen (paragraph 3 below), 'Undertaking Felix' was still being contemplated. But Hitler was not now relying solely on the cooperation of General Franco. On 9th May 1941, as part of the programme of securing the West of Europe during 'Undertaking Barbarossa', the High Command of the Armed Forces had prepared a plan for the seizure of the Atlantic coast of Spain and Portugal. This operation was known as 'Isabella'. Fresh orders concerning 'Undertaking Isabella' were issued on 20th June 1941, two days before the launching of 'Undertaking Barbarossa'.

whether she is prepared to cooperate in driving the British from Gibraltar or not.

The possibility of exerting strong pressure on Turkey and Iran improves the prospect of making direct or indirect use of these countries in the struggle against England.

B. This situation, which will be created by the victorious conclusion of the campaign in the East, can confront the Armed Forces with the following strategic tasks for the late autumn of 1941 and the winter of 1941–2:

1. The *newly conquered territories in the East* must be organized, made secure and, in full cooperation with the Armed Forces, exploited economically.

The strength of the security forces required in Russia can only be forecast with certainty at a later date. In all probability, however, about sixty divisions and one Air Fleet will be sufficient, with allied and friendly forces, for our further duties in the East.

2. The *struggle against the British positions in the Mediterranean and in Western Asia* will be continued by converging attacks launched from Libya through Egypt, from Bulgaria through Turkey, and in certain circumstances also from Transcaucasia through Iran.

(*a*) In *North Africa* it is important that Tobruk should be eliminated and conditions thereby established for the continuation of the German–Italian attack on the Suez Canal. This attack should be planned for about November on the understanding that the German Africa Corps will be by then brought to the highest possible efficiency in personnel and equipment and with adequate reserves of all kinds under its own hand (by the conversion of 5th Light Division into a full armoured division), so that it is not necessary to move further large German formations to North Africa.

The preparations for the attack require that the tempo of transport be quickened by all means available, including the employment of ports in French North Africa and, when possible, the new sea route from Southern Greece.

It will be the duty of the Navy, in cooperation with the Italian Navy, to arrange for the necessary tonnage by chartering French and neutral shipping.

The possibility of moving German motor torpedo boats to the Mediterranean will be examined.

The Italian Navy will be afforded all support in improving unloading facilities in North African ports.

Commander-in-Chief Air Force will transfer to the Africa Corps sufficient air units and anti-aircraft artillery for the operation, as these become superfluous in the East. He will also reinforce Italian protection of seaborne convoys by the use of German air formations.

In order to coordinate the handling of transport, the Supply and Transport Office of the Armed Forces Overseas [*Heimatstab Ubersee*] has been established, which will work on the lines laid down by the High Command of the Armed Forces, in cooperation with the German General at Italian Armed Forces Headquarters, and with Commander Armed Forces South-east.

(b) In view of the expected British reinforcement of the Near and Middle East, especially for the defence of the Suez Canal, a German operation *from Bulgaria through Turkey* will be planned, with the aim of attacking the British position on the Suez Canal from the East also.

To this end plans must be made to assemble in Bulgaria as soon as possible sufficient forces to render Turkey politically amenable or to overpower her resistance.

(c) If the collapse of the Soviet Union has created the necessary conditions, preparations will be made for the dispatch of a motorized expeditionary force *from*

Transcaucasia against Iraq, in conjunction with operations mentioned in paragraph (*b*) above.

(*d*) Exploitation of the Arab Freedom Movement. The situation of the English in the Middle East will be rendered more precarious, in the event of major German operations, if more British forces are tied down *at the right moment* by civil commotion or revolt. All military, political, and propaganda measures to this end must be closely coordinated during the preparatory period. As central agency abroad I nominate *Special Staff F*, which is to take part in all plans and actions in the Arab area, whose headquarters are to be in the area of the Commander Armed Forces Southeast. The most competent available experts and agents will be made available to it.

The Chief of the High Command of the Armed Forces will specify the duties of Special Staff F, in agreement with the Foreign Minister where political questions are involved.*

3. *Closing of the Western Entrance to the Mediterranean by the elimination of Gibraltar:*

Preparations for 'Undertaking Felix', already planned, will be resumed to the fullest extent even during the course of operations in the east. It may be assumed that unoccupied French territory may also be used, if not for German troop movements, then at least for the movement of supplies. The cooperation of French naval and air forces is also within the bounds of possibility.

After the capture of Gibraltar only such forces will be moved to Spanish Morocco as are necessary to protect the Straits.

The defence of the seaboard of North and West Africa,

---

* For *Sonderstab F*, under Air Force General Felmy, see Directive No. 30 above. On the failure of Rashid Ali's revolt, Felmy had returned to Germany. His 'Special Staff' was reconstituted by a separate order dated 21st June 1941.

the elimination of English possessions in West Africa, and the recovery of the areas controlled by de Gaulle, will be the tasks of the French who will be granted such reinforcements as the situation requires. The use of West African bases by the Navy and Air Force, and possibly also the occupation of the Atlantic Islands, will be facilitated by our control of the Straits.

4. In addition to these contemplated operations against the British position in the Mediterranean, the 'Siege of England' must be resumed with the utmost intensity by the Navy and Air Force after the conclusion of the campaign in the East.

All weapons and equipment required for this purpose will be given priority in the general armaments programme. At the same time German Air Defences will be strengthened to the maximum. Preparations for the invasion of England will serve the double purpose of tying down English forces at home and of bringing about a final English collapse through a landing in England.

C. The time at which the operations planned in the Mediterranean and the Near East can be undertaken cannot yet be foreseen. The strongest operational effect would be achieved by a simultaneous attack on Gibraltar, Egypt, and Palestine.

Whether this will, in fact, be possible depends upon a number of factors which cannot, at the moment, be foreseen, but chiefly on the power of the Air Force to provide the forces necessary for the simultaneous support of these three operations.

D. I request Commanders-in-Chief to begin the planning and organization of these operations as outlined above and to keep me informed of the results so that I may issue final directives before the campaign in the East is over.

signed: WARLIMONT

32a

The German attack on Russia, thanks to its suddenness, was immediately successful, and Hitler was confident of a quick, total victory. On 14th July 1941 he issued a supplement to Directive No. 32 which looked forward to a substantial reduction in both Army and Navy.

The Führer and Supreme
Commander of the Armed Forces

Führer Headquarters,
14th July 1941.
13 copies

On the basis of my intentions for the future prosecution of the war, as stated in Directive 32, I issue the following general instructions concerning personnel and equipment:

1. *General:*

Our military mastery of the European continent after the overthrow of Russia will make it possible considerably to reduce the strength of the *Army*. Within the limits of this reduced Army, the relative strength of the armoured forces will be greatly increased.

The manning and equipment of the *Navy* will be limited to what is essential for the direct prosecution of the war against England and, should the occasion arise, against America.

The *main effort of equipment* will be devoted to the *Air Force*, which will be greatly strengthened.

2. *Manpower:*

The future strength of the Army will be laid down by me, after receiving proposals from Commander-in-Chief Army.

The Replacement Army will be reduced to conform with the diminished strength of the Army.

The Chief of the High Command of the Armed Forces

will decide, in accordance with my directives, on the employment of the manpower which will become available for the Armed Forces as a whole and for the armaments industry.

The Class of 1922 will be called up at the latest possible date, and will be distributed by the High Command of the Armed Forces in accordance with the future tasks of the various branches of the Armed Forces.

3. *Arms and Equipment:*

(a) *The Armed Forces as a whole.*

The arming and equipment of troops will be reduced to the requirements of the situation in the field, without reference to existing establishment scales.

All formations not intended for actual combat (security, guard, construction, and similar units) will be armed basically with captured weapons and second line equipment.

All requests for 'general Armed Forces equipment' will be immediately reduced or rejected in relation to available supplies, need, and wear and tear. Continued manufacture of such weapons as can be proved to be necessary will be decided in agreement with the Minister for Armaments and Munitions.

Plant (buildings and machine tools) already in use will not be expanded unless it can be shown that existing equipment cannot be put to full use by the introduction of shift working.

Work on all such permanent buildings for industry and the Armed Forces as are intended for use in peacetime rather than for the *immediate* prosecution of the war and for the production of arms, will be halted. Construction directly necessary for the conduct of the war and for armaments will remain subject to the regulations of the General Plenipotentiary for Building. Buildings erected by civilian contractors will be limited by him to such as are most essential to the war effort.

Contracts of all kinds which do not comply with these principles will be immediately withdrawn.

The manpower, raw materials, and plant released by these measures will be made available for the main tasks of equipment and placed, as soon as possible, at the disposal of the Minister of Armaments and Munitions for use elsewhere.

(b) *Army*:

The extension of arms and equipment and the production of new weapons, munitions, and equipment will be related, with immediate effect, to the smaller forces which are contemplated for the future. Where orders have been placed for more than six months ahead all contracts beyond that period will be cancelled. Current deliveries will only continue if their immediate cancellation would be uneconomic.

The following are exceptions to these limitations:

The tank programme for the motorized forces (which are to be considerably reinforced) including the provision of special weapons and tanks of the heaviest type.

The new programme for heavy anti-tank guns, including their tractors and ammunition.

The programme for additional equipment for expeditionary forces, which will include four further armoured divisions for employment in the tropics, drawn from the overall strength of the armoured forces.

Preparations for the manufacture of equipment unrelated to these programmes will be halted.

The Army's programme for anti-aircraft guns is to be coordinated with that of the Air Force, and represents a single unified scheme from the manufacturing point of view. All available plant will be fully employed in order to achieve the delivery targets which I have laid down.

(*c*) *Navy:*

The Navy will continue its submarine programme. Construction will be limited to what is directly connected with this programme. Expansion of the armaments programme over and above this is to be stopped.

(*d*) *Air Force:*

The overall armaments programme will concentrate on carrying out the expanded '*Air Armaments programme*' which I have approved. Its realization up to the spring of 1942 is of decisive importance for the whole war effort. For this purpose all available manpower from the Armed Forces and industry will be employed. The allocation of aluminium to the Air Force will be increased as far as possible.

The speed of the programme, and the extent to which it can be fulfilled, will be linked to the increased production of light metals and mineral oil.

4. The *programme for powder and explosives* will concentrate upon the requirements of the Air Force (bombs and anti-aircraft ammunition) at the expense of the requirements of the Army. Buildings will be restricted to the barest essentials and confined to the simplest type of construction.

Production of explosives will be limited to the existing basis.

5. It is particularly important to ensure supplies of *raw materials and mineral oil.* Coal production and the extension of the light metal, artificial rubber, substitute materials, and liquid fuel industries will be supported by the Armed Forces in every way, particularly by the release of miners and specialist workers. The construction of the necessary plans for the extended air armaments industry will be developed simultaneously.

6. The allocation of manpower, raw materials, and plant will be made in accordance with these principles.

7. The Chief of the High Command of the Armed Forces will issue the necessary orders for the Armed Forces, and the

Minister for Armaments and Munitions for his sector, in mutual agreement.

signed: ADOLF HITLER

33

This and the succeeding directives point the way of the German advance in Russia.

The Führer and Supreme	Führer Headquarters,
Commander of the Armed Forces	19th July 1941.
	13 copies

Directive No. 33
Continuation of the war in the East

1. The second series of battles in the East has ended, along the whole front, with the breach of the Stalin Line and the deep thrust of the armoured forces. In the area of Army Group Centre, mopping up of the strong enemy forces which still remain between the motorized formations will still require considerable time.

The northern flank of Army Group South is restricted in its freedom of movement and effectiveness by the fortress of Kiev and the Russian 5th Army in its rear.

2. The aim of the next operations must be to prevent any further sizeable enemy forces from withdrawing into the depths of Russia, and to wipe them out.

Plans will be made for this as follows:

(a) South-eastern Front:

The most important object is, by concentric attacks, to destroy the enemy 12th and 6th Armies while they are still west of the Dnieper. The main Rumanian forces will support these operations in the south.

The enemy 5th Army can also be quickly and decisively defeated and annihilated by cooperation

GERMAN ATTACK ON RUSSIA 1941

MURMANSK

ARCHANGEL

FINLAND

L. ONEGA

PERIOD JUNE – SEPT.
1941
PERIOD OCT – DEC.

L. LADOGA

REVAL

LENINGRAD

L. PEIPUS

BALTIC SEA

0   300
MILES

RIGA

KALININ

ARMY
GROUP
"C"

SMOLENSK

MOSCOW

R. VOLGA

WARSAW

MINSK

ARMY
GROUP
"B"

TULA

BRYANSK

BREST
LITOVSK

OREL

LUBLIN

KURSK

VORONEZH

LEMBERG

KIEV

KHARKOV

KREMENCHUG

STALINGRAD

ARMY
GROUP
"A"

ODESSA

ROSTOV

KERCH
STRAITS

SEBASTOPOL

TUAPSE

CASPIAN SEA

BULGARIA

BLACK   SEA

between forces on the south flank of Army Group Centre and the northern flank of Army Group South.

While infantry divisions of Army Group Centre move southward, other forces, chiefly motorized, after carrying out the tasks assigned to them, securing their lines of communication and providing cover in the direction of Moscow, will advance south-eastwards in order to cut off the withdrawal of enemy forces which have crossed to the further bank of the Dnieper, to prevent their withdrawal deeper into Russia, and to destroy them.

(b) *Central Part of the Eastern Front:*

After the destruction of the many pockets of enemy troops which have been surrounded and the establishment of lines of communication, Army Group Centre, while continuing to advance to Moscow with infantry formations, will use these motorized units which are not employed in the rear of the Dnieper line to cut communications between Moscow and Leningrad, and so cover the right flank of the advance on Leningrad by Army Group North.

(c) *Northern Part of the Eastern Front:*

The advance on Leningrad will be resumed only when 18th Army has made contact with 4th Armoured Group and the extensive flank in the east is adequately protected by 16th Army. At the same time Army Group North must endeavour to prevent Russian forces still in action in Estonia from withdrawing to Leningrad.

Early capture of the Baltic Islands, which might be used as bases by the Soviet Navy, is desirable.

(d) *Finnish Front:*

It remains the task of the main Finnish forces, reinforced by most of 163rd Division, to attack the enemy opposing them with the main weight of attack east of Lake Ladoga and, later, in conjunction with Army Group North, to destroy them.

The object of the attack under the direction of XXXVI Corps and the Mountain Corps remains as already directed, except that stronger support from the air cannot be expected for the moment and operations may therefore have to be temporarily delayed.

3. The task of the *Air Force* is, in particular, as forces become available from the Central front, to support operations on the South-eastern front at their most important point by bringing air and anti-aircraft units into action, and, if necessary, by early reinforcement or regrouping.

The attack on Moscow by the bomber forces of 2nd Air Fleet, temporarily reinforced by bomber forces from the West, will be carried out as soon as possible as 'reprisal for Russian attacks on Bucharest and Helsinki'.

4. The *Navy* will continue to ensure the free passage of sea-borne traffic, especially of supplies for the land forces, as far as enemy activity at sea and in the air allows. Further, with the increasing threat to enemy bases, appropriate steps are to be taken to prevent the escape of enemy ships to Swedish ports, where they would be interned.

As naval forces in the Baltic become free, motor torpedo boats and minesweepers – one flotilla of each to start with – will be transferred to the Mediterranean.

To support German operations in Finland, which might be hampered by the arrival of enemy reinforcements by sea, a few submarines will be transferred to the Arctic Ocean.

5. All three branches of the Armed Forces in the West and North will bear in mind the possibility of British attacks on the Channel Islands and the Norwegian coast. Plans must be made for the quick transfer of air forces from the West to all parts of Norway.

signed: ADOLF HITLER

33a

<table>
<tr><td>The Chief of the High
Command of the Armed Forces</td><td>Führer Headquarters,
23rd July 1941.
14 copies</td></tr>
</table>

Supplement to Directive No. 33

After a report by Commander-in-Chief Army, the Führer on 22nd July issued the following orders to amplify and extend Directive 33.

1. *Southern Part of the Eastern Front:*

The enemy forces which are still west of the Dnieper must be decisively defeated and dispersed. As soon as the state of operations and of supplies allows, 1st and 2nd Armoured Groups will be concentrated under command of 4th Tank Army and, with the support of infantry and mounted divisions, will occupy the Kharkov industrial area and thrust forward across the Don to Caucasia.

The bulk of the infantry divisions will then occupy the Ukraine, the Crimea, and the area of Central Russia up to the Don. The security of the area immediately south-west of the Bug is to be left to the Rumanian Army.

2. *Central Part of the Eastern Front:*

After mopping-up operations around Smolensk and on the southern flank, Army Group Centre, whose infantry formations drawn from both its armies are strong enough for the purpose, will defeat such enemy forces as remain between Smolensk and Moscow, by an advance on the left flank if possible. It will then capture Moscow.

3rd Armoured Group will come under temporary command of Army Group North to secure its right flank and to surround the enemy in the Leningrad area.

For the further task of thrusting forward to the Volga,

the mobile forces of 3rd Armoured Group will probably be once more available.

3. *Northern Part of the Eastern Front:*
The subordination to it of 3rd Armoured Group will enable Army Group North to employ strong forces of infantry for an attack in the direction of Leningrad, and to avoid expending its mobile forces in frontal attacks over difficult terrain.

Enemy forces still in action in Estonia will be destroyed. Their embarkation and withdrawal across the Narva towards Leningrad will be prevented.

3rd Armoured Group is to be returned to Army Group Centre on the completion of its task.

4. The High Command of the Army will plan *further operations* so that large parts of Army Group North, including 4th Armoured Group and some of the infantry formations of Army Group South, may be moved back to Germany as soon as the situation allows.

3rd Armoured Group will be rendered fully operational by drawing upon 4th Armoured Group for equipment and personnel. 1st and 2nd Armoured Groups will, if necessary, supply themselves by merging units.

5. The orders given for *Navy* and *Air Force* in Directive 33 remain valid.

In addition they are to ease the situation of the Mountain Corps: the *Navy*, by the determined employment of its forces in the Arctic Ocean (now reinforced); the Air Force, by the transfer of several dive-bomber groups to the Finnish theatre once the fighting around Smolensk is over. This will also reduce the temptation for England to intervene in the fighting along the Arctic coast.

6. The troops available for *securing the conquered Eastern territories* will, in view of the size of this area, be sufficient for their duties only if the occupying power meets resistance, not by legal punishment of the guilty, but by striking such terror into the population that it loses all will to resist.

The Commanders concerned are to be held responsible,

together with the troops at their disposal, for quiet conditions in their areas. They will contrive to maintain order, not by requesting reinforcements, but by employing suitably draconian methods.

signed: KEITEL

34

By the end of July 1941 the German armies had penetrated deeply into Russia; but now they began to meet tougher resistance, especially in the centre of the front, opposite Moscow, where Army Group Centre, under General von Bock, was opposed by the Russian Army Group of General Timoshenko. At this point a serious difference of opinion broke out between Hitler and the Commander-in-Chief of the Army, General von Brauchitsch. Brauchitsch wished to concentrate on the destruction of Timoshenko's Army Group and the capture of Moscow. Hitler insisted that Moscow could wait while more sweeping victories were to be won in the North, in the Leningrad area, and in the South, towards the Caucasus. These new conditions, and Hitler's change of strategy in respect of the Moscow front, are shown in Directive No. 34 and in the supplement to it.

The Führer and Supreme Führer Headquarters,
Commander of the Armed Forces 30th July 1941.
  14 copies

Directive No. 34

The development of the situation in the last few days, the appearance of strong enemy forces on the front and to the flanks of Army Group Centre, the supply position, and the need to give 2nd and 3rd Armoured Groups about ten days to rehabilitate their units, make it necessary to postpone *for the moment* the further tasks and objectives laid down in

Directive 33 of 19th July and in the supplement of 23rd July.

I therefore order as follows:

I. 1. In the *Northern Sector* of the Eastern front the main attack will continue between Lake Ilmen and Narva towards Leningrad, with the aim of encircling Leningrad and making contact with the Finnish Army.

North of Lake Ilmen this attack will be covered in the Volkhov sector; South of Lake Ilmen it will be carried north-eastwards only so far as is required to protect the right flank of the attack north of the lake. The situation around Velikiye Luki will have been previously cleared up. All forces not required for these operations will be transferred to take part in the flank attacking north of Lake Ilmen. The intended thrust by 3rd Armoured Group against the high ground around Valdai will be postponed until armoured formations are fully ready for action. Instead, the left flank of Army Group Centre will advance sufficiently far north-eastwards to afford protection to the right flank of Army Group North.

Estonia must first of all be mopped up by all the forces of 18th Army; only then may divisions advance towards Leningrad.

2. Army Group *Centre* will go over to the defensive, taking advantage of suitable terrain.

Attacks with limited objectives may still be mounted in so far as they are necessary to secure favourable spring-boards for our offensive against Soviet 21st Army.

2nd and 3rd Armoured Groups will be withdrawn from the front line for quick rehabilitation as soon as the situation allows.

3. Operations on the *South-eastern front* will, for the present, be conducted only by formations of Army Group South.

Their objective must be to destroy the strong enemy forces west of the Dnieper and, in addition, by securing bridge-heads near to the south of Kiev, to establish the conditions necessary for bringing 1st Armoured Group later to the eastern bank of the Dnieper.

The 5th Red Army, fighting in the marshland north-west of Kiev, must be brought to battle west of the Dnieper and annihilated. Any danger that it might break through to the north across the Pripet must be countered in good time.

4. *Finnish Front:*

The attack in the direction of Kandalaksha will be halted. The threat to the flank of the Mountain Corps from the Motovski Bight is to be eliminated. Only so many forces are to be left with XXXVI Corps as are necessary for defence and to give the impression of further offensive preparations.

In the area of III (Finnish) Corps an attempt will be made to cut the Murmansk railway, particularly towards Louhi. All forces suitable for this attack will be moved to this area; other available forces will be transferred to the Karelian Army. Should difficulties of terrain bring the offensive to a standstill in the area of the III (Finnish) Corps too, the German forces will be withdrawn and employed with the Karelian Army. This applies particularly to mobile units, tanks, and heavy artillery.

The 6th Mountain Division will join the Mountain Corps, using all available transport routes. The Foreign Office will settle whether the railway through Sweden to Narvik may also be used.

II. *Air Force.*

1. *North-eastern Front:*

Air Force will switch the main weight of air attack to the North-eastern front by attaching the bulk of VIII Air Corps to 1st Air Fleet. These reinforcements will be moved up in time to go into action at the beginning of the offensive by Army Group North and at its vital point (early morning 6th August).

2. *Centre:*

The task of such units of the Air Force as remain with

Army Group Centre is to afford such fighter-cover as is absolutely necessary on the 2nd and 9th Army fronts and to support possible local attacks. Attacks on Moscow will continue.

3. *South-eastern Front:*

Tasks as already laid down. It is not proposed to reduce the strength of the air forces with Army Group South.

4. *Finland:*

The main task of 5th Air Fleet is to support the Mountain Corps. The offensive by III Finnish Corps will also be supported at favourable points.

Preparations are to be made for the employment of forces in support of the Karelian Army should this be necessary.

signed: ADOLF HITLER

34a

The High Command
of the Armed Forces

Führer Headquarters,
12th August 1941.
14 copies

Supplement to Directive No. 34

The Führer has issued the following orders for the prosecution of operations in the East, supplementary to Directive 34:

1. *South-eastern Front:*

Through the battle of annihilation at Uman, Army Group South has won definite superiority over the enemy and freedom to undertake extensive operations on the further side of the Dnieper. As soon as it has gained a firm foothold east of the river, and has ensured the safety of its communications in the rear, it will possess the necessary strength, with corresponding action by allied forces and the cooperation of the Rumanian Army, to achieve with its own forces the far-reaching objectives which lie ahead of it.

Its next task is:

(*a*) To prevent the establishment by the enemy of a planned defensive front behind the Dnieper.

For this purpose the largest possible portion of enemy forces still west of the Dnieper must be destroyed, and bridgeheads across the Dnieper won as soon as possible.

(*b*) To occupy the Crimean peninsula, which is particularly dangerous as an enemy air base against the Rumanian oilfields.

(*c*) To occupy the Donets area and the industrial area of Kharkov.

The battle for the Crimean peninsula may require mountain troops. The possibility of their use later, across the Kerch straits, in the direction of Batum, will be considered.

The attack on the city of Kiev itself will be halted. It is proposed to destroy the city by incendiary bombs and gunfire as soon as the supply position allows.

This entails a large number of tasks for the *Air Force*. These cannot be carried out simultaneously, but must be accomplished one after another through the largest possible concentration of forces. Such concentrations will be achieved by the addition of dive-bomber units, first in the battles between Kanev and Boguslav, and then for the purpose of securing a bridgehead over the Dnieper.

2. *Central Part of the Eastern Front:*

The most important task here is to eliminate the enemy flanking positions, projecting deeply to the west, with which he is holding down large forces of infantry on both flanks of Army Group Centre. For this purpose close cooperation in timing and direction on the southern flank, between the adjoining flanks of Army Group South and Army Group Centre, is particularly important. The Russian 5th Army must be deprived of any further power to operate by cutting the roads to Ovruch and Mozyr, by which it obtains supplies and reinforcements, and then finally annihilated.

On the northern flank the enemy must be defeated as soon as possible by the employment of mobile forces west of Toropets. The left flank of Army Group Centre will then be moved as far northwards as is necessary to relieve Army Group North of anxiety about its right flank and to enable it to transfer infantry divisions to take part in the attack on Leningrad.

Apart from this, efforts will be made beforehand to move some one division (102nd Division) to Army Group North in reserve.

Only after these threats to our ranks have been entirely overcome and armoured formations have been rehabilitated will it be possible to continue the offensive, on a wide front and with echeloning of both flanks, against the strong enemy forces which have been concentrated for the defence of Moscow. The object of operations must then be to deprive the enemy, before the coming of winter, of his government, armament, and traffic centre around Moscow, and thus prevent the rebuilding of his defeated forces and the orderly working of government control.

Before the beginning of this attack on Moscow operations against Leningrad must be concluded, and the aircraft from 2nd Air Fleet which are at present attached to 1st Air Fleet must again be available to 2nd Air Fleet.

3. *North-eastern Front:*

The attack which is now in progress should result in the encirclement of Leningrad and a junction with the Finnish forces.

With regard to cooperation by the *Air Force*, it should be a principle, as far as the position of our own airfields allows, always, if possible, to concentrate on a single point, in order to secure the utmost effect.

As soon as the situation allows, enemy air and naval bases

on Dagö and Ösel will be eliminated by a combined operation by Army, Naval, and Air Forces.

It is urgently necessary that enemy airfields from which attacks on Berlin are evidently being made should be destroyed.

The Army is responsible for the coordinated planning of operations.

The Chief of the High Command of the Armed Forces.
signed: KEITEL

35

In August the dispute between Hitler and Brauchitsch became acute. Hitler insisted on his own strategy. On 15th August he ordered Army Group Centre to go over to the defensive, while Army Group North was to be reinforced with armour and to press ahead to capture Leningrad: 'the resumption of the offensive against Moscow cannot be considered till that has been done'. On 18th August Brauchitsch submitted his views. Hitler replied tersely on 21st August that 'the Army's proposal of 18th August for the further conduct of operations in the East is not in accordance with my intentions'; and he gave his own orders. 'The most important aim to be achieved before the onset of winter', he wrote, 'is not to capture Moscow, but to seize the Crimea and the industrial and coal region on the Donets, and to cut off the Russian oil supply from the Caucasus area. In the north, the aim is to cut off Leningrad and to join with the Finns.' In order to achieve these results Army Group Centre was to stay on the defensive in front of Moscow, and to lend its right flank to a concentric movement, with Army Group South, to push the Russian 5th Army back across the Dnieper and occupy the Crimea. Its left flank was similarly to join with the right wing of Army Group North. 'Only by cutting off Leningrad, joining the Finns, and annihilating the Russian 5th Army, will proper conditions be created, and enough forces liberated to attack the Timoshenko Army

Group with good prospects of defeating it, as envisaged in the Supplement to Directive No. 34 of 12th August.' Having thus imposed his will, Hitler issued his Directive No. 35.

The Führer and Supreme   Führer Headquarters,
Commander of the Armed Forces   6th September 1941.
                                          10 copies

Directive No. 35

Combined with the progressive encirclement of the Leningrad area, the initial successes against the enemy forces in the area between the flanks of Army Groups South and Centre have provided favourable conditions for a decisive operation against the Timoshenko Army Group which is attacking on the Central front.* This Army Group must be defeated and annihilated in the limited time which remains before the onset of winter weather. For this purpose it is necessary to concentrate all the forces of the Army and Air Force which can be spared on the flanks and which can be brought up in time.

On the basis of the report of Commander-in-Chief Army, I issue the following orders for the preparation and execution of these operations:

1. *On the Southern sector of the front* the aim is the annihilation of the enemy forces in the triangle Kremenchug–Kiev–Konotop by the forces of Army Group South which are advancing northward across the Dnieper, acting in conjunction with the attack by the southern flank of Army Group Centre. As soon as the completion of this task allows, those formations of 2nd and 6th Armies, and of 2nd Armoured Group, which have become free, will be reformed for the new operation.

Beginning about 10th September at latest, the motorized forces of Army Group South, reinforced by infantry

---

* A later order (19th September 1941) gave to this intended attack the cover-name '*Taifun* (Typhoon)'.

divisions, and supported at the main point of attack by 4th Air Fleet, will make a surprise movement from the bridgehead secured by 17th Army north-westwards on and beyond Lubny. At the same time 17th Army is to gain ground in the direction of Poltava and Kharkov.

The offensive against the Crimea from the lower Dnieper will continue, with support from 4th Air Fleet; so will – so far as available forces permit – the offensive from the Dniepropetrovsk bridgehead.* An advance by motorized forces south of the lower Dnieper towards Melitopol would be of substantial advantage for the mission of 11th Army.

2. On the *Central front*, the operation against the Timoshenko Army Group will be planned so that the attack can be begun at the earliest possible moment (end of September) with the aim of destroying the enemy forces located in the area east of Smolensk by a pincer movement in the general direction of Vyazma, with strong *concentrations* of armour on the flanks.

For this purpose mobile focal points are to be established with *motorized units* as follows:

On the southern flank (probably in the area south-east of Roslavl, the direction of the thrust being north-east), from the available forces of Army Group Centre and 5th and 2nd Armoured Divisions, which will be released for the purpose.

In the 9th Army sector (the thrust being probably towards Bjeloj), by bringing the strongest possible forces from the area of Army Group North.

Only when Army Group Timoshenko has been defeated in these highly coordinated and closely encircling operations

* On 19th September 1941 the passage 'as will . . . Dniepropetrovsk bridgehead' was deleted by a teleprinter message signed by Warlimont, on behalf of the Chief of the High Command of the Armed Forces. The message added, 'The Führer wishes all motorized divisions to be added to 1st Armoured Group for the attack from the bridgehead of Kremenchug, since forces of 4th Air Fleet are not available to support an attack from the Dniepropetrovsk bridgehead.'

of annihilation will our central Army be able to begin the advance on Moscow with its right flank on the Oka and its left on the Upper Volga.

The *Air Force* will support the offensive with the 2nd Air Fleet, which will be reinforced at the appropriate time, especially from the north-east area. It will concentrate on the flanks and will employ the bulk of its dive-bomber units (VIII Air Corps) in support of the motorized forces on both flanks.

3. On the *North-eastern front*, in conjunction with the Finnish Corps attacking on the Karelian peninsula, we must (after the capture of Schlusselburg) so surround the enemy forces fighting in the Leningrad area that by 15th September at the latest substantial units of the motorized forces and of 1st Air Fleet, especially VIII Air Corps, will be available for service on the Central front. Before this, efforts will be made to encircle Leningrad more closely, in particular in the east, and, should weather permit, a large-scale air attack on Leningrad will be carried out. It is particularly important in this connexion to destroy the water supply.

In order to assist the Finnish advance beyond the fortifications along the old Russo-Finnish frontier, as well as to narrow the battle area and eliminate enemy air bases, forces of Army Group North will move north across the Neva sector as soon as possible.

With Finnish cooperation, the Bay of Kronstadt will be so completely closed by mine-laying and artillery that enemy forces will be unable to escape into the Baltic to Hangö and the Baltic Islands.

As soon as the necessary forces can be made available, the battle area around Leningrad is to be covered to the eastward and on the lower Volkhov. The link-up with the Karelian Army on the Svir will only take place when the destruction of the enemy around Leningrad is assured.

4. As regards *further operations* it is intended that the offensive towards Moscow by Army Group Centre should be covered by a flank guard composed of available motorized

forces in the Army Group South sector and advancing in a
general north-easterly direction, and that forces from Army
Group North should be moved forward on both sides of
Lake Ilmen to cover the northern flank and to maintain
contact with the Finnish Karelian Army.

5. Any saving of time and consequent advance of the time-
table will be to the advantage of the whole operation and its
preparation.

signed: ADOLF HITLER

36

Meanwhile, the German forces in the far north, in Norway,
were seeking, in cooperation with the Finns, to contribute to
the success of the war against Russia. For the Finns, the aim
was the recovery of territory lost to Russia in the winter of
1939-40, when the Russians, as part of their westward expansion in the period of the Russo-German Treaty, made war on
Finland. The Germans sought to protect their supplies of
nickel from Petsamo in northern Finland and to capture
the Murmansk railway which, running from Murmansk on
the Arctic Ocean, through Kandalaksha, on the White Sea,
to Leningrad, was one of the main routes used to convey
the arms and equipment brought by British Arctic convoys.

The Führer and Supreme   Führer Headquarters,
Commander of the Armed Forces   22nd September 1941.
                                          12 copies

Directive No. 36

I. Owing to unusual difficulties of the terrain, defective lines
of communications, and the continual arrival of Russian
reinforcements in Karelia and Lapland, the weak forces of
Army High Command Norway and 5th Air Fleet have not
so far succeeded, in spite of immense efforts and the bravest
actions, in reaching the Murmansk railway. The interruption

by the enemy of our sea communications along the Arctic coast has still further reduced the likelihood that the Mountain Corps will reach Murmansk this year.

We have, however, succeeded in tying down strong enemy forces and in drawing them away from the main Russian front, in driving back the enemy across the former Finnish frontier at all points, and in eliminating, so far, all threats to North Finland, and above all to the nickel mines.

II. The ultimate aim of our operations in Northern and Central Finland remains constant. It is to destroy the enemy forces around Murmansk and along the Murmansk railway.

The importance of this area lies in the nickel mines which are vital for the German war effort. The enemy realizes this importance. It is likely that the English will deploy strong air forces around Murmansk and Kandalaksha and may perhaps even commit Canadian or Norwegian troops there, and that they will send as much war material as possible to Murmansk. We must expect air attacks, even in winter, against the nickel mines and the homes of the miners. Our own efforts must correspond with the greatness of this danger.

III. I therefore order as follows:

 1. *Army High Command Norway*.

(*a*) The attacks in the sector of III (Finnish) Army Corps will be halted and the forces thus released transferred to XXXVI Army Corps.

(*b*) All preparations are to be made by XXXVI Army Corps for resumption of the attack towards Kandalaksha in the first half of October with the aim of at least cutting Murmansk off from its rail communications by the time winter sets in. Moreover, the question whether the continuation of this attack in the winter will have greater prospects of success than in the autumn is to be considered.

The Finnish High Command will be requested to

transfer 163rd Division, by rail via Rovaniemi, to the High Command of the Army at the proper time.

(c) The offensive of the *Mountain Corps* towards Murmansk is to be halted for the time being and the northern flank will advance only so far as is required to improve the position and to mislead the enemy. On the other hand it is necessary, in the light of the tasks assigned to the Navy, at least to occupy the western end of the Fisherman's Peninsula* before the beginning of the winter and thereby to prevent the enemy from hampering access to the port of Liinahamari by artillery and motor torpedo boats.

The collection of intelligence and planning for this attack will begin at once and the result will be reported as soon as possible. Special weapons suitable for use against targets on land and at sea, which are still lacking, will be provided.

Whether the plan of Army High Command Norway for the winter can be carried out can only be decided later. This plan is to leave two reinforced mountain divisions in the Petsamo area and to allow 2nd Mountain Division to rest in the Rovaniemi area. If possible this will be done. It is also planned to relieve 3rd Mountain Division by 5th Mountain Division or by a newly raised mountain division.

(d) Numbers of lorries will be bought or hired in Sweden in order to shift the supply route of the Mountain Corps to the Arctic Highway. If this transport is not sufficient, reinforcements will be brought from home.

(e) I have instructed Reichsminister Dr Todt to construct a field railway from Rovaniemi along the Arctic Highway to Petsamo by the ruthless employment of Russian prisoners of war.

---

* i.e. the Rybachiy Peninsula, which juts into the Arctic Ocean on the Russo-Finnish border, close to the Arctic port of Petsamo.

(f) For the resumption of the attack on Murmansk, all modern weapons suitable for use in the tundra will be supplied.

2. *Navy:*

It is the task of the Navy to attack enemy supplies moving to Murmansk even in winter, and particularly at times when air operations are more or less crippled.

For this purpose a suitable subsidiary *base* for light naval forces will be established – preferably in Petsamo Bay – in case we succeed in capturing the western part of the Fisherman's Peninsula. The flow of supplies by sea to Kirkenes and Petsamo, even should it be interrupted for a time, must be constantly attempted.

Coastal defences in the bays of Petsamo and Kirkenes will be strengthened so that they are capable of meeting attacks even by heavy enemy ships.

3. *Air Force:*

It is of decisive importance that 5th Air Fleet should remain in North Norway with strong forces suitable for action in winter.

These forces are to be large enough to give effective support to the attack on Kandalaksha and the capture of the western part of the Fisherman's Peninsula up to the beginning of the bad weather. Meanwhile it is necessary to make continuous attacks on the enemy's shipping and rear communications as well as his supply and equipment depots.

These attacks are to be continued throughout the period of bad weather whenever opportunity offers and to be extended particularly to shipping and bases under construction.

Air Force ground establishments must therefore remain, as far as possible, in Northern Norway and Finland and must be protected against the winter by all possible means.

Protection against enemy air attack of our own camps and communications and, above all, of the nickel mines and the naval base which is to be established must be ensured.

Ground organizations and supplies will be increased so

that, when the time comes, the resumption of the attack on Murmansk can be supported by considerably stronger air forces than hitherto.

signed: ADOLF HITLER

37

The Führer and Supreme Commander of the Armed Forces

Führer Headquarters, 10th October 1941.

13 copies

Directive No. 37

The sudden favourable developments of the situation in the Eastern theatre, together with reports from Army High Command Norway on the state of the forces there and on the possibilities of further operations in Finland, have led me to issue the following orders:

1. After the defeat or destruction of the main Russian forces in the principal theatre of operations, there will be no compelling reason to tie down Russian forces in Finland by continued attacks. The strength and offensive power of the available German formations are inadequate, in view of the lateness of the season, to capture Murmansk or the Fisherman's Peninsula or to cut the Murmansk railway in Central Finland before the onset of winter.

The *most important task*, therefore, is to hold what we have gained, to protect the Petsamo nickel fields from attack by land, air, or sea, and to make all preparations – beginning while it is still winter – for the final capture of Murmansk, the Fisherman's Peninsula, and the Murmansk railway next year.

The *time-table* will be as follows:

(a) Army formations to go over to the defensive in favourable, easily defended positions. Winter accommodation to be erected and preparations made for winter warfare.

(*b*) Relief and reinforcement of troops.

(*c*) In *winter*, a concentric attack against the Murmansk railway, as follows:

> With Finnish forces from the south towards Bielo-morsk–Kem and if possible towards Louhi.

> With German forces from the Verman sector towards Kandalaksha.

(*d*) At a favourable moment the capture of the Fisherman's Peninsula, if possible in its entirety, and an attack on Murmansk.

These operations must be so timed that it is possible to concentrate all attacking forces at *one point*.

2. *The next duty of Army High Command Norway* will be, while ensuring the defence of all areas which do not call for the employment of large forces, so to distribute forces that those formations which have been heavily engaged for a long time past can rest and be equipped for winter warfare, or, where necessary, be relieved by reinforcements and withdrawn. In this connexion –

(*a*) 2nd and 3rd Mountain Divisions of the *Mountain Corps* will be relieved by the reinforced 6th Mountain Division. One mountain division will remain in Northern Finland, the second will be moved to the Rovaniemi area and south of it. Their transfer home is planned to coincide with the arrival of 5th Mountain Division (about January 1942).

> After that, a further mountain division, newly raised or reorganized, will relieve the division which remains in Northern Finland.

(*b*) 163rd Infantry Division will come under command of XXXVI Corps as soon as it is clear that it is not required for a concentric attack on the south shore of Lake Ladoga between the Karelian Army and Army Group North.

> *Personnel* of 169th and 163rd Infantry Divisions will

if possible be relieved in the course of the winter by divisions from Norway or from home.

3. *All reliefs*, including those of the mountain divisions, will be carried through so as to ensure that the bulk of heavy weapons, equipment, horses, and draught animals remain on the spot. That is to say, only troops and their personal weapons will be exchanged. This will save time and shipping space.

4. *SS Formations*. It is intended to relieve SS 9th Regiment, at present under command of 2nd Mountain Division, by an SS Regiment consisting of Norwegians and Finns and, by reinforcing it with one Austrian SS Regiment, to convert SS Battle Group North into a mountain brigade. The execution of this plan will be coordinated by the High Command of the Armed Forces with the other plans for exchanges of staffs and units.

5. As the Finnish High Command intends to undertake a complete reorganization of the Army on the conclusion of the present operation, the German and Finnish forces in *III Finnish Corps* will be exchanged for one another (6th Finnish Division against SS Battle Group North). It is then proposed to bring the sector held by III Finnish Corps under the command of Field Marshal Mannerheim.

Field Marshal Mannerheim will be requested to place at least a few small Finnish formations under command of the German Forces attacking Kandalaksha before the beginning of the new operations.

6. The *Air Force* will carry out the following tasks in the Finnish theatre, as far as weather allows:

(a) It will keep the coasts of Northern Norway and Finland under observation to protect our own sea traffic and to attack that of the enemy.

(b) It will provide air defences, particularly for the Petsamo nickel area, ports at which supplies are unloaded, and naval bases.

(c) It will reconnoitre the area of future operations and

will constantly attack the enemy supply base at Murmansk and movements to it by sea or rail.

(d) It will make preparations for the employment of stronger forces in support of forthcoming operations.

7. The task of the *Navy* will be to attack enemy supplies going by sea to Murmansk and to protect our own traffic in the Arctic Ocean within the limits of its forces.

To this end light naval forces are to be strengthened as soon as possible and motor torpedo boats to be brought up.

Kirkenes will be developed as a subsidiary base.

In order to protect our own coastal traffic it is desirable to bring up further coastal batteries. The Chief of the High Command of the Armed Forces will issue the necessary orders. Kirkenes and Petsamo will be reinforced, beyond the establishment already laid down, by one battery each of 21 cm. guns. One 28 cm. battery will be established at Vardö. After the capture of the Fisherman's Peninsula, an extra-heavy battery will be established there.

8. *Cooperation* between Army High Command Norway, Navy, and Air Force must be particularly close in the ensuing months in order to counteract any possible operations against our front or against our sea flank. In order to simplify this cooperation the Navy will appoint a *Naval Commander* North and the Air Force, after withdrawing Headquarters 5th Air Fleet to Norway, will appoint an *Air Force Commander* North.

9. *Operation Orders* will be issued by the Chief of the High Command of the Armed Forces.* Through him there should be submitted to me:

(a) By Army High Command Norway:
Time-table for regrouping.
Plans for re-equipment in order that all troops may be

---

* Two such operational orders were issued, on the basis of this directive, on 7th and 21st November 1941.

capable of operating in the tundra and in the forests
of Eastern Karelia.

Plans for operations and requests for army troops as
reinforcements.

Proposals for the exchange of staffs.

(*b*) By the Navy and Air Force: Their detailed plans.

10. Where Directive 36 is altered by these orders it becomes invalid.

signed: ADOLF HITLER

38

While the Germans advanced in Russia, their victims in the
Balkans began to stir again and the British were recovering
from their defeats in the Eastern Mediterranean. All through
the autumn there were ominous signs in the Mediterranean,
and in November 1941 the British resumed their advance in
North Africa which had been halted and driven back as a
result of the diversion of forces to Greece. To counter this
Hitler decided, at the end of October, to transfer a whole Air
Corps to the Central Mediterranean. On 2nd December he
gave the orders in the form of a directive.

The Führer and Supreme   Führer Headquarters,
Commander of the Armed Forces   2nd December 1941.
                                         17 copies

Directive No. 38

1. In order to secure and extend our own position in the
Mediterranean, and to establish a *focus of Axis strength in
Central Mediterranean*, I order, in agreement with the Duce,
that part of the German Air Force no longer required in the
East be transferred to the South Italian and North African
areas, in the strength of about one Air Corps with the
necessary anti-aircraft defences.

Apart from the immediate effect of this movement on the war in the Mediterranean and North Africa, efforts will be made to ensure that it has a considerable effect upon further developments in the Mediterranean area as a whole.

2. I appoint Field Marshal *Kesselring* to command all forces employed in these operations. He is also appointed Commander-in-Chief South.

His *tasks* are:

To secure mastery of the air and sea in the area between Southern Italy and North Africa in order to secure communications with Libya and Cyrenaica and, in particular, to keep Malta in subjection.

To cooperate with German and allied forces engaged in North Africa.

To paralyse enemy traffic through the Mediterranean and British supplies to Tobruk and Malta, in close cooperation with the German and Italian naval forces available for this task.

3. *Commander-in-Chief South* will be under the orders of the Duce, whose general instructions he will receive through the Commando Supremo. In all Air Force matters Commander-in-Chief Air Force will deal direct with Commander-in-Chief South. In important matters the High Command of the Armed Forces is to be simultaneously informed.

4. *The following will be subordinate to Commander-in-Chief South:*

   (a) All units of the German Air Force stationed in the Mediterranean and North African areas;

   (b) the air and anti-aircraft units put at his disposal for the execution of his tasks by the Italian Armed Forces.

5. German *naval forces* in the Central Mediterranean remain under command of Commander-in-Chief Navy.

For the execution of the tasks assigned to him, Commander-in-Chief South is authorized to issue directives to the German Admiral with the Italian Naval High Command

and, if necessary, to Naval Group South (for the Eastern Mediterranean). Operation orders will be issued by the Naval Headquarters concerned in agreement with Commander-in-Chief South.

Requests by Commander-in-Chief South for combined operations by *allied* naval forces will be made exclusively to the German Admiral with the Italian Naval High Command.

6. The duties of Commander Armed Forces South-east and of the German General at the headquarters of the Italian Armed Forces remain unchanged.

signed: ADOLF HITLER

39

Meanwhile, the Russian winter had come. Hitler had been confident of completing his *Blitzkrieg* against Russia in one summer campaign. He had reckoned on capturing Leningrad and Moscow and occupying the whole Caucasian area. On 29th September he was still so confident that he issued an order on 'the future of Leningrad'. He had decided 'to have Leningrad wiped from the face of the earth'. The German Navy had asked that the shipyards and harbour installations might be preserved for its own use, but Hitler was adamant: his intention was 'to close in on the city and blast it to the ground' by artillery fire and air bombardment. The population would disappear with it: 'in this war for existence we have no interest in keeping even part of this great city's population'. We know that he intended the same fate for Moscow. But in fact not even Leningrad was captured. November found Hitler still at loggerheads with his generals, he insisting that Moscow must now be taken before the end of the year, they demanding that their armies be allowed to dig in for the winter. Hitler's will prevailed and, in spite of the intense cold, Army Group Centre attacked on 4th December. The attack failed, and two days later Hitler yielded not to persuasion but to objective facts. The *Blitzkrieg* had failed: the war in the East, as in the West, was to be a long war.

The Führer and Supreme Commander of the Armed Forces

Führer Headquarters, 8th December 1941. 14 copies

Directive No. 39

The severe winter weather which has come surprisingly early in the East, and the consequent difficulties in bringing up supplies, compel us to abandon immediately all major offensive operations and to go over to the defensive.

The way in which these defensive operations are to be carried out will be decided in accordance with the purpose which they are intended to serve, viz.:

(*a*) To hold areas which are of great operational or economic importance to the enemy.

(*b*) To enable forces in the East to rest and recuperate as much as possible.

(*c*) Thus to establish conditions suitable for the resumption of large-scale offensive operations in 1942.

My detailed orders are as follows:

I. *Army:*

1. The main body of the Army in the East will, as soon as possible, go over to the defensive along a lightly tenable front to be fixed by Commander-in-Chief Army. Thereafter the rehabilitation of troops is to begin, armoured and motorized divisions being withdrawn first.

2. Where the front has been withdrawn without being forced by the enemy, rear areas will be established in advance which offer troops better living conditions and defensive possibilities than the former positions.

To allow the enemy access to important lateral lines of communication can create danger for other sectors of the front not yet fortified. In such cases the timing of with-

The number of small supply ships being built in Germany and occupied countries (particularly for use across the Black Sea and in the Aegean) must be still further increased even at the expense of all not absolutely essential claims and security measures.

IV. The *replacement of personnel* of the Armed Forces for 1942 must be ensured even in the event of heavy casualties. As the Class of 1922 will not be sufficient alone for this purpose, drastic steps are necessary.

I therefore order:

1. All Armed Forces troops which can be released from Germany or from special employment (e.g. Military Mission Rumania) will be made available, by wholesale redeployment, to the fighting front.

Younger soldiers who are serving at home or in rear areas will take the place of older fighting soldiers.

2. The movement of forces between the Eastern and Western theatres will be made on the following principles:

Divisions of the second and third wave and armoured divisions in the West, if fully fit for action, will relieve divisions in the East which have been exhausted by particularly heavy fighting. We are justified in risking a purely temporary weakening of our forces in France during the winter.

Battle-tried officers, non-commissioned officers, and men from the divisions in the East which are to be relieved may be posted to these divisions in the West.

Beyond this I will decide whether divisions in the West which cannot be employed in the East as full formations should be disbanded and employed to reinforce seasoned divisions on the Eastern front. This decision will be reached when the Army's general plans for reorganization and regrouping are submitted to me.

At all events the strength of the Army in the West must be maintained so that it is capable of coastal defence and of carrying out 'Undertaking Attila'.

3. Young workers classified as essential will be released from their employment on a large scale and will be replaced by prisoners and Russian civilian workers, employed in groups. The High Command of the Armed Forces will issue special orders in this respect.

signed: ADOLF HITLER

40

The failure of his *Blitzkrieg* against Russia was a very serious blow to Hitler. It had also precipitated a serious clash with his own generals. On 16th December 1941 he gave orders for defensive positions to be held throughout the winter along the whole Eastern front. Three days later he removed General Brauchitsch from his post as Commander-in-Chief of the Army and himself took over supreme command of the Army. General Halder, the Chief of Staff of the Army, and another critic of his strategy, became his immediate subordinate. From now on Hitler intended to have no trouble from his generals; he would impose his will in order to carry the German Army through the Russian winter to victory in 1942.

This serious blow in the East was mitigated, but not offset, by the appearance, at the same time, of a new ally. On 7th December 1941, the day before Hitler called off his offensive against Moscow, Japan burst into the war by smashing the American fleet at Pearl Harbour from the air. Thereafter, by a series of brilliant aggressions, the Japanese captured control of South-east Asia from Britain and America. This could be seen as a triumph for the policy laid down in Hitler's Directive No. 24. But if the Japanese onslaught added to the difficulties of Britain, it also ranged America on Britain's side. The ultimate threat to Hitler's Western front was thereby greatly increased, and with his main forces unexpectedly immobilized in the East, he became increasingly concerned for the security of the long European coastline from the

North Cape to the Dardanelles. Already the populations of occupied countries were stirring: in September the anti-German attitude of the Norwegian people had been declared to have 'assumed intolerable proportions' and new measures of severity had been introduced. At the same time partisan activity had begun throughout the Balkans. It was partly to deal with this last threat that Hitler had transferred an air corps to the Mediterranean. On 14th December he issued new orders for defence of the whole Atlantic coastline, which was 'ultimately to be built into a "new West Wall"', in order that we can be sure of repelling any landing attempt, however strong, with the minimum number of permanently stationed troops'. By March the danger of such attempts was greater and called forth a special Führer Directive.

The Führer and Supreme
Commander of the Armed Forces

Führer Headquarters,
23rd March 1942.
25 copies

Directive No. 40
Ref. Competence of Commanders in coastal areas.

I. *General Considerations:*

The coastline of Europe will, in the coming months, be exposed to the danger of an enemy landing in force.

The time and place of the landing operations will not be dictated to the enemy by operational considerations alone. Failure in other theatres of war, obligations to allies, and political considerations may persuade him to take decisions which appear unlikely from a purely military point of view.

Even enemy *landings with limited objectives* can interfere seriously with our own plans if they result in the enemy gaining any kind of foothold on the coast. They can interrupt our coastal sea traffic, and pin down strong forces of our Army and Air Force, which will therefore have to be withdrawn from areas of crucial importance. It would be particularly dangerous should the enemy succeed in capturing our airfields or in establishing his own in areas which he has occupied.

The many important military and industrial establishments on the coast or in its neighbourhood, some of them equipped with particularly valuable plant, may moreover tempt the enemy *to undertake surprise attacks of a local nature*.

Particular attention must be paid to English *preparations for landings* on the open coast, for which they have at their disposal many armoured landing craft, built to carry armoured fighting vehicles and heavy weapons. The possibility of *parachute and airborne attacks* on a large scale must also be envisaged.

II. *General operational instructions for coastal defence:*

1. *Coastal defence is a task for all Armed Forces*, calling for particularly close and complete cooperation by all units.

2. The intelligence service, as well as the day-to-day reconnaissance by the *Navy* and the *Air Force*, must strive to obtain early information of enemy *readiness and approach preparations* for a landing operation.

All suitable sea and air forces will then concentrate on enemy points of embarkation and convoys, with the aim of destroying the enemy as far from the coast as possible.

It is however possible that the enemy, by skilful camouflage and by taking advantage of unpredictable weather conditions, may achieve a completely surprise attack. *All troops* who may be exposed to such surprise attacks must be in *a state of permanent readiness*.

One of the most important duties of Commanding Officers will be to overcome the lack of vigilance among the troops which, as experience has shown, increases with the passage of time.

3. *In defending the coast* – and this includes *coastal waters* within range of medium coastal artillery – *responsibility for the planning and implementation of defensive measures* must, as recent battle experience dictates, lie unequivocally and unreservedly in the hands of a single Commander.

The Commander responsible must make use of all available forces and weapons of the branches of the Armed Forces, of organizations and units outside the Armed Forces, and of our civil headquarters in the area, for the destruction of enemy transports and landing forces. He will use them so that the attack collapses *if possible before it can reach the coast, at the latest on the coast itself.*

Enemy forces which have landed must be destroyed or thrown back into the sea by immediate counter-attack. All personnel bearing arms – irrespective to which branch of the Armed Forces or to which non-service organization they may belong – will be employed for this. Moreover, the required working capacity of the naval shore supply establishments must be guaranteed, in so far as they are not involved in the land fighting themselves. The same applies to the readiness for action of the Air Force ground staff and the anti-aircraft defence of airfields.

No headquarters or formation is to initiate withdrawal in such circumstances. All German troops stationed on or near the coast must be armed and trained for battle.

The enemy must be prevented from securing a foothold on all islands which could present a threat to the mainland or coastal shipping.

4. *The distribution of forces and the extension of defensive works* must be so carried out that our strongest defence points are situated in those sectors most likely to be chosen by the enemy for landings (fortified areas).

Other coastal sectors which may be threatened by small-scale surprise attacks will be defended by a series of strong-points, supported if possible by the coastal batteries. All military and industrial plant of importance to the war effort will be included within these strong-points.

The same principles will apply to off-shore islands.

Less threatened sectors will be kept under observation.

5. *The division of the coast into sectors* will be decided by the three services in mutual agreement, or, should the situation demand it, by the responsible Commander (referred to

here in paragraph III, 1), whose decision will be final.

6. *The fortified areas and strong-points* must be able, by proper distribution of forces, by completion of all-round defence, and by their supply situation, to hold out for some time even against superior enemy forces.

Fortified areas and strong-points will be defended to the last man. They must never be forced to surrender from lack of ammunition, rations, or water.

7. The responsible Commander (referred to here in paragraph III, 1) will issue orders for keeping the coast under constant observation, and ensure that reconnaissance reports from all services are quickly evaluated, coordinated, and transmitted to the headquarters and civilian authorities concerned.

As soon as there is any evidence that an operation by the enemy is imminent, the Commander is authorized to issue the necessary instructions for coordinated and complementary reconnaissance on sea and land.

8. There can be no question of peacetime privileges for any headquarters or formation of the Armed Forces in coastal areas, or for non-military organizations and units. Their accommodation, security precautions, equipment, immediate readiness for action, and the use they make of the terrain, will be entirely dependent upon the necessity of meeting any enemy attack as swiftly and in as great strength as possible. Where the military situation requires it, the civilian population will be immediately evacuated.

III. *Competence of Commanders.*

1. The following are responsible for the preparation and execution of coastal defence in the *areas under German Command*:

    (*a*) In the Eastern area of operations (excluding Finland): The Army Commanders appointed by High Command of the Army.

    (*b*) In the coastal area of Army High Command Lapland:

Commander-in-Chief Army High Command Lapland.

(c) In Norway:

Commander Armed Forces Norway.

(d) In Denmark:

The Commander of German troops in Denmark.

(e) In the occupied Western territories (including the Netherlands):

Commander-in-Chief West.

For coastal defence the responsible Commanders in (d) and (e) will be directly subordinate to the High Command of the Armed Forces.

(f) In the Balkans (including the occupied islands):

Commander Armed Forces South-east.

(g) In the Baltic territories and the Ukraine:

Commander Armed Forces Baltic Territories and Ukraine.

(h) In the Home theatre of war: the Commanding Admirals.

2. The Commanders named in paragraph III, 1 will have for these tasks *full powers of command* over the staffs commanding all Armed Forces, the German civil authorities, and the non-military units and organizations in their area.

In exercising their authority they will issue the necessary tactical, administrative, and supply instructions, and will ensure that they are complied with. In all matters relating to land fighting, training of units will follow their ruling, and all necessary information will be put at their disposal.

3. Among the orders to be given and measures to be taken, the following must *be given first place*.

(a) The inclusion within fortified areas or strong-points of all important military and industrial establishments connected with defence, particularly those of the Navy (submarine bases) and the Air Force.

(b) The coordination of coastal reconnaissance.

(c) The defence of fortified areas and strong-points by infantry.

(*d*) The defence by infantry of all isolated positions outside the fortified areas and strong-points – e.g. coastal look-out points and air-attack warning-posts.

(*e*) Artillery defence against land targets. (The Navy has priority in the installation of new batteries, or the conversion of existing batteries.)

(*f*) The defensive readiness, development, and supply facilities of installations, as well as of isolated positions away from these installations. (This includes being equipped with all weapons needed for defence: mines, hand-grenades, flame-throwers, barbed-wire, etc.)

(*g*) The signals network.

(*h*) Methods for ensuring that troops are always on the alert, and that infantry and gunnery training is being carried out in accordance with the special defence requirements.

4. *The same authority is conferred upon local commanders up to sector commanders*, in so far as they are responsible for the defence of a part of the coast.

The Commanders designated in paragraph III, 1 will, in general, appoint Commanders of *Army Divisions* employed in coastal defence as local Commanders with full powers. In Crete the 'Fortress Commandant Crete' will appoint them.

As far as their other duties allow, local Commandants or Commanders of the Air Force and Navy will be made responsible for the general defence of individual sectors or sub-sectors, particularly Air and Naval strong-points.

5. *All naval and air units employed in strategic warfare* are subordinate to the Navy or Air Force. In the event of enemy attacks on the coast, however, they are required to comply, in so far as tactical considerations allow, with the orders of the Commanders responsible for defence. They must therefore be included in the distribution of such information as they require for their duties, and close liaison will be maintained with their headquarters.

IV. *Special duties of the branches of the Armed Forces in the field of coastal defence.*

1. *Navy.*
(*a*) Organization and protection of coastal traffic.
(*b*) Training and employment of all coastal artillery against targets at sea.
(*c*) Employment of naval forces.

2. *Air Force.*
(*a*) Air defence of coastal areas. The use against enemy landings of suitable and available anti-aircraft guns, under the orders of the commander responsible for local defence, will not be affected.
(*b*) The completion of ground organizations and their protection against air attack and surprise attack by land; the latter in cases where airfields are not included in the coastal defences and are therefore insufficiently protected.
(*c*) Operational employment of air forces. Attention will be paid to the duplication of command implied by these special duties.

V. Orders and instructions which run contrary to this directive are cancelled from 1st April 1942.

New operation orders, which will be issued by Commanders on the basis of my directive, are to be submitted to me through the High Command of the Armed Forces.

signed: ADOLF HITLER

41

When the campaigning season in Russia opened again, the Germans had suffered heavily, and lost some ground, in the winter months; but Hitler was prepared to launch a new offensive. As before, he was prepared to stand still before Moscow, and concentrate on Leningrad and the Caucasus.

The Führer and Supreme   Führer Headquarters,
Commander of the Armed Forces   5th April 1942.
                                                14 copies

Directive No. 41

The winter battle in Russia is nearing its end. Thanks to the unequalled courage and self-sacrificing devotion of our soldiers on the Eastern front, German arms have achieved a great defensive success.

The enemy has suffered severe losses in men and material. In an effort to exploit what appeared to him to be early successes, he has expended during the winter the bulk of reserves intended for later operations.

As soon as the weather and the state of the terrain allows, we must seize the initiative again, and through the superiority of German leadership and the German soldier force our will upon the enemy.

Our aim is to wipe out the entire defence potential remaining to the Soviets, and to cut them off, as far as possible, from their most important centres of war industry.

All available forces, German and allied, will be employed in this task. At the same time, the security of occupied territories in Western and Northern Europe, *especially along the coast*, will be ensured in all circumstances.

I. *General Plan*

In pursuit of the original plan for the Eastern campaign, the armies of the Central sector will stand fast, those in the *North* will capture Leningrad and link up with the Finns, while those on the *southern flank* will break through into the Caucasus.

In view of conditions prevailing at the end of winter, the availability of troops and resources, and transport problems, these aims can be achieved only one at a time.

First, therefore, all available forces will be concentrated on the *main operations in the Southern sector*, with the aim of destroying the enemy before the Don, in order to secure the Caucasian oilfields and the passes through the Caucasus mountains themselves.

The final encirclement of Leningrad and the occupation of Ingermanland may be undertaken as soon as conditions in that area permit, or sufficient forces can be made available from other theatres.

II. *Conduct of operations*

A. *The first task* of the Army and Air Force, when the period of thaw with its muddy ground conditions is over, will be to establish the preliminary conditions for carrying out our main operation.

This calls for *mopping-up and consolidation on the whole Eastern front* and in the rear areas so that the greatest possible forces may be released for the main operation. The other sectors of the front must be able to meet any attack with the smallest possible expenditure of manpower.

Wherever, for this purpose, *offensive operations with limited objectives* are to be carried out, in accordance with my orders, every effort will be made to ensure that all available forces of the Army and Air Force are ready to go into action in overwhelming strength, in order to achieve rapid and decisive success. Only thus shall we be able, even before the beginning of the big spring offensive, to make our troops confident in the certainty of victory, and to instil into the enemy a sense of his own hopeless inferiority.

B. The next task will be a mopping-up operation in the *Kerch peninsula on the Crimea* and the capture of *Sevastopol*. The Air Force, and later the Navy, will have the task of preparing these operations, and hindering enemy supply traffic in the Black Sea and the Kerch Straits as energetically as possible.

In the *Southern area*, the enemy forces which have broken through on both sides of *Izyum* will be cut off along the course of the Donets river and destroyed.

Final decision concerning the mopping-up still necessary

in the *Central and Northern sectors* of the Eastern front must
await conclusion of the present fighting and of the muddy
season. The necessary forces, however, must be provided,
as soon as the situation allows, by thinning out front-line
troops.

C. *The main operation on the Eastern front.*

The purpose is, as already stated, to occupy the Caucasus
front by decisively attacking and destroying Russian forces
stationed in the Voronezh area to the south, west, or north
of the Don. Because of the manner in which the available
formations must be brought up, this operation can be carried
out in a series of consecutive, but coordinated and complementary, attacks. Therefore these attacks must be so syn-
chronized from north to south that each individual offensive
is carried out by the largest possible concentration of army,
and particularly of air, forces which can be assured at the
decisive points.

Experience has sufficiently shown that the Russians are
not very vulnerable to operational encircling movements. It
is therefore of decisive importance that, as in the double
battle of Vyazma–Bryansk, individual breaches of the front
should take the form of close pincer movements.

We must avoid closing the pincers too late, thus giving the
enemy the possibility of avoiding destruction.

It must not happen that, by advancing too quickly and too
far, armoured and motorized formations lose connexion
with the infantry following them; or that they lose the
opportunity of supporting the hard-pressed, forward-
fighting infantry by direct attacks on the rear of the encircled Russian armies.

Therefore, apart from the main object of the operation, in
each individual case, we must be absolutely sure to annihilate
the enemy by the method of attack and by the direction of
the forces used.

The general operation will begin with an overall attack
and, if possible, a breakthrough from the area south of Orel

in the direction of Voronezh. Of the two armoured and motorized formations forming the pincers, the *northern* will be in greater strength than the southern. The object of this breakthrough is the capture of Voronezh itself. While certain infantry divisions will immediately establish a strong defensive front between the Orel area, from which the attack will be launched, and Voronezh, armoured and motorized formations are to continue the attack south from Voronezh, with their left flank on the River Don, in support of a second breakthrough to take place towards the east, from the general area of Kharkov. Here too the primary objective is not simply to break the Russian front but, in cooperation with the motorized forces thrusting down the Don, to destroy the enemy armies.

The third attack in the course of these operations will be so conducted that formations thrusting down the Don can link up in the Stalingrad area with forces advancing from the Taganrog–Artelnovsk area between the lower waters of the Don and Voroshilovgrad across the Donets to the east. These forces should finally establish contact with the armoured forces advancing on Stalingrad.

Should opportunities arise during these operations, particularly by the capture of undemolished bridges, to establish bridgeheads to the east or south of the Don, advantage will be taken of them. In any event, every effort will be made to reach Stalingrad itself, or at least to bring the city under fire from heavy artillery so that it may no longer be of any use as an industrial or communications centre.

It would be particularly desirable if we could secure either undamaged bridges in Rostov itself or other bridgeheads south of the Don for later operations.

In order to prevent large numbers of Russian forces north of the Don from escaping southwards across the river, it is important that the right flank of our forces advancing east from the Taganrog area should be strengthened by armoured and motorized troops. These will, if necessary, be formed from improvised units.

According to the progress made in these attacks, we must not only provide strong protection for the north-east flank of the operation; we must immediately set about establishing positions along the Don. In this matter, anti-tank defences are especially important. These positions will from the first be prepared with a view to their eventual occupation in winter, for which they will be fully equipped.

In the first instance, units of our allies will be used to hold the Don front, which will become longer and longer as the attack proceeds. German forces will provide a strong supporting force between Orel and the Don, and in the Stalingrad strip. For the rest, individual German divisions will also remain available as reserves behind the Don front.

Allied troops will be mainly disposed so that the Hungarians are farthest north, then the Italians, and the Rumanians furthest to the south-east.

D. *The swift progress of the movements* across the Don to the south, in order to attain the operational objectives, is essential, in consideration of the season.

III. *Air Force*.

Apart from giving direct support to the Army, the task of the Air Force will be to cover the deployment of forces in the Army Group South area *by strengthening air defences*. This applies particularly to railway bridges across the Dnieper.

If *enemy forces are seen to be concentrating*, the principal roads and railways serving the concentration area will be brought under continuous attack well in the enemy's rear. A first priority will be the destruction of railway bridges across the Don.

At the opening of operations, the *enemy Air Force* and its ground organization in the theatre of operations will be attacked and destroyed by a concentrated effort of all available forces.

The possibility of a *hasty transfer of Air Force units* to

the Central and Northern fronts must be borne in mind, and the necessary ground organization for this maintained as far as possible.

IV. *Navy*.

In the *Black Sea* it is the principal duty of the Navy, in so far as our combat and escort forces and our tonnage allow, to assist in supplying the Army and Air Force by sea.

Because the battle potential of the Russian Black Sea fleet is still unbroken it is particularly important that the light naval forces to be moved to the Black Sea should be ready for action there as soon as possible.

The Baltic will be protected by blockading Russian naval forces in the inner waters of the Gulf of Finland.

V. My basic order to *ensure secrecy** is once again to be brought to the attention of all staffs concerned in these preparations. In this connexion the attitude to be adopted to our allies will be laid down in special instructions.

VI. *The preparations planned by the various branches of the Armed Forces*, and their time-tables, will be notified to me through the High Command of the Armed Forces.

signed: ADOLF HITLER

42

Fears of a second front in the West now caused the Germans to revive their old projects of occupying, or at least being ready to occupy, Mediterranean France (see Directive 19) and Spain (Directive 32, note 1). It will be noted that there is no question now of cooperation with Franco in respect of Spain. His name,

---

* This was an order issued by Hitler on 11th January 1940, after two German Air Force officers had allowed the secret orders for the Western offensive to fall into Allied hands. It strictly limited access to secret material.

since his 'great refusal' of the previous winter, could no longer be uttered in Hitler's presence.

The Führer   Führer Headquarters.
                                              29th May 1942.
                                              6 copies

Directive No. 42
Instructions for operations against unoccupied France and the Iberian Peninsula

(previously known as 'Attila' and 'Isabella')

I. *The development of the situation in unoccupied France*, or in the French possessions in North Africa, may render it necessary in future to occupy the *whole* of French territory.

Likewise we must reckon on possible enemy attempts to seize the *Iberian Peninsula*, which will call for immediate counter-measures on our part.

II. *Because of the continual shifting of our forces in the West*, and the consequent changes in the readiness for battle of our formations there, *only general principles can be given for carrying out these operations*. Similarly, the situation with regard to manpower and equipment makes it impossible to keep forces and material permanently available for these operations.

Therefore the directives already issued for 'Attila' and 'Isabella' are cancelled with immediate effect. *Improvised plans for both operations* will, however, be made so that they can still be carried out at very short notice.

III. *Occupation of unoccupied France in cooperation with Italian Forces* (cover name 'Anton' (most secret). Day of commencement of operations, A-day).

1. *The object of the operation* is to break the powers of resistance of unoccupied France and to occupy the country.

It will therefore be the task of the *German forces*, without weakening coastal defence, with quickly formed and very mobile forces, to seize by surprise such objectives as are important for defence, and thus to eliminate the possibility of French resistance. It will be particularly important to seize quickly the larger French garrison towns, railway junctions, dumps of supplies, munitions and arms, airfields, and the seat of the Government, Vichy.

It will be the task of *the Italians* to occupy the French Mediterranean coast (and Corsica) and, by blockading naval bases, particularly Toulon, to prevent the French Home Fleet and merchant vessels in Mediterranean ports from passing over to the enemy. The Italians will be supported in this by German naval and air forces in the Mediterranean.

The Italians may also, if the situation requires, have to take action in Tunisia. A force for this purpose is now being formed.

2. *The High Command of the Army* (*Army Group D*) will make all necessary preparations in view of the forces available.

The special forces required to support the Army in particular tasks (e.g. the occupation of Air Force establishments, the elimination of signals centres, and sabotage) are to be formed by the branches of the Armed Forces and by the departments of the High Command of the Armed Forces, upon request of, and in agreement with, the High Command of the Army.

3. It will be the task of the Air Force to give direct support to ground operations in France and, in cooperation with the Italians, to eliminate such French air forces as remain in France.

If 7th Air Division and the necessary transport are available, advantage will be taken of all possibilities of airborne landings.

In order that the Air Force may be used for this purpose, the necessary ground organization is to be set up at once in occupied France.

IV. *First counter-measures against an enemy assault on the Iberian Peninsula* (cover name 'Ilona' (most secret). Day of crossing the frontier, I-day).

1. *The first aim of our counter-measures* will be to occupy the southern passes of the Pyrenees and thus establish the conditions necessary for future operations. Any threat to the strategically important ports on the Atlantic Coast of France will be met by securing the harbours on the northern coast of Spain.

2. *Negotiations and preliminary discussions* with the Spanish and other non-German authorities concerning these plans are forbidden.

V. *The High Commands of the branches of the Armed Forces* will report by 10th June concerning both operations, as follows:

(*a*) Proposed strength of forces.
(*b*) Proposals on general lines for carrying out operations.
(*c*) Time required before operations can begin.
(*d*) Demands or requests to the Italians, and possible ways of supporting them (see III, 1, sub-section 3).

The necessary discussions with the Italians will then be authorized by the High Command of the Armed Forces.

signed: ADOLF HITLER

43

Projects for a second front in Europe, insistently demanded by Russia, were indeed being worked out in London; but apart from commando raids (such as that on St Nazaire in March) nothing was yet practical. Indeed, the early summer months of 1942 were months of German success on all fronts. In Russia the Germans swept forward to the Crimea; in the Mediterranean the British remained static in the African desert while Rommel was reinforced; and the new German air power in the Mediterranean nearly succeeded in starving Malta, the most essential British fortress, into submission. On 26th May Rommel forestalled the British and launched a heavy attack. On 21st June he captured Tobruk, thought impregnable, with its garrison of 25,000 men, and shortly afterwards entered Egypt, intent on destroying the whole British position in the Middle East. On 1st July Churchill's strategy was challenged in Parliament. In these circumstances Hitler was confident. 'Our rapid and great victories', he wrote on 9th July, might well confront Britain with the dilemma of either launching a full-scale invasion now or 'seeing Russia eliminated as a political and military factor'. He therefore gave new orders for readiness along the Atlantic coast, and promised that, 'in the event of an enemy landing, I personally will proceed to the West and assume charge of operations there.' But the threat clearly did not alarm him. Such landings would be premature and could be dealt with. Meanwhile his eyes were turned to the East where he looked forward, at last, to final victory. His headquarters were deep in the Ukraine. His public speeches and private table-talk breathed confidence. The next three directives illustrate his plans for continuing the Russian campaign to final success in 1942.

The Führer

Führer Headquarters,
11th July 1942.
5 copies

Directive No. 43
Continuation of operations from the Crimea

1. After clearing the Kerch peninsula and capturing Sevastopol, *the first task of 11th Army* will be, while ensuring the defence of the Crimea, to make all *preparations* for the main body of the army to cross the Kerch strait by the middle of August at the latest.* The aim of this operation

---

* This was changed by teleprinter two days later to 'by the beginning of August'.

will be to thrust forward on either side of the western foothills of the Caucasus in a south-easterly and easterly direction.

The operation will be known by the cover-name 'Blücher'
(most secret), and the day of the landing will be known as
'Bl-day'.

2. The operation will *be executed* on the following lines:

In accordance with the proposals of 11th Army, the crossing is to be planned so that the strongest possible forces are
landed in the rear of enemy coast defences.

The high ground north of Novorossiysk will then be captured. The ports of Anapa and Novorossiysk will be occupied, thereby eliminating bases for the enemy fleet.

After that, the operation will continue to the north of the
Caucasus, its main thrust in a general easterly direction. In
this connexion it is specially important that the Maykop area
be quickly occupied. The decision whether small forces
should also be landed on the coast road along the Black Sea
in the Tuapse area can only later be taken.

For this operation 11th Army is to keep the bulk of the
medium and field artillery (flat trajectory and howitzer)
mortar batteries up to 21 cm. mortars inclusive, and some of
the heavy projector detachments.

3. *The Navy* will take immediate steps to secure the
necessary shipping for the crossing, in accordance with
detailed Army requirements.

To meet this need, suitable shipping, apart from vessels
already available in the Black Sea and the Sea of Azov and
those which may be brought in for the operation, will be
chartered or bought from the Bulgarians and Rumanians.

During the actual operation, the Navy will support the
landing forces during the crossing, and protect them with all
available means against action by enemy sea forces.

Naval units detailed to cover the crossing of the landing
forces will come under command of 11th Army during the
operation.

4. The task of the *Air Force* in preparing the operation is

THE BATTLE IN
SOUTH RUSSIA 1942

FRONT, APRIL 1942
+++++MAXIMUM GERMAN GAINS

MURMANSK

ARCHANGEL

LENINGRAD

KALININ
MOSCOW
VYAZMA
SMOLENSK
MINSK
BRYANSK
OREL
KURSK   VORONEZH
KIEV R. DNIEPER
KHARKOV   R. DON
R. DONETZ
STALINGRAD
STALINO
ODESSA   ROSTOV

R. VOLGA

BULGARIA
SEVASTOPOL   KERCH
STRAITS   MAIKOP
TUAPSE   NALCHIK   GROZNY
Black   Sea
TIFLIS

Caspian   Sea

0   300
MILES

the overall elimination of enemy naval forces and harbours in the Black Sea.

During the operation its task, apart from immediate support of the landing forces, will be to prevent enemy naval forces from interfering with the crossing.

Preparations are to be made so that the Army forces landed on the Temryuk peninsula may be supplied for several days by air.

The possibility of using parachute and airborne troops is to be investigated. If possible, 7th Airborne Division will not be involved in these operations, or at least only in small part. It may be advantageous to employ units of 22nd Infantry Division as airborne troops.

5. The enemy is to be *deceived into believing* that large forces of 11th Army are being moved from the Crimea to the area north of the Sea of Azov. For this purpose a large-scale movement by road and rail will be undertaken towards the north, while the actual concentration for 'Undertaking Blücher' will be concealed by night marches.

The High Command of the Armed Forces will support this deception by suitable means.

6. The following *special operations* (*Abwehr* II*) have been prepared. These special operations are to be examined by the General Staff of the Army with Foreign Intelligence, Security II [Abwehr II], and, if approved, to be included in 'Operation Blücher'.

(*a*) Parachute drop of a commando detachment in the Maykop area to protect oil installations ('Undertaking Schamil').

(*b*) Sabotage operations against the triangle of railways

---

* *Abwehr* II (in full, *Amt Ausland*, *Abwehr*, *Abteilung II*) was the section of the Armed Forces Foreign Intelligence Service which specialized in sabotage and subversion. The Brandenburg Training Regiment (*Lehrregiment Brandenburg*) was a unit under its orders.

Krasnodar–Kropotkin–Tikhoretsk, and against the bridges over the Kuban in that area.

(c) Participation of a light engineer company of the Brandenburg Training Regiment, raised for operations of this kind, in attacks on enemy ports and coastal installations.

7. *Details* for the preparation and conduct of the operation will be worked out by the Army General Staff in conjunction with the Navy and Air Force.

I am to be informed daily through High Command of the Armed Forces, Operations Staff, on the state of preparations (provision of shipping) and the forces to be used.

signed: ADOLF HITLER

44

The Führer

Führer Headquarters,
21st July 1942.
8 copies

Directive No. 44
Operations in Northern Finland

1. The unexpectedly rapid and favourable development of the *operations against the Timoshenko Army Group* entitle us to assume that we may soon succeed in depriving Soviet Russia of the Caucasus, with her most important source of oil, and of a valuable line of communication for the delivery of English and American supplies.

This, coupled with the loss of the entire Donets industrial area, will strike a blow at the Soviet Union which would have immeasurable consequences.

2. We must now *cut the northern supply route* which links Soviet Russia with the Anglo-Saxon powers. This is principally the *Murmansk railway*, along which by far the largest proportion of supplies from America and England were delivered during the winter months. The importance of this

supply route will increase further when the season and weather conditions prevent successful operations against northern convoys.

3. 20th Mountain Army therefore proposes, in cooperation with 5th Air Fleet, to prepare an offensive this autumn *to seize the Murmansk railway near Kandalaksha.*

For this, we can assume –

(*a*) Leningrad will be captured in September at the latest, and Finnish forces thereby released.

(*b*) 5th Mountain Division will have moved to Finland by the end of September.

The undertaking has been allotted the cover-name of '*Lachsfang* [Salmon-Trap]'. Day of attack will be called 'L-day'.

4. It is desirable that the attack by 20th Mountain Army should be coordinated with *a Finnish advance on Belomorsk.*

Liaison Staff North will ascertain the intentions of the Finnish Command for this attack, in conjunction with 20th Mountain Army.

5. *The most important task of 20th Mountain Army* remains the complete protection of the Finnish nickel production.

It must once again be stressed, with the greatest emphasis, that without deliveries of Finnish nickel Germany could probably no longer manufacture the high-grade steel necessary above all for aircraft and submarine engines. This could have decisive effects upon the outcome of the war.

20th Mountain Army must therefore be at all times ready to send reinforcements to Mountain Corps Norway as required for the fulfilment of these tasks.

Similarly, the Air Force 5th Air Fleet will, in the event of an attack upon the nickel mines, renounce all other duties and concentrate on the defence of the area.

6. '*Undertaking Meadowland* [*Wiesengrund*]'* will not

---

* This was the project to capture the 'Fisherman's Peninsula'. See above, Directive 37, paragraph 1(*d*).

take place this year. Preparations for this operation will, however, continue and be reinforced, so that it can be executed in the spring of 1943 at short notice (about eight weeks).

Particular attention will be paid to the development and strengthening of air and supply bases, because these are essential both for the success of 'Meadowland' and for meeting a major enemy offensive in the north.

7. 20th Mountain Army and Commander-in-Chief Air Force will inform me of their intentions as soon as possible.

Liaison Staffs North will report on Finnish plans for the attack on Belomorsk.

signed: ADOLF HITLER

45

The Führer

Führer Headquarters,
23rd July 1942.
6 copies

Directive No. 45
Continuation of 'Operation Brunswick [Braunschweig]'*

I. In a campaign which has lasted little more than three weeks, the broad objectives outlined by me for the southern flank of the Eastern front have been largely achieved. Only weak enemy forces from the Timoshenko Army Group have succeeded in avoiding encirclement and reaching the further bank of the Don. We must expect them to be reinforced from the Caucasus.

A further concentration of enemy forces is taking place in the Stalingrad area, which the enemy will probably defend tenaciously.

---

* This was the cover-name given to the Caucasus offensive.
T—G

II. *Aims of future operations.*

A. *Army.*

1. The next task of Army Group A is to encircle enemy forces which have escaped across the Don in the area south and south-east of Rostov, and to destroy them.

For this purpose strong fast-moving forces are to move from the bridgeheads which will be established in the Konstantinovskaia–Tsymlyanskaya area, in a general south-westerly direction towards Tikhoretsk. Infantry, light infantry, and mountain divisions will cross the Don in the Rostov area.

In addition, the task of cutting the Tikhoretsk–Stalingrad railway line with advanced spearheads remains unchanged.

Two armoured formations of Army Group A (including 24th Armoured Division) will come under command of Army Group B for further operations south-eastwards.

Infantry division 'Greater Germany [*Grossdeutschland*]' is not to advance beyond the Manych sector.* Preparations will be made to move it to the west.

2. *After the destruction of enemy forces* south of the Don, the most important task of Army Group A will be to occupy the entire eastern coastline of the Black Sea, thereby eliminating the Black Sea ports and the enemy Black Sea fleet.

For this purpose the formations of 11th Army already designated (Rumanian Mountain Corps) will be brought across the Kerch Straits as soon as the advance of the main body of Army Group A becomes effective, and will then push south-east along the Black Sea coastal road.

A *further force* composed of all remaining mountain and light infantry divisions will force a passage of the Kuban, and occupy the high ground around Maykop and Armavir.

In the further advance of this force, reinforced at a suitable time by mountain units, towards and across the western

---

* This passage, and the previous sentence, were originally slightly different. They are here printed as amended on the following day.

part of the Caucasus, all practical passes are to be used, so that the Black Sea coast may be occupied in conjunction with 11th Army.

3. *At the same time* a force composed chiefly of fast-moving formations will give flank cover in the east and capture the Groznyy area. Detachments will block the military road between Osetia and Groznyy, if possible at the top of the passes.

Thereafter the Baku area will be occupied by a thrust along the Caspian coast.

The Army Group may expect the subsequent arrival of the Italian Alpine Corps.

These operations by Army Group A will be known by the cover name '*Edelweiss*'. Security: Most Secret.

4. The task of Army Group B is, as previously laid down, to develop the Don defences and, by a thrust forward to Stalingrad, to smash the enemy forces concentrated there, to occupy the town, and to block the land communications between the Don and the Volga as well as the Don itself.

Closely connected with this, fast-moving forces will advance along the Volga with the task of thrusting through to Astrakhan and blocking the main course of the Volga in the same way.

These operations by Army Group B will be known by the cover-name 'Heron [*Fischreiher*]'. Security: Most Secret.

B. *Air Force.*

The task of the Air Force is, primarily, to give strong support to the land forces crossing the Don, and to the advance of the eastern group along the railway to Tikhoretsk, and to concentrate its forces on the destruction of the Timoshenko Army Group.

In addition, the operations of Army Group B against Stalingrad and the western part of Astrakhan will be supported. The early destruction of the city of Stalingrad is especially important. Attacks will also be made, as opportunity affords, on Astrakhan. Shipping on the Lower Volga should be harassed by mine-laying.

During further operations the Air Force is to concentrate on cooperating with the forces advancing on the Black Sea ports, and, apart from giving direct support to the Army, to assist the Navy in preventing enemy naval forces from interfering.

Secondly, sufficient forces must be allocated to cooperate with the thrust on Baku via Groznyy.

In view of *the decisive importance of the Caucasus oilfields* for the further prosecution of the war, air attacks against their refineries and storage tanks, and against ports used for oil shipments on the Black Sea, will only be carried out if the operations of the Army make them absolutely essential. But in order to block enemy supplies of oil from the Caucasus as soon as possible, it is especially important to cut the railways and pipelines still being used for this purpose and to harass shipping on the Caspian at an early date.

C. *Navy*.

It will be the task of the Navy, besides giving direct support to the Army in the crossing of the Kerch Straits, to harass enemy sea action against our coastal operations with all the forces available in the Black Sea.

To facilitate Army Supply, some naval ferries will be brought through the Kerch Straits to the Don, as soon as possible.

In addition, Commander-in-Chief Navy will make preparation for transferring light forces to the Caspian Sea to harass enemy shipping (oil tankers and communications with the Anglo-Saxons in Iran).

III. The local operations now being prepared *in the Central and Northern Army Group* areas should be carried out as far as possible in quick succession. Their result must be the maximum disruption and disintegration of enemy commands and forces.

Army Group North is preparing to capture Leningrad by the beginning of September. Cover-name: 'Fire Magic' [*Feuerzauber*]'.* For this, they will be reinforced by five divisions from 11th Army, by heavy and extra-heavy artillery and by such other Army troops as may be necessary.

Two German and two Rumanian divisions will remain in the Crimea for the present. 22nd Division, as already ordered, will revert to Commander Armed Forces South-east.

IV. In handling and re-transmitting this Directive and orders arising from it, I draw particular attention to my order on *secrecy* of 12th August.

signed: ADOLF HITLER

46

One of the greatest problems of the German Army in Russia was the partisan activity organized by the communist party in the large areas behind the front. The following directive deals with this problem.

The Führer

Führer Headquarters,
18th August 1942.
30 copies

Directive No. 46
Instructions for intensified action against banditry in the East

A. *General Considerations*
I. In recent months *banditry in the East* has assumed intolerable proportions, and threatens to become a serious danger to supplies for the front and to the economic exploitation of the country.

---

* On 31st July 1942 this cover-name was changed to '*Nordlicht* (Northern Light)'.

By the beginning of winter these bandit gangs must be substantially exterminated, so that order may be restored behind the Eastern front and severe disadvantages to our winter operations avoided.

The following measures are necessary:

1. Rapid, drastic, and active operations against the bandits by the coordination of all available forces of the Armed Forces, the SS, and Police which are suitable for the purpose.

2. The concentration of all propaganda, economic, and political measures on the necessity of combating banditry.

II. The following *general principles* will be borne in mind by all concerned in formulating military, police, and economic measures:

1. The fight against banditry is as much *a matter of strategy* as the fight against the enemy at the front. It will therefore be organized and carried out by the same staffs.

2. The destruction of the bandits calls for *active operations and the most rigorous measures* against all members of gangs or those guilty of supporting them. Operation orders for action against bandits will follow.

3. The confidence of the local population in German authority must be gained by *handling them strictly but justly*.

4. A necessary condition for the destruction of bandit gangs is *the assurance to the local population of the minimum requirements of life*. Should this fail, or – what is particularly important – should available supplies not be fairly distributed, the result will be that more recruits will join the bandits.

5. In this struggle against the bandits the *cooperation of the local population* is indispensable. Deserving persons should not be parsimoniously treated; rewards should be really attractive. On the other hand, reprisals for action in support of the bandits must be all the more severe.

6. *Misplaced confidence in the native population*, particularly in those working for the German authorities, must be strictly guarded against. Even though the majority of the population is opposed to the bandits, there are always spies

to be reckoned with, whose task is to inform the bandits of all action contemplated against them.

B. *Command and responsibility*

1. *The Reichsführer SS and the Chief of the German Police.**

The Reichsführer SS and Chief of the German Police is the central authority for the collection and evaluation of all information concerning action against bandits.

In addition, the Reichsführer SS has the sole responsibility for combating banditry in the *Reich Commissioners' territories*. Commanders of the Armed Forces will support him in his tasks arising from this by coordinating their measures, and by transferring such staffs, command communications, and supplies as are needed. In so far as is allowed by military security duties, which will be carried out locally as actively as possible, Higher SS and Police Leaders† will if necessary assume temporary command of forces of the Armed Forces for use in their operations.

The closest liaison between Higher SS and Police Leaders and Commanders of the Armed Forces is an essential condition of success.

2. *Army.*

The Chief of the Army General Staff is solely responsible for action against bandits in *operational areas*. In carrying out this task, police units stationed in the area of operations, as well as the Army units engaged, will come under the Army Commanders concerned. The latter will entrust the command of individual operations to Army Commanders, or to Higher SS and Police Leaders, according to the situation,

---

* i.e. Heinrich Himmler.

† *Höhere SS- und Polizeiführer* were Himmler's deputies in occupied countries.

the forces engaged, and the seniority of the officers concerned.

C. *Available Forces*

1. *Forces of the Reichsführer SS.*

The Police and SS formations available and allocated for operations against bandits are intended primarily for *active* operations. Their employment in other security duties is to be avoided. Efforts will be made to reinforce Police and SS formations in the East, and to transfer to the threatened areas a considerable number of establishments of the Reichsführer SS at present employed elsewhere. Formations still at the front, but indispensable for operations against bandits in the rear areas, will be withdrawn from the Army as soon as possible, and placed at the disposal of the Reichsführer SS for duty in their proper areas.

2. *Army Forces.*

In order to reinforce the garrisons of the vast eastern territories behind the fighting front, I order as follows:

(*a*) When the General Government* becomes a Home Forces area, two reserve divisions will move to the General Government.

(*b*) A total of five reserve divisions will be moved to the spheres of Commander Armed Forces Baltic Territories and Commander Armed Forces Ukraine by 15th October 1942.

(*c*) All formations, units, staffs, establishments, and schools of the Field Army not serving under the Commander of the Replacement Army will be withdrawn by 1st October 1942 from the General Government and transferred to the territories of the Reich Commissioners or to the area of operations. Any necessary exceptions will be approved by the Chief of the High Command of the Armed Forces.

(*d*) The final target is to transfer by the end of October a

---

* i.e. German-occupied Poland.

replacement force of 50,000 men formed from the Reserve Army.

(e) The necessary operation orders concerning paragraphs (a) to (d) will be issued by the Chief of the High Command of the Armed Forces.

3. *Air Force*.

Commander-in-Chief Air Force will arrange for the transfer of Air Force establishments to the areas threatened by bandits, in order to reinforce the garrison in the eastern territories.

4. *Units formed from the native population*.

Native units made up of local people who have particularly distinguished themselves in action against the bandits are to be maintained and extended,* provided they are completely reliable and are volunteers. They will not take part in fighting at the front, nor will *émigrés* or members of the former intelligentsia be enrolled in them.

The Army General Staff will issue general directions covering the internal organization of these units, where this has not already been done. In matters of rank, uniforms, and training, these directions will follow the general lines laid down for the Turkoman formations.† They will then be approved by the Chief of the High Command of the Armed Forces. The wearing of German badges of rank, the *Hohetisabzeichen* [the Eagle and Swastika], and German military shoulder-straps is forbidden. The dependents of these men are to be provided for. Ration scales for them will be laid down corresponding to the duties they are required to perform. These people will receive preferential treatment in

---

* On 23rd June 1943 Hitler ordered that there be no further extension of such native units, and the words 'and extended' were struck out of this paragraph.

† German-controlled formations raised from Russian Turkestan and the Caucasus.

the form of grants of land, which should be as liberal as possible within the limits of local circumstances.

5. *Other forces.*

The arming of the Reich Labour Service, railwaymen, foresters, agricultural overseers, etc., will, where required, be improved. They should be able to *defend themselves with the most effective weapons available.*

There must be no German in the area threatened by bandits who is not engaged, actively or passively, in the fight against them.

signed: ADOLF HITLER

47

Partisan activity was not confined to German-occupied Russia. It was also becoming a major problem to the Germans in Western and Southern Europe, where it was supplied and organized from Britain and from the British headquarters in the Middle East. On 18th October 1942 Hitler would issue what he called a 'sharp order' (afterwards referred to as the 'extermination order') requiring that 'sabotage troops of the British and their hirelings', whether in uniform or not, whether with or without arms, be 'killed to the last man in battle or in flight', or, if captured indirectly, handed over to the SS. British activities of this kind, said Hitler, were merely the Russian methods under a different name: against both these 'a war of extermination' must be fought.

But partisan activity behind his lines was only the beginning of Hitler's troubles. The summer of 1942, which he had entered with such confidence, ended in disillusion. While the German armies in Russia were bombarding Leningrad and advancing, against increasing opposition, to the Caucasus, and while Rommel was consolidating his position in Egypt, a global strategy of counter-attack was being devised between Washington, London, and Moscow, and at the beginning of winter the blows were delivered. In North Africa, at the beginning of November, the British Eighth Army launched its well-prepared attack and won the great victory of El Alamein, the beginning of Rommel's doom. Thereafter the British advance into Libya was swift. In Russia, at the same time, General Paulus's 6th Army, having hammered in vain at Stalingrad, found itself exposed to Russian counter-attack on both its flanks. Hitler, who had now dismissed his Army Chief of Staff, General Halder, for refusing to share his faith in continual advance, forbade Paulus to withdraw and, in consequence, the whole 6th Army was surrounded and trapped between the Don and the Volga. Paulus attempted to break out, but was ordered by Hitler to stand firm. On 12th December an attempt to relieve 6th Army failed and the siege began. Meanwhile, the other German objectives had not been reached. The Russians still held a base for their Black Sea Fleet; they still held Baku and its Caspian oilfields; they still held Leningrad.

Finally, the long-feared blow from the West had fallen. On 8th November, immediately after Rommel's defeat in Egypt, the Anglo-American forces landed in Morocco and Algeria and seized Casablanca and Algiers. Admiral Darlan, the Vichy Minister of Marine, who happened to be in Algiers, promptly changed sides and ordered the French fleet in Toulon to come over. Hitler reacted at once. 'Operation Attila' (see above, Directive 19) was put in force; Vichy France was occupied; and the French fleet, to avoid seizure by the Germans, was scuttled in Toulon harbour. Thanks to prompt measures, and Vichy compliance, the Germans were able to prevent the Allied seizure of Tunisia, towards which Rommel would retreat from Libya. But the whole balance of power in the Mediterranean was now changed – and changed at a time when the Germans had been halted, surrounded, and frozen in the East.

It was in these circumstances that Hitler issued his next directive. It reflects his continued anxiety over the Balkans: the vulnerable flank which he had been obliged to close before undertaking his Russian campaign, and which, now that that campaign was in jeopardy, was exposed again.

The Führer

Führer Headquarters,
28th December 1942.
24 copies

Directive No. 47
Command and defence measures in the South-east

I. The situation in the Mediterranean makes it possible that an attack may be made, in the foreseeable future, on Crete and on German and Italian bases in the Aegean Sea and the Balkan peninsula.

It must be expected that this attack will be supported by risings in the Western Balkan countries.

The increasing influence of the Anglo-Saxon powers on *the attitude of Turkey* also calls for fresh vigilance.

II. As a result of this situation and of developments in North Africa, I transfer the defence of the South-east area, including off-shore islands, to *Commander Armed Forces South-east* who will be directly subordinate to me as Commander-in-Chief South-east (Army Group E).

The principles laid down for coastal defence in Directive No. 40 will apply here.

The military forces of our allies will, as far as is necessary, come under direct tactical command of Commander-in-Chief South-east only in the event of enemy attack.

The naval and air forces of our Allies will, in such an event, come under tactical command of the headquarters of the corresponding German services.

This command organization will become effective upon the issue of special orders.

In *preparing* for a defensive battle of this kind, Commander-in-Chief South-east will have the following tasks:

1. *Preparation of coastal defences* with main emphasis in the Dodecanese, Crete, and the Peloponnese, which will be developed as fortresses (with the exception of Mytilene and Chios).

2. The final pacification of the hinterland and the destruction of rebels and bandits of all kinds, in conjunction with Italian 2nd Army.

3. *The preparation of all necessary measures* to meet an enemy attack on the Balkans which is helped or condoned by Turkey. This will be carried out in agreement with the Bulgarian High Command.

In addition, Commander-in-Chief South-east will control in the German sphere –

Unified sea transport and its protection in the Aegean Sea, including Crete.

Supplies by land and sea for all German forces stationed in the South-east, in accordance with their requirements and the transport available.

Decisions on all questions which may arise in the three services concerning the coordinated control of *transport and communications* in the occupied area of the South-east.

III. *Organization of Command*

A. *In the German sphere:*

1. *Commander-in-Chief South-east* is the highest representative of the forces in the South-east, and will exercise full powers in all areas occupied by German troops.

He will supervise the civil administration which has been set up by the various Commanders and by the Commandant of Fortress Crete.

Commander Armed Forces South-east will cease to be subordinate to Commander-in-Chief South from 1st January 1943.

2. The following are subordinate to Commander-in-Chief South-east:

(a) In the area of Croatia, '*The German General Plenipotentiary in Croatia*' (apart from his duties as Military Attaché), and '*The Commander of German Troops in Croatia*'.

(b) In the area of Old Serbia, the '*Commanding General Serbia*'.

(c) In the Salonika area, and in the islands of Lemnos, Mytilene, Chios, and Strati, as well as for the neutral zone near Turkey in Thrace, the '*Commander Salonika –Aegean*'.

(d) For the Piraeus port area, the billeting areas, and the area occupied by German troops in Attica, as well as the island of Melos, the '*Commander Southern Greece*'.

(e) For the Crete area, '*the Commandant of Fortress Crete*'.

(f) '*The Admiral Aegean*' in all matters concerning coastal defence.

(g) The '*Military Attaché in Sofia*', where duties beyond those of an Attaché are concerned.

For the *Navy*, the present distinction between Naval Group South and the German Naval Headquarters in Italy will be retained.

3. *Air Force.*

(a) *Conduct of Air Warfare.*

(1) *The conduct of air operations in the whole Mediterranean area*, with the exception of the French Mediterranean coast, *remains the responsibility of Commander-in-Chief South*. He will receive directives for operations as follows:

    (i) In the Central Mediterranean, from the Italian Supreme Command.

    (ii) In the Eastern Mediterranean and Balkans, from Commander-in-Chief Air Force, in accordance with my instructions. Commander-in-Chief Air Force and Italian Supreme Command will agree upon basic plans for air warfare.

(2) In order to ensure coordinated operations, particularly in coastal defence, and coordinate control in the Eastern Mediterranean and Balkan areas, Commander-in-Chief South will appoint a staff to cooperate with

Commander-in-Chief South-east for air operations in this area. Its duties will also be to prepare ground establishments in the Balkans and common action with our allies in the case of an enemy attack.

(*b*) *Air Defence*.

(1) Air Defence in the Central Mediterranean is the responsibility of Commander-in-Chief South under the Italian Supreme Command.

(2) In the Balkan area air defence is the responsibility of Commander-in-Chief South-east in accordance with the directives of Commander-in-Chief South, thereby assuring that air operations in the Eastern Mediterranean are also under unified command.*

B. *Preparations* for action and the pacification of the area will be made in close cooperation with *our allies*. Liaison officers will be exchanged, where this has not already been done.

The following general principles apply:

1. *Italy:*

(*a*) *Army:* Regulations regarded as necessary for the Italian theatre will be submitted to the High Command of the Armed Forces, who will obtain the agreement of the Italian Supreme Command. The latter will then issue the necessary orders to the Italian armies stationed in the South-east.

(*b*) *Navy:* Orders proposed by Commander-in-Chief Navy Group South for the Italian Admiral in the Dodecanese concerning preparatory measures will be forwarded, in the form of draft orders, by Navy Group

---

* On 1st June 1943, as the result of the conversion of X Flying Corps to Air Force Command South, under the direct command of Commander-in-Chief Air Force, this whole paragraph (III. A.3) was changed and the air war in the whole eastern Mediterranean area was placed under the control of Commander-in-Chief Air Force (instead of under Commander-in-Chief South), cooperating with the Italian Supreme Command.

South to the Naval Staff, which will obtain the agreement of the Italian Naval High Command for the issue
of corresponding orders. The Italian Naval High
Command will then issue such orders, after obtaining
the approval of the Italian Supreme Command.

(c) *Air Force:* Regulations regarded as necessary for the
Italian Air Force in the South-east area will be submitted to Commander-in-Chief South, who, after
securing the approval of the Italian Supreme Command, will agree on them with the High Command of
the Italian Air Force, and will ensure their publication
in an order.

2. *Bulgaria:* Every effort will be made to secure a similar
procedure with the Bulgarian forces. (The outcome of conversations with the Bulgarians is still awaited.)

3. *Croatia:* Cooperation with Croatia and the employment of the Croatian forces will continue as hitherto. Commander-in-Chief South-east and the German naval and air
force commands have the duty to ensure unified defence
preparations for the whole South-eastern area, and are
entitled to examine all measures directed to this end.

IV. Commander-in-Chief South-east has all *the powers of a
territorial commander* over the three branches of the Armed
Forces and the Waffen-SS in those parts of Croatia, Serbia,
and Greece (including the Greek Islands) occupied by
German troops.

Areas occupied exclusively by German troops are *operational areas*. Commander-in-Chief South-east will exercise
full powers in them through his subordinate commanders.

Those parts of Croatia which are occupied by German
troops, or in which German troops are operating, will also be
regarded as operational areas.

In those parts of the *Italian* occupation area in which German troops are stationed, Commander-in-Chief South-east
will exercise powers of command over all branches of the

Armed Forces in so far as the military requirements of the German forces demand.

For the delimitation of powers between Commander-in-Chief South-east and '*the Plenipotentiary of the Reich for Greece*' see Appendix.*

V. Directive No. 31 of 9th June 1941 and OKW/WFSt/Op. No. 551743/42 g. K. Chefs. of 13th October 1942† are hereby cancelled.

signed: ADOLF HITLER

48

The German disasters of November 1942 changed the character of the war. Hitherto the pace had been dictated by Germany; from now on it was dictated by the Allies. In the East the whole German 6th Army of General Paulus was gradually starved into surrender, and by the end of January 1943 its resistance was over. Hitler was outraged when Paulus himself surrendered instead of committing suicide, and declared three days of national mourning for the loss of the army. When spring came, it was no longer a question of continuing the advance, as in 1942: Hitler's orders were to be ready for resumed Russian attacks, and to protect a German retreat by leaving devastation behind. In Africa the British Eighth Army cleared the Germans out of Libya and captured Tripoli on 23rd January 1943; in Tunisia Rommel was able to make a stand with reinforcements from Italy, but by 12th May Tunis and Bizerta had fallen and the Axis no longer had an inch of territory in Africa. Allied landings on the Mediterranean coast

---

* This appendix is not here printed. The Plenipotentiary for Greece, appointed on 28th April 1941, represented the political, economic, and cultural interests of Germany in Greece.

† This was a previous order concerning unified command in the Mediterranean.

were now expected, and further orders were given to strengthen its defences everywhere, but especially in the Peloponnese, where the blow was most regularly expected. By this
time the Italians were demoralized, and on 19th May a
'Führer-directive' was drafted on the assumption that they
would no longer be able to contribute to the defence of Greece:
the Germans would have to rely on themselves and the Bulgarians alone. This directive seems never to have been sent.
On 10th July the blow fell, not in Greece, but in Sicily. In
just over a month the whole island was occupied. Meanwhile,
on 25th July, Mussolini was overthrown by a palace-revolution
and the attitude of the new Italian government of Marshal
Badoglio, though it professed loyalty to the old Axis, was unpredictable. It was in these delicate circumstances that Hitler,
on 26th July, issued his next directive, which still presumed
that the Allies would land in Greece.

The Führer   Führer Headquarters,
                                          26th July, 1943.
                                            17 copies

Directive No. 48
Command and defence measures in the South-east

I. *The enemy's measures in the Eastern Mediterranean*, in conjunction with the attack on Sicily, indicate that he will shortly
begin landing operations against our strong line in the
Aegean, Peloponnese–Crete–Rhodes, and against the west
coast of Greece with offshore Ionian islands.

Should the operations of the enemy extend from Sicily to
the mainland of Southern Italy, we must also reckon with an
assault on the east coast of the Adriatic, north of the straits
of Otranto.

The enemy's conduct of operations is also based on the
bandit movement, which is increasingly organized by him in
the interior of the South-east area.

Turkey's neutrality is at present beyond question, but
needs continuous watching.

II. In view of this situation, *the Command in the South-eastern* area will be rearranged in agreement with our Italian allies on the following general lines:

A. *Army*

1. Commander-in-Chief South-east will assume command of 11th Italian Army from 00.00 hours 27th July 1943.

2. German formations at present posted, or to be posted, in this Army area will come under tactical command of 11th Italian Army and of the headquarters designated by it, with the proviso that uniform command of all German and Italian troops in the Peloponnese will be assumed by German LXVIII Army Corps, and that Italian VIII Army Corps will move to the area north of the Corinth canal.

German units directly employed in coastal defence will come under command of the responsible Italian divisions in their sectors.

3. German units temporarily committed in Albania, Montenegro, and those coastal areas of Croatia under Italian occupation will come under the tactical command of Italian Army Group East or of 2nd Italian Army.

B. *Navy and Air Force.*

The principles already laid down for exerting influence on our allies through the Navy and Air Force remain in operation. In this connexion Admiral Aegean will ensure that all measures for coastal defence taken by the Navy in the coastal areas occupied by 11th Italian Army comply with German requirements.

III. *The most important task of Commander-in-Chief South-east* is to make defensive preparations for the coast of Greece, on the islands and on the mainland. An essential preliminary is to destroy the bandit gangs in Greece, Serbia, and Croatia and thus open up the supply lines, in particular the main railway lines, to ensure to our forces the necessary freedom of movement in rear areas.

In matters of coastal defence, only German plans for

manning and development are to be applied, even where Italian formations are concerned.

To stiffen the Italians in the most threatened coastal sectors, German Fortification Battalions and, where these do not suffice, units of German divisions held in reserve will be stationed on or near the coast. We must also demand that important Italian coastal batteries and other key points be reinforced by racial Germans.

Where German formations are not strong enough to form an effective operational reserve, Italian units will be brought under German command and interspersed with German units.

Airfields near the coast will be defended by German forces.

In the siting and construction of all defensive positions, and in the reconnaissance for movement and concentration of troops, the likelihood of enemy air superiority will be borne in mind.

In the rear areas the most urgent task of Commander-in-Chief South-east is to destroy the bandits in Serbia and Croatia, with special emphasis on lines of communication to Greece.

Through close cooperation with Italian Army Group East and the 2nd Italian Army, and by transferring German forces where necessary, we must ensure that operations against the bandits in their areas are also carried out with the utmost intensity; and, in particular, that gangs of bandits near the coast, who could be exceptionally dangerous in the event of an enemy landing, are annihilated. Moreover, the Army Group must be constantly prepared to intervene, with as strong German forces as possible, in order to defend the coast in the Italian area, should the situation so demand.

IV. The disposition of forces proposed by Commander-in-Chief South-east in his memo of 26th July 1943 is approved in principle. Details will be the subject of special orders.

Orders concerning Army reinforcements will follow.

In addition, it is intended in the next few months to concentrate an operational army along the Belgrade–Larissa railway line. It will consist of:

Two Armoured or Armoured Grenadier Divisions
Two Mountain Divisions
Two Light Infantry Divisions

which will be moved from the East.

V.

A. 1. Greek territory occupied by German forces and by the 7th Bulgarian Division, including the islands and the neutral zone in Thrace, will be *an operational area*. Commander-in-Chief South-east will exercise full powers in this area, and is authorized to delegate his powers to *Military Commander Greece*.

His powers will be defined by the Chief of the High Command of the Armed Forces in a special instruction, on the general principle that, as the military situation demands, all non-military German authorities posted, or to be posted, in Greece will be subordinate to Commander-in-Chief South-east and will be incorporated in the Staff of Military Commander Greece. The authority of senior officials of the Ministries of the Reich for issuing technical instructions is not affected by this: but these instructions will be transmitted through the Military Commander.

2. Pending a final settlement with the Foreign Office, the Plenipotentiary of the Reich accredited to the Greek government is excluded from this arrangement, as is Minister Neubacher, whose special duties and powers remain for the present unchanged. Instructions to the Military Commander will ensure the closest cooperation between him and these authorities.

3. Commander-in-Chief South-east should influence the military administration of the Italian-occupied areas only in so far as the military situation requires. If agreement cannot be reached with local Italian authorities, appropriate

application is to be made to the High Command of the Armed Forces.

B. 1. In the Serbian and Croatian area of operations, *Commander-in-Chief South-east* will delegate his executive powers to the 'Military Commander South-east', who for this purpose, in Croatia, will make use of the Commander of the German troops in Croatia.

2. The overwhelming importance of Serbia for the entire conduct of the war in the South-east requires that all German authorities should be coordinated. Non-military authorities stationed in Serbia will therefore be subordinate to the Military Commander South-east and incorporated in his staff.

The authority of senior officials of the Ministries of the Reich for issuing technical instructions is not affected by this, but these instructions will be transmitted through the Military Commander.

The Chief of the High Command of the Armed Forces will issue orders on distribution of duties.

3. The Commander of German troops in Croatia and the German General Plenipotentiary in Croatia will retain their command competences and duties as heretofore.

VI. The Chief of the High Command of the Armed Forces will issue, on my behalf, the necessary instructions for the incorporation of staffs and headquarters, and for the provision of supplies.

Regulations not conforming with this directive are cancelled.

signed: ADOLF HITLER

49

For over a month the Badoglio Government in Italy outwardly preserved the alliance with Germany. But secretly Badoglio was seeking to make peace and his agent was negotiating with the Western allies in Lisbon. Meanwhile, the Germans were making immediate preparations for the defection which they expected but did not wish to provoke. A series of plans were drawn up, which were to be carried out on the release of the code word '*Alarich* (Alaric)', later changed to '*Achse* (Axis)'. Italian positions in France and throughout the Balkans were to be taken over; important installations and positions in Italy were to be seized; the Italian fleet was to be captured; and German forces were to take up new defensive positions. These details originally formed the substance of Directive No. 49. But in fact this directive was never issued and the text does not survive. Instead, on 31st July 1943, a series of individual orders were issued, dealing with separate areas and problems. Then, on 3rd September, the Allied forces crossed from Sicily, now completely conquered, to the mainland of Italy. Five days later Badoglio's surrender to the West was confirmed. Hitler's response was dramatic. On the same day the code word 'Axis' was released. Four days later a party of German parachutists landed on the rock in the Abruzzi where the fallen Mussolini was imprisoned and carried him off by air to join his rescuer. Under Hitler's protection, Mussolini now became the puppet-ruler of German-occupied Italy.

50

The fall of Mussolini and the defection of the Italian Government was the greatest political blow which Hitler had suffered. From now on the 'Rome–Berlin' Axis, which had been the basis of the revolution in Europe since 1936, did not exist. Moreover, it was likely to begin a rot among the satellites. On the Eastern front the German armies were now being pushed relentlessly back. In July and August the Russians won three great battles at Kursk, Orel, and Kharkov, and by September the Germans were in retreat along the whole front from Moscow to the Black Sea. On 25th September the Russians recovered Smolensk. The Northern front remained static, but with such evidence of German defeat, and with the example of Italy before them, the loyalty of the Finns might well be doubted; and it was with this in mind that Hitler issued his Directive No. 50.

The Führer   Führer Headquarters,
                                              28th September 1943.
                                              10 copies

Directive No. 50

Concerning the preparations for the withdrawal of 20th Mountain Army to Northern Finland and Northern Norway

1. The situation in the Army Group North sector is completely stabilized, and there is no prospect of a withdrawal on this front. The most dangerously threatened sector operationally, around Velikiye Luki, is being continually reinforced. Nevertheless, a secondary position is now being developed behind Lake Peipus and the Narva, in case of unfavourable developments, particularly in Finland itself.

2. It is our duty to bear in mind the possibility that Finland may drop out of the war or collapse.

3. In that case it will be the immediate task of 20th Mountain Army to continue to hold the Northern area, which is vital to our war industry, by moving back the front to a line running through Karesuando, Ivalo, and the sector at present held by XIX (Mountain) Corps. 230th and 270th Infantry Divisions will come under its command in due course.

It would then be especially important to defend against ground and air attack the Kolosjoki nickel mines, which would be particularly threatened.

It is impossible to say at present how long this task may be practical.

4. The exceptional difficulty of moving troops and making war under these conditions entails early preparations, which are likely to be lengthy. They will cover the following points:

(*a*) Construction and maintenance of roads likely to be used for troop movements. Establishment of staging-posts.

(*b*) Preparation of supplies for the Army should it withdraw.

(*c*) Plans to destroy establishments of value to the enemy in the areas to be evacuated.

(*d*) Storage of supplies.

(*e*) Preparation for billeting troops after they have withdrawn to their future area of operations.

(*f*) Preparations for signals traffic.

The appropriate preparations to be made by 20th Mountain Army in immediate consultation with the Commander Armed Forces Norway must apply to all seasons of the year. They should assume the worst, i.e. that it may be impossible to move those troops not required for holding the Northern area by sea from Finnish ports.

5. If the measures ordered cannot be carried out inconspicuously, they are to be explained to our own troops, and to the Finns, as concerned exclusively with the development of communications between Norway and Finland. These communications will enable divisions to be moved from the Reserve of Commander Armed Forces Norway to Finland, even in winter if necessary. The number of officers to be informed of the further reasons for these preparations will be restricted to a minimum. If exchange of correspondence or verbal exchange is necessary between Commander Armed Forces Norway and 20th Mountain Army, it must be routed via Germany, not via Sweden.

6. 20th Mountain Army is to submit to the High Command of the Armed Forces (Operations Staff) a short memorandum on the conduct of the proposed operation, with special reference to supplies.

The progress of preparations ordered in paragraph 4 will be reported by 20th Mountain Army and Commander Armed Forces Norway by 1st December 1943.

signed: ADOLF HITLER

51

Hitler had good grounds for concern in the East; but the immediate danger lay in the West. In 1941 he had turned his back on Britain as powerless to thwart him, though obstinately unwilling to recognize its impotence. Now, when his *Blitz-krieg* against Russia, which should have been over two years ago, had foundered, and his armies were already being thrown back, when his Mediterranean defences had been pierced and his ally had deserted him, he had to admit that an even greater, and closer, menace threatened him in his rear. The 'powerless' West was rising up against him with a vengeance. Directive No. 51, issued as the third Russian winter descended to freeze operations in the East, betrays a new note of hysteria as the 'Two-Front War', which Hitler had always promised to avoid, became a dreadful reality.

The Führer   Führer Headquarters,
                                     3rd November 1943.
                                     27 copies.

Directive No. 51

The hard and costly struggle against Bolshevism during the last two and a half years, which has involved the bulk of our military strength in the East, has demanded extreme exertions. The greatness of the danger and the general situation demanded it. But the situation has since changed. The danger in the East remains, but a greater danger now appears in the West: an Anglo-Saxon landing! In the East, the vast extent of the territory makes it possible for us to lose ground, even on a large scale, without a fatal blow being dealt to the nervous system of Germany.

It is very different in the West! Should the enemy succeed in breaching our defences on a wide front here, the immediate consequences would be unpredictable. Everything indicates that the enemy will launch an offensive against the Western front of Europe, at the latest in the spring, perhaps even earlier.

I can therefore no longer take responsibility for further weakening the West, in favour of other theatres of war. I have therefore decided to reinforce its defences, particularly those places from which the long-range bombardment of England will begin. For it is here that the enemy must and will attack, and it is here – unless all indications are misleading – that the decisive battle against the landing forces will be fought.

Holding and diversionary attacks are to be expected on other fronts. A large-scale attack on Denmark is also not out of the question. From a naval point of view such an attack would be more difficult to deliver, nor could it be as effectively supported by air, but if successful, its political and operational repercussions would be very great.

At the beginning of the battle the whole offensive strength of the enemy is bound to be thrown against our forces holding the coast-line. Only by intensive construction, which means straining our available manpower and materials at home and in the occupied territories to the limit, can we strengthen our coastal defences in the short time which probably remains.

The ground weapons which will shortly reach Denmark and the occupied areas in the West (heavy anti-tank guns, immobile tanks to be sunk in emplacements, coastal artillery, artillery against landing troops, mines, etc.) will be concentrated at strong-points in the most threatened areas on the coast. Because of this, we must face the fact that the defences of less threatened sectors cannot be improved in the near future.

Should the enemy, by assembling all his forces, succeed in landing, he must be met with a counter-attack delivered with all our weight. The problem will be by the rapid concentration of adequate forces and material, and by intensive training, to form the large units available to us into an offensive reserve of high fighting quality, attacking power, and mobility, whose counter-attack will prevent the enemy from exploiting the landing, and throw him back into the sea.

Moreover, careful and detailed emergency plans must be drawn up so that everything we have in Germany, and in the coastal areas which have not been attacked, and which is in any way capable of action, is hurled immediately against the invading enemy.

The Air Force and Navy must go into action against the heavy attacks which we must expect by air and sea with all the forces at their disposal, regardless of the losses.

I therefore order as follows:

A. *Army*.

1. *The Chief of the Army General Staff and the Inspector General of Armoured Forces* will submit to me without delay a plan for the distribution, within the next three months, of weapons, tanks, self-propelled guns, motor vehicles, and ammunition on the Western front and in Denmark, in accordance with the requirements of the new situation.

The plan will rest on the following basic principles:

(a) All armoured and Armoured Grenadier divisions in the West will be assured of adequate mobility, and each will be equipped with 93 Mark IV tanks or self-propelled guns, and with strong anti-tank weapons by the end of December 1943.

The 20th Air Force Field Division will be converted into an effective mobile offensive formation by the allocation of self-propelled artillery before the end of 1943.

SS Armoured Grenadier Division 'H.J.' [Hitler Youth], 21st Armoured Division, and the infantry and reserve divisions stationed in Jutland will be brought up to full armed strength with speed.

(b) There will be a further reinforcement with Mk IV self-propelled guns and heavy anti-tank guns of armoured divisions in reserve in the West and in Denmark, and of the self-propelled artillery training unit in Denmark.

(c) A monthly allocation of a hundred heavy anti-tank guns Mks 40 and 43 (of which half will be mobile), for the months of November and December, in addition to the heavy anti-tank guns, will be made to the newly raised formations in the West.

(d) An increased allocation of weapons (including about 1,000 machine-guns) will be made to improve the equipment of ground forces engaged in coastal defence in the West and in Denmark, and to coordinate the equipment of units which are to be withdrawn from sectors not under attack.

(e) A liberal supply of short-range anti-tank weapons will be granted to formations stationed in threatened areas.

(f) The fire-power in artillery and anti-tank guns of formations stationed in Denmark, and on the coasts of occupied territories in the West, will be increased, and Army artillery will be strengthened.

2. No units or formations stationed in the West and in Denmark, nor any of the newly raised self-propelled armoured artillery or anti-tank units in the West, will be withdrawn to other fronts without my approval.

The Chief of the Army General Staff and the Inspector General of Armoured Forces will report to me, through the High Command of the Armed Forces (Operations Staff), when the equipment of armoured units, self-propelled artillery units, and light anti-tank units and companies is complete.

3. *Commander-in-Chief West* will decide which additional formations from sectors of the front that have not been under attack can be moved up and made capable of an offensive role, by a time-table of exercises in the field and similar training measures. In this connexion, I insist that areas unlikely to be threatened should be ruthlessly stripped of all

except the smallest forces essential for guard duties. In areas from which these reserves are drawn, units will be formed from security and emergency forces for duties of surveillance and protection. Our labour units employed on construction will open the lines of communication which will probably be destroyed by the enemy, employing for this the help of the local population on an extensive scale.

4. The Commander of German troops in Denmark will adopt the measures outlined in paragraph 3 for the area under his command.

5. The Chief of Army Equipment and Commander of the Replacement Army will raise battle groups of regimental strength in the Home Defence area from training depots, troops under instruction, army schools, training battalions and recuperative establishments. These will form security and engineer-construction battalions, and will be ready, on receipt of special orders, to move within forty-eight hours of being called up.

In addition, all further personnel available will be incorporated in infantry units and equipped with such weapons as are available, so that they may immediately replace the heavy casualties to be expected.

B. *Air Force.*

In view of the new situation, the offensive and defensive power of formations of the Air Force stationed in the West and in Denmark will be increased. Plans will be drawn up to ensure that all forces available and suitable for defensive operations will be taken from flying units and mobile anti-aircraft artillery units engaged in Home Defence, from schools and training units in the Home Defence area, and will be employed in the West, and if necessary in Denmark.

Ground establishments in Southern Norway, Denmark, North-western Germany, and the West will be organized and supplied so that, by the largest possible degree of decentralization, our own units are not exposed to enemy bombing at the beginning of large-scale operations, and the weight of the enemy attack will be effectively broken up. This applies particularly to our fighter forces, whose ability to go into action must be increased by the establishment of a number of emergency airfields. Particular attention will be paid to good camouflage. In this connexion also I expect all possible forces to be made available for action regardless of the circumstances, by stripping less threatened areas of their troops.

C. *Navy*.

The Navy will draw up plans for bringing into action naval forces capable of attacking the enemy landing fleet with all their strength.* Coastal defences under construction will be completed with all possible speed, and the establishment of additional coastal batteries and the laying of further obstacles on the flanks will be considered.

Preparations will be made for the employment of all ranks capable of fighting, from schools, training establishments, and other land establishments, so that they may be deployed with the least possible delay, if only on security duties, in the battle area where enemy landings have taken place.

In the naval plans for strengthening defences in the West, special attention will be given to defence against enemy landings in Norway or Denmark. In this connexion, I attach particular importance to plans for using large numbers of submarines in the northern sea areas. A temporary diminution of submarine forces in the Atlantic must be accepted.

D. *SS*.

The Reichsführer SS will test the preparedness of units of the Waffen-SS and Police for operational, security, and guard duties. Preparations will be made to raise battle-trained formations for operational and security duties from

---

* Such a report was presented on 13th November by the Commander-in-Chief Navy, Admiral Doenitz, who had replaced Admiral Raeder in this capacity on 30th January 1943.

training, reserve, and recuperative establishments, and from schools and other units in the Home Defence Area.

E. Commanders-in-Chief of the branches of the Armed Forces, the Reichsführer SS, the Chief of the Army General Staff, Commander-in-Chief West, the Chief of Army Equipment and Commanding General of Replacement Army, the Inspector-General of Armoured Forces, and the Commander of German troops in Denmark will report to me by the 15th November the steps taken, and those which they propose to take.

I expect all staffs concerned to exert every effort during the time which still remains in preparation for the expected decisive battle in the West.

All those responsible will ensure that time and manpower are not wasted in dealing with questions of jurisdiction, but that they are employed in increasing our powers of defence and attack.

signed: ADOLF HITLER

I CANADIAN
II BRITISH
ARMY

BRUSSELS
SEPT. 3 1944

BERLIN
MAY 2 1945

JULY 3
1944

LONDON

INVADED
JUNE 6, 1944

I U.S.ARMY
II BRITISH
ARMY

9TH U.S.A.

3RD U.S.A.

PARIS

PARIS
LIBERATED
AUG.25
1944

I.FR.
ARMY

7TH
U.S.ARMY

R. PO

VIENNA
APRIL
13, 1945.

INVADED
AUG.15
1944

NAPLES
OCT. I
1943

U.S.5TH C.
B. 5TH C.

ALGIERS

RABAT
NOV. 8
1942

ORAN
NOV. 8
1942

BONE
NOV. 12
1942

U.S. 7TH
ARMY

BRITISH
8TH ARMY

SEPT. 3
1943

SICILY
JULY 9.10.
1943.

BRITISH
8TH ARMY

0   300
MILES

BEURAT
DEC.28
1942

BENGHAZI
NOV. 20
1942

HITLER'S DEFENSIVE

MURMANSK

ARCHANGEL

R. VOLGA

● MOSCOW

SMOLENSK

MINSK

VORONEZH

GERMAN FORCES
SURRENDER
FEB. 2 1943

● STALINGRAD

KIEV

● KHARKOV

NOV. 6
1943

ROSTOV

KERCH
STRAITS

TUAPSE

ODESSA
APRIL 10.
1944

ATHENS
OCT. 14
1944

────── ALLIES ADVANCE
- - - - RUSSIAN ADVANCE

ALAMEIN
OCT. 23
NOV. 4
1942

CAMPAIGNS

Part II

The Defensive War

52

Directive No. 51 was the last of Hitler's numbered directives. As the tone of that directive sufficiently indicates, Hitler had lost the initiative and general strategic control was slipping from his hands. Whether consciously for this reason or not, he now ceased to issue *Weisungen* and his orders to the various theatres take the form of special orders on particular subjects. Nevertheless, the substance of these orders remains similar to those of the directives, and continues to illustrate Hitler's attempts to control the course of the war.

Directive No. 51 was followed by several supplementary orders concerning the same problem: the expected landings in the West. On 12th December Hitler ordered Keitel to issue a list of general conclusions drawn from previous experience of fighting against 'the Anglo-Saxons', and on 27th December, believing that the troop concentrations in Southern England were nearing completion, so that landings might take place as early as mid-February, he ordered troops to concentrate on the front held by 15th Army and the right flank of 7th Army (the Cotentin peninsula in Normandy), where he expected the main attack. Next day he issued orders forbidding the withdrawal of personnel or material from the areas commanded by Commander-in-Chief West (i.e. the whole area of France, Belgium, and Holland) and Commander Armed Forces Denmark. On 17th January 1944 he empowered Commander-in-Chief West to declare any area he chose a 'battle area' in which all civilian authorities were under his orders.

The landing which Hitler so feared was indeed being prepared, though not so early as he supposed: the date chosen for the Anglo-American 'Operation Overlord' was May 1944. The immediate operational problem in Western Europe was therefore still the problem of Italy, where fierce fighting was in progress. On 4th October 1943 Hitler had decided not to withdraw to the positions originally envisaged in Northern Italy, but, while fighting delaying actions in the South, to prepare a firm defence, the '*Winterstellung*', along the line of the rivers Garigliano and Rapido, below the monastery of Monte Cassino, in the West and the river Sangro, running into the Adriatic near Ortona, in the East. By the end of the year the Allies had reached this line, which was strongly defended both by Nature and by art. They had occupied Ortona and crossed the Rapido; but they were unable to make headway against the formidable German position at Monte Cassino. They therefore attempted to encircle it by making, on 21st January 1944, a seaborne landing behind the German lines at Nettuno, near Anzio, south of Rome. By 25th January this position was consolidated and it seemed that the '*Winterstellung*' would be turned and the battle for Rome would begin. In these circumstances Hitler sent the following message to Field-Marshal Kesselring to whom, on 19th January, he had given 'unlimited authority' over all services, and the SS, in his area.

Teleprint.   28th January 1944.

From: High Command of the Armed Forces, Operations Staff.

To: Commander-in-Chief South-west, Field Marshal Kesselring.

Within the next few days the 'Battle for Rome' will begin. It will be decisive for the defence of Central Italy and for the fate of 10th Army.

But the significance of this struggle goes even beyond that, because the landing at Nettuno marked the opening of the invasion of Europe planned for 1944.

The purpose of the enemy is to hold down large German forces as far away as possible from the bases in England where the main invasion forces are still standing ready, to wear down the German forces, and to gain experience for future operations.

Of the significance of the battle which 14th Army is about to give, every one of its soldiers must be thoroughly aware.

It is not sufficient to give clear and tactically correct orders. All officers and men of the Army, the Air Force, and the Naval forces must be penetrated by a fanatical will to end this battle victoriously, and never to relax until the last enemy soldier has been destroyed or thrown back into the sea. The battle must be fought in a spirit of holy hatred for an enemy who is conducting a pitiless war of extermination against the German people, who is prepared to adopt any means to this end, and who, without any higher ethical purpose, seeks only the annihilation of Germany and, with her, of European culture.

The fight must be hard and merciless, not only against the enemy, but against all officers and units who fail in this decisive hour.

The enemy must be forced to recognize, as he did in the fighting in Sicily, on the Rapido river, and at Ortona, that the fighting strength of Germany is unbroken, and that the great invasion of 1944 is a hazardous enterprise which will be drowned in the blood of Anglo-Saxon soldiers.

signed: ADOLF HITLER

53

The Allied landing at Anzio did not achieve its main purpose. The western end of the German '*Winterstellung*' was not turned. Hitler ordered large reinforcements into central Italy and on 14th February ordered a heavy counter-attack at Anzio, which stayed but did not dislodge the bridgehead. Thereafter the position remained static. Meanwhile, the imminent landing on the Atlantic coast continued to exercise Hitler, who sought to strengthen defences everywhere. On 19th January he had designated a number of areas from Holland to the Gironde estuary in South-west France as 'fortresses', and had issued special instructions for their defence. On 3rd March the Channel Islands were similarly converted into fortresses.

But it was not only in the West that the shrivelling German empire needed fortresses. In the East the Russian armies were now preparing to move forward on all fronts, and the inland cities of the Baltic states, of Eastern Poland, and of the Ukraine were as exposed as the beaches of Western Europe. On 8th March Hitler issued an order defining two classes of fortresses. Four appendices (not printed here) gave or demanded further details. One of them gave a list of the new 'fortified areas' in the East: a chain of cities stretching from Reval [Tallin], on the Baltic, to Nikolayev, near Odessa, on the Black Sea. One of them was Vinnitsa in the Ukraine, which less than two years ago had been the 'Führer Headquarters' for the conquest of all Russia.

The Führer.　　　　　　　　　　Führer Headquarters,
High Command of the Army.　　　8th March, 1944.

Führer Order No. 11
(*Commandants of Fortified Areas and Battle Commandants*)

In view of various incidents, I issue the following orders:
1. A distinction will be made between 'Fortified Areas' [*feste Plätze*], each under a 'Fortified Area Commandant', and 'Local Strong-points' [*Ortsstützpunkte*], each under a 'Battle Commandant'.

The '*Fortified Areas*' will fulfil the function of fortresses in former historical times. They will ensure that the enemy does not occupy these areas of decisive operational importance. They will allow themselves to be surrounded, thereby holding down the largest possible number of enemy forces, and establishing conditions favourable for successful counter-attacks.

'*Local Strong-points*' are strong-points deep in the battle area, which will be tenaciously defended in the event of enemy penetration. By being included in the main line of battle they will act as a reserve of defence and, should the enemy break through, as hinges and corner-stones for the front, forming positions from which counter-attacks can be launched.

2. Each '*Fortified Area Commandant*' should be a specially selected, hardened soldier, preferably of General's rank. He will be appointed by the Army Group concerned. Fortified Area Commandants will be personally responsible to the Commander-in-Chief of the Army Group.

Fortified Area Commandants will pledge their honour as soldiers to carry out their duties to the last.

Only the Commander-in-Chief of an Army Group in person may, with my approval, relieve the Fortified Area Commandant of his duties, and perhaps order the surrender of the fortified area.

Fortified Area Commandants *are subordinate* to the Commander of the Army Group, or Army, in whose sector the fortified area is situated. Further delegation of command to General Officers commanding formations will not take place.

Apart from the garrison and its security forces, all persons within a fortified area, or who have been collected there, are *under the orders* of the Commandant, irrespective of whether they are soldiers or civilians, and without regard to their rank or appointment.

The Fortified Area Commandant has the *military rights* and disciplinary powers of a Commanding General. In the performance of his duties he will have at his disposal mobile courts martial and civilian courts.

The *staff of Fortified Area Commandants* will be appointed by the Army Group concerned. The Chiefs of Staff will be appointed by High Command of the Army, in accordance with suggestions made by the Army Group.

3. The *garrison* of a fortified area comprises:

> the security garrison, and
> the general garrison.

The security garrison must be inside the fortified area at all times. Its strength will be laid down by Commander-in-Chief Army Group, and will be determined by the size of the area and the tasks to be fulfilled (preparation and completion of defences, holding the fortified area against raids or local attacks by the enemy).

The general garrison must be made available to the Commandant of the fortified area in sufficient time for the men to have taken up defensive positions and be installed when a full-scale enemy attack threatens. Its strength will be laid down by Commander-in-Chief Army Group, in accordance with the size of the fortified area and the task which is to be performed (total defence of the fortified area).

4. *The 'Battle Commandant'* comes under the orders of the local forces commander. He will be appointed by him, will be subordinate to him, and will receive operation orders from him. His rank will depend upon the importance of the position in the battle area and the strength of the garrison. His duties call for specially energetic officers whose qualities have been proved in crisis.

5. *The strength of the garrisons* of a 'Local Strong-point' will be determined by the importance of the position and the forces available. It will receive its orders from the authorities to which the Battle Commandant is subordinate.

6. *The duties* of 'Fortified Area Commanders' and 'Battle Commandants' as well as a list of fortified areas, and of reports on them submitted by Army Groups, are contained in the appendices.

7. All previous orders concerning Battle Commandants are hereby cancelled.

signed: ADOLF HITLER

54

The 'fortresses' in the East were intended to hold the Russian advance roughly on the old Russian frontier – the frontier of 1938. In April Hitler still believed that this might be done.

Telegram.
High Command of the Army.   2nd April 1944.

Operation Order No. 7
*Directive for further operations by Army Group A,
Army Group South, and Army Group Centre*

1. The Russian offensive in the south of the Eastern front
has passed its climax. The Russians have exhausted and
divided their forces.

The time has now come to bring the Russian advance to a
final standstill.

For this reason I have introduced measures of a most
varied kind. It is now imperative, while holding firm to the
Crimea, to hold or win back the following line:

Dniester to north-east of Kishinev–Jassy–Targul Neamt –
the Eastern exit from the Carpathians between Targul
Neamt and Kolomyya – Ternopol–Brody–Kovel.

2. For the present, *Army Group A* will hold the line
Tiligulski–Liman–Dniester around Dubosari, until we can
assume that the Crimea can be supplied independently of
Odessa. No more will be done than to prepare for the retreat
to the Dniester line. After closing the gap between 8th Army
and the Carpathians, the strongest possible forces will be
switched quickly from the right flank to the left flank of the
Army Group. Rumanian forces must be made mobile and
deployed forward by us in every way possible.

Rumanian forces will be disposed in accordance with the
terrain, so that chiefly German troops occupy the sectors in
danger of enemy tank attack.

It is particularly important that the heavy anti-tank guns
which I have placed at the disposal of the Rumanians should
reach them as early as possible, and be brought into position
in the most threatened areas. They will be manned by German gun-crews. This may be a question of hours. The Army
Group is fully responsible for this, and will employ a special
staff to deal with it.

3. The chief task of *Army Group South* is to free the surrounded 1st Tank Army. 1st Tank Army must continue to break through to the north-west.

An offensive force of great striking power will be formed in the area south-east of Lemberg* from available and newly arriving formations. This force must advance south-west at the earliest possible moment, in strong concentration, in order to annihilate the enemy forces which have broken through in the Stanislav area, and to re-establish connexion with 1st Tank Army. In general, I am in agreement with the plans of Field Marshal von Manstein.

After contact has been established with 1st Tank Army, the line originally laid down will finally be secured by local attacks; contact will be made with Army Group Centre, south of Kovel; and a unified front will be established. The Hungarian forces which have been raised in Hungary will come under command of Army Group South. It is important here, too, to put them in the front line along with German formations to stiffen them. Rigorous orders are necessary here.

4. *For Army Group Centre*, I am in full agreement with the heavy concentration around Brest.†

The first task of Army Group Centre is to fight its way out of Kovel and establish contact with Army Group South.

signed: ADOLF HITLER

55

While hoping to stay the Russian advance in the East, Hitler had one last hope of striking a decisive blow at the great arsenal from which he apprehended the final assault: Britain. German scientists had long been working on flying bombs and rockets, and Hitler had boasted of having in reserve a 'secret weapon'

---

* i.e. Lwów in Southern Poland.
† i.e. Brest-Litovsk in Eastern Poland.

which would redress the failing balance for Germany. The nature of this 'secret weapon' was not unknown to the British who, in 1943–44, by bombing the factories where it was being developed, held up its manufacture. But by 1st December 1943 the German programme was complete and on that date Hitler approved orders 'to prepare and carry out long-range warfare against England with all the special weapons involved therein'. The Commander-in-Chief West was authorized to take all the necessary measures, and heavily fortified sites were constructed in Northern France from which to fire the missiles. A further order was issued on 23rd December, and definite instructions were issued by Hitler in May 1944.

Führer Order of 16th May 1944
Ref.: *Employment of long-range weapons against England.*

High Command of the Armed Forces

Führer Headquarters,
16th May 1944.

The Führer has ordered:

1. *The long-range bombardment of England* will begin in *the middle of June*. The *exact date* will be set by Commander-in-Chief West, who will also control the bombardment with the help of LXV Army Corps and 3rd Air Fleet.

2. The following weapons will be employed:

(*a*) Fzg. 76.*
(*b*) Fzg. 76 launched from HE. 111.
(*c*) Long-range artillery.
(*d*) Bomber forces of 3rd Air Fleet.

3. *Method:*

(*a*) Against *the main target*, London.

---

* This was the original name given to the long-range missiles (pilotless planes) built by the Fieseler aircraft factory in Kassel. It was later known as *Vergeltungswaffe* (Reprisal weapon) 1, or V-1.

The bombardment will open like a thunderclap by night with Fzg. 76, combined with bombs (mostly incendiary) from the bomber forces, and a sudden long-range artillery attack against towns within range. It will continue with persistent harassing fire by night on London. When weather conditions make enemy air activity impossible, firing can also take place by day. This harassing fire, mingled with bombardments of varying length and intensity, will be calculated so that the supply of ammunition is always related to our capacities for production and transport. In addition, six hundred Fzg. 76 will be regarded as a reserve of the High Command of the Armed Forces, to be fired only with the approval of the High Command of the Armed Forces.

 (*b*) Orders will be given in due course for *switching fire to other targets*.

 4. *Bomber planes of the Air Force will cooperate* to the exclusion of other tasks, at least at the beginning of the bombardment. Fighter and anti-aircraft defence of firing-points and dumps will be completed and organized at the beginning of the bombardment. All preparations will be made on the assumption that communications with the firing-points will come under heavy enemy attack and may be destroyed.

 5. The orders laid down for secrecy in paragraph 7 of the order of 25th December 1943 No. 663082/43 for Senior Commanders will apply.

 The Chief of the High Command of the Armed Forces.

signed: KEITEL

56

The long-range bombardment of London had been arranged for mid-June. Before that time had arrived, the long-expected Allied landing took place. On 6th June 'the Anglo-Saxons' invaded the Continent of Europe with the greatest force ever delivered across the sea. All Hitler's preparations failed 'to hurl it back into the sea'. At once orders were issued to launch the 'secret weapons'. V-1 flying bombs began to reach the London area on 13th June, and for the next three months, in spite of increasingly effective counter-measures, they continued to fall. They were followed, from 8th September, by 'V-2' rockets. But they did not turn the scale, or affect the prosecution of the war in Normandy.

Meanwhile, Hitler was concerned with the problem of shipping-space. This had been a serious problem for the last year, and on 30th May 1943 Hitler had appointed Karl Kaufmann, Gauleiter of Hamburg, as Reich Commissioner of Maritime Shipping, responsible to himself. On 12th July he placed all questions of maritime shipping for the Armed Forces under the control of the Navy.

The Führer

Führer Headquarters,
12th July 1944.

Developments in the military situation make shipping traffic increasingly dependent upon naval operations, and call therefore for close coordination within the Armed Forces in all matters affecting shipping.

I therefore order as follows:

1. Commander-in-Chief Navy will assume responsibility within the Armed Forces for uniformity of handling in all matters concerning shipping movements.

2. The duties and responsibilities of the Reich Commissioner for Shipping, as laid down in my order of 30th May 1942, are not affected by this.

3. Commander-in-Chief Navy will take over command of all movements by sea in areas cut off from Germany by enemy action, in basic conformity with my order on sea traffic of 25th October 1943.

4. The Chief of the High Command of the Armed Forces

will issue operation orders in consultation with Commander-
in-Chief Navy and the Reich Commissioner for Shipping.*

signed: ADOLF HITLER

57

A few days after the Anglo-American landings in Normandy,
the Russians launched their summer offensive. In the North
they broke through the Finnish 'Mannerheim Line', captured
Vyborg [Viipuri], and reopened the Murmansk railway. In the
centre they surrounded and captured the German 'fortified
areas' and swept forward through Lithuania to the frontier of
East Prussia. In the south they smashed the German front and
advanced through Poland to the Vistula. By mid-July, with
the Western Allies firmly established in France and the
Russians rapidly advancing in the East, Hitler had to reckon
with the invasion of Germany; and an invasion of Germany
would not only be a threat to the Reich, it might well lead to
the immediate overthrow of the régime and the Party which,
in the hour of defeat, was widely detested not only by the
people but also – what was far more dangerous – in the Army
itself. Faced by such a threat, the Party resolved to defend
itself and tighten its control.

Already, on 31st May, Martin Bormann, the Party Chan-
cellor and now the most powerful figure at Hitler's side, had
sent out, from the Führer Headquarters, a circular letter to all
Gauleiters, outlining 'the task of the Party in case of an
invasion'.

The invaders, wrote Bormann, would try to mobilize 'all
defeatist elements and enemies of the government in and
behind the area of operation'; they would make it their prime
business 'to smash the Party'. Therefore the Party must be
prepared, and must prepare the people, 'psychologically and
materially', to survive the test; it must 'prove its capacity for

---

* These orders were issued on 22nd July 1944.

leadership'; and its leaders must go fully armed, 'in soldierly fashion, to the very centres of action'. Now, when the invasion of the Reich seemed imminent, Hitler signed two complementary decrees delimiting the authority of Party and Army, and defining Party control, in such an event. The decrees (*a* and *b* below) were not yet published: they were held in reserve against the hour of danger. Meanwhile, an order signed by Keitel (No. 58 below) was issued on 19th July.

(*a*)

Decree of the Führer on the exercise of command in an area of operations within the Reich

of 13th July 1944

In the event of enemy forces advancing into the territory of the German Reich, I order as follows:

I

The state and local civil authorities will continue to carry out their duties in the area of operations.

II

1. The military Commander-in-Chief, to whom I delegate plenary powers, will address his demands concerning civil matters arising out of the military situation to the Reich Commissioner for Defence in the area of operations.

2. In the immediate battle areas, whose limits will be defined by the Commander-in-Chief in agreement with the Reich Commissioner for Defence in the area of operations, senior military commanders are empowered to issue direct to civilian authorities of the State, and to local authorities, such instructions as are necessary for carrying out their respective operational duties. Should unforeseen events call for immediate action, and the Reich Commissioner for Defence in the area of operations not be available, the Commander-in-Chief has the same powers throughout the

area of operations. The Reich Commissioner for Defence in the area of operations will be informed by the quickest means of the measures which have been taken.

3. I shall nominate the Reich Commissioner for Defence in the area of operations.

III

1. The Reich Commissioner for Defence in the area of operations has the task of advising the military Commander-in-Chief in all matters of civil administration, including economic affairs. He can issue the necessary instructions to the state and local civil authorities.

2. Should the Reich Commissioner for Defence in the area of operations have any requests to make, he will refer, in police matters, to the competent Higher SS and Police Leaders; in railroad and inland shipping matters, to the Plenipotentiary of the Reich Minister for Transport; in matters of sea traffic, to the deputy of the Reich Commissioner for Shipping; and in matters of armament and war production, to the competent Chairman of the Armaments Committee of the Reich Minister for Armaments and War Production.

IV

Reich Commissioners for Defence, whose districts lie wholly or partly in the area of operations, will appoint a liaison officer who will be attached to the Reich Commissioner for Defence in the area of operations in an advisory capacity.

V

The Reich Commissioner for Defence in the area of operations will carry out the task assigned to him with the officials placed at his disposal in his capacity as Reich Commissioner for Defence. On the proposal of highest authorities of the Reich, experts in special fields may be attached to him by the Plenipotentiary General for the Administration

of the Reich, in agreement with the Head of the Party
Chancery and the High Command of the Armed Forces.

VI

The Reich Commissioner for Defence in the area of operations may delegate the execution of his duties in the area of
a subordinate commander to the Reich Commissioner for
Defence in that area. In this case the subordinate commander must first have been granted plenary powers by the
Commander-in-Chief. In putting forward requests the Commissioner will apply to the regional authorities in his area in
accordance with paragraph III subparagraph 2.

VII

The Reich Minister of the Interior will issue the necessary
legal and administrative orders for the implementation of
this decree.

Führer Headquarters. 13th July 1944.
The Führer.
signed: ADOLF HITLER

The Reich Minister and Chief of the Reich Chancery.
signed: DR LAMMERS

The Chief of the High Command of the Armed Forces.
signed: KEITEL

(b)

*Decree of the Führer on cooperation between the Party and the
Armed Forces in an area of operations within the Reich*

13th July 1944

In the event of enemy forces penetrating into the territory
of the German Reich, I order as follows:

I

The National Socialist Party, its branches and associated

organizations, will continue to carry out their duties in the area of operations.

II

1. The military Commander-in-Chief, to whom I delegate plenary powers, will address his demands on matters arising out of the military situation which concern the National Socialist Party, its branches and associated organizations, to the Gauleiter for the area.

2. In the immediate battle areas, whose limits will be defined by the Commander-in-Chief in agreement with the Reich Commissioner for Defence in the area of operations, senior military commanders are empowered to issue direct to the National Socialist Party, its branches and associated organizations, such instructions as are necessary for carrying out their respective operational duties. Should unforeseen events call for immediate action, and the Gauleiter in the area of operations be not available, the Commander-in-Chief has the same powers throughout the area of operations. The Gauleiter in the area of operations will be informed by the quickest means of the measures which have been taken.

3. I shall nominate the Gauleiter for the area of operations.

III

The Gauleiter for the area of operations has the task of advising the military Commander-in-Chief in matters concerning the National Socialist Party, its branches and associated organizations.

IV

Gauleiters whose districts lie wholly or partly in the area of operations will appoint a liaison officer, who will be attached to the Gauleiter for the area of operations, in an advisory capacity.

V

The Gauleiter for the area of operations will carry out the tasks assigned to him, using all available resources of the National Socialist Party, its branches and associated organizations.

VI

The Gauleiter for the area of operations may delegate the execution of his duties in the area of a subordinate commander to the Gauleiter for that area. In this case the subordinate commander must first have been granted plenary powers by the Commander-in-Chief.

VII

The Chief of the Party Chancery will issue the necessary instructions for the implementation of this decree.

The Führer.
signed: ADOLF HITLER
The Chief of the Party Chancery.
signed: M. BORMANN
The Chief of the High Command of the Armed Forces.
signed: KEITEL

58

The Chief of the High Command of the Armed Forces

Führer Headquarters,
19th July 1944.
100 copies

Order of Chief of the High Command of the Armed Forces concerning preparations for the defence of the Reich

Subject: *Preparations for the Defence of the Reich.*

Regulations hitherto issued for the defence of the coasts

and frontiers of the Reich are summarized and supplemented as follows:

As basic principle, it must be observed that the Armed Forces staffs must confine themselves exclusively, in making these preparations, to matters of a purely military nature. Other questions, for example, the mobilization of all resources in the Home theatre, the direction of manpower and, particularly, measures for the evacuation of the German civilian population, are the responsibility of the Party alone. Corresponding measures in the economic sphere are the responsibility of the Ministries concerned. The necessary cooperation must be pursued relentlessly, with the sole aim of achieving the highest efficiency, regardless of questions of jurisdiction.

I. *Organization of Command*

1. The Chief of Army Equipment and of the Replacement Army is responsible for making preparations to defend the Home theatre of war in all matters concerning the Army and general service matters. Commanders of Military Districts will act in accordance with his directives. In matters concerning the Navy and Air Force, preparations are the responsibility of Commander-in-Chief Navy and Commander-in-Chief Air Force respectively.

2. Basic rules for preparations to defend the Reich will be issued by the High Command of the Armed Forces (Operations Staff). Supplementary directives concerning service matters in general will be issued by the various branches of the High Command of the Armed Forces. Rules in matters of supply and rations will be issued by Army General Staff, Quartermaster General.

3. The responsibility of Commanding Admirals for preparation and execution of the defence measures for the coasts against enemy landings, as laid down in Directive 40, remains fully valid.

4. The existing orders dealing with the following remain in force:

(a) Action against parachute and airborne troops in the Home theatre of war.

(b) Action against individuals landing by parachute.

(c) Action against mines dropped from the air in inland waterways.

(d) Protection of buildings and plant important from the military point of view, and for the war effort.

5. Should military operations overlap parts of any particular Military District, special local orders will lay down the areas in which direction of operations *on the ground* come under command of the Army in the field, and cease to be the responsibility of the Chief of Army Equipment and of the Replacement Army.

Instructions on these lines have already been issued in respect of the General Government* and Military District I.

6. The defence of the Home theatre of war depends upon the preparedness of all sections of the population, at whose head stand the Gauleiters and the Reich Commissioners for Defence in the different provinces of the Reich. These officials have been notified of their special duties in the defence of the Reich in a circular letter from the Chief of the Party Chancery.†

Commanders of Military Districts will support and further in every way the initiative displayed by the Gauleiters and Reich Commissioners for Defence; they will decide, in the closest cooperation with them, and with the civilian authorities, the appropriate measures to be taken in matters involving the Armed Forces; prepare common measures to be taken in time-table form; and ensure that all concerned are given timely notice of measures taken by the Armed Forces.

II. *Tasks*

In the preparatory measures for defending the Home

---

* i.e. The 'General Government' area of Poland.

† The reference is to Bormann's circular mentioned in the introduction to No. 57 above.

theatre of war, Commanders of Military Districts will include all command staffs, troops, offices, and establishments of the Armed Forces and Waffen SS in the area of their command. They will also include additional forces placed at the disposal of Gauleiters and Higher SS and Police Leaders. Command staffs, troops, offices, and establishments of the Navy and Air Force will only be included in so far as the fulfilment of their own duties (paragraph I.1) is not thereby prejudiced.

The tasks embrace essentially these:

1. An appreciation of the accommodation, strength, mobility, and armament of the forces available for operations.

2. Plans for concentrating these forces, for chain of command, for placing forces on the alert, and for equipment and movements.

3. Plans for embodying and training the German civilian reserves which have been made available by the Party authorities.

The regulations already issued in respect of coastal areas and occupied territories are now extended to apply to the entire Home theatre of war.

4. Release of leading personalities of the Party and State from military service, in cooperation with the Gauleiters and Reich Commissioners for Defence.

5. Preparations for installations in planned defensive works, and for other tasks relating to defence and the primary tasks in battle.

In siting defensive works, Commanders of Military Districts are responsible for location, for instruction, and for the final form which they will take. The *construction* will in general be handed over to the Reich Commissioners for Defence, in their capacity as Gauleiters.

6. (a) Preparations, in cooperation with Reich Commissioners for Defence, for moving prisoners of war to the rear.

(b) Instructions on the measures to be employed for moving foreign labour to the rear – this is the task of the Reichsführer SS.

(c) Instructions on the measures (to be prepared by the Gauleiter alone) for evacuating the German civil population.

7. (a) *Preparations* for dispersal and evacuation, obstruction and demolition in the *military* sphere.

(b) *At the request* of Reich Commissioners for Defence, cooperation with them in making a time-table of preparations for dispersal, evacuation, obstruction, and demolition in the civilian sphere. These are tasks of the Reich Commissioners for Defence, acting on the directives of the Reich Ministries. The Military Commanders also have the duty of preparing support for the Reich Commissioners for Defence when they eventually execute these measures.

8. The instruction of Reich Commissioners for Defence and the senior Party officials – in the immediately threatened provinces, down to District Leader – concerning the condition of military preparedness and, eventually, of the military situation.

9. Preparation in the supply field.

III. *Supplementary regulations*

1. The broad instructions given above are of value only as a guide. Preparations will be confined, in every case, to the most restricted number of persons, in order to exclude unnecessary commotion among the civilian population. Should it prove impossible to carry out preparations of this kind without their having an undesirable effect upon the population, the preparations will be temporarily abandoned.*

2. The necessary regulations for carrying out these measures will be issued by the responsible commands.

---

* This last sentence was deleted by an order issued on 28th July 1944.

Where these regulations include general instructions of a fundamental nature, they will be submitted to the High Command of the Armed Forces (Operations Staff) before being issued.

3. These orders apply, in essentials, for the preparation of defence in the operational zones of the Alpine Approaches and on the Adriatic Coast, with the proviso that those tasks for which Commanders of Military Districts would be responsible in the Home theatre of war will here be the responsibility, respectively, of Commander Operations Area Alpine Approaches, and Commander Operations Area Adriatic Coast, in accordance with the directives from Commander-in-Chief South-west.

signed: KEITEL

59

The day after the issue of Keitel's order the tension between Party and Army, which Hitler and Bormann apprehended, broke out in a dramatic form. At the Führer Headquarters, now at Rastenburg in East Prussia, a long-prepared Army conspiracy ended in the attempt to assassinate Hitler, during a staff conference, with a carefully placed time-bomb. The bomb exploded and Hitler was presumed to be dead. After a period of tension, during which several high officers exposed themselves as supporters of the conspirators, Hitler's survival became known and the struggle for power was won by the Party which, from now on, tightened its control over all departments. Especially it tightened its grip on the Army, at once the most suspect and the most dangerous body in the State. Numerous changes were made in the command of the Army, many generals and other officers were arrested by the SS, and most of them executed, with or without trial. One very important change was in the command of the Replacement Army to which a key position had just been assigned in the event of invasion of the Reich. Its commander, General

Fromm, had been compromised in the Plot. He was instantly removed and replaced by the most formidable of Hitler's paladins, the Reichsführer SS, Heinrich Himmler. Fromm was afterwards hanged. There were changes too, in the West, and Field Marshal Rommel, who had been sent there after his defeat in Africa, but had been won over by the conspirators, was ordered to commit suicide to avoid the inconvenience of a trial. But the most vulnerable front, at this moment, was in the North-east, where the invader was closest to German soil. Here, on 23rd July, Hitler ordered a reorganization of the command, appointing as Commander-in-Chief the one general whom he trusted as a convinced Nazi. This was General Schörner, whom he would shortly make a field marshal (No. 59 below). Next day he ordered the distribution of his suspended orders concerning the authority of Army and Party in the event of invasion (No. 57 above). These were to 'become applicable in the event of enemy penetration into Reich territory, whether from the East or from the West or in any other theatre of war'.

The Führer

Führer Headquarters,
23rd July 1944.
70 copies

Ref.: *Reorganization of command authority in the area of Army Group North.*

I. I appoint Colonel General *Schörner* as Commander-in-Chief of Army Group North. I empower him to employ in the overall area under his command all available forces and materials of the Armed Forces and the Waffen SS, of non-military organizations and formations, of Party and civilian authorities, in order to repel enemy attacks and preserve our Baltic territories [*Ostland*].

All those bearing arms, irrespective of the branch of the Armed Forces to which they belong, or the non-military organization of which they may be members, are to be directed uniformly to this end. At the same time the fighting ability of our naval forces, and the supply traffic for which they are responsible, as well as of the Air Force, must be guaranteed.

Naval forces and operational air force units come under the command of the Navy and the Air Force respectively. They are, however, expected to comply with the requirements of Commander-in-Chief Army Group North, in so far as their tactical situation allows.

II. The entire area of Army Group North (i.e. Reich Commissariat Baltic Territories, excluding those parts of the Commissariat General in Lithuania which come into the area of Army Group Centre) will be an area of operations.

Commander Armed Forces Baltic Territories is subordinate to Commander-in-Chief Army Group North, in all respects.

III. The civil administration in the operational area of Army Group North, and the relations of the military authorities to the civil administration, remain as heretofore.

IV. I leave the Reich Commissioner Baltic Territories in the civil sphere, and Commander-in-Chief Army Group North in the military sphere, free to take such measures for withdrawal and evacuation as they consider proper and necessary in the light of the situation at the front.

The arrests which are now being carried out by the Higher SS and Police Leader Baltic Territories, under the plenary powers which I have delegated to him, must not be prejudiced by any measures of this kind.

I reserve to myself the right to give orders for the evacuation of the Estonian oil refining district.

signed: ADOLF HITLER

60

Hitler's orders, released on 24th July, had referred to an invasion of Germany 'whether from the East or from the West or in any other theatre of war'. The other theatre was in the South; and indeed, by now, invasion from the south seemed almost as likely. For in Italy, too, after the failure at Anzio, General Alexander had prepared a great summer offensive which began on 11th May. A week later, Cassino at last fell to the Polish Corps, and thereafter, though stubbornly resisted, the advance was general. On 4th June the Allies entered Rome, and although their forces in Italy were weakened, a month later, by the diversion of seven divisions for a landing on the Mediterranean coast of France, by the end of July they were established on the line of the river Arno in the West and held Ancona in the East. The Germans held a long prepared position, known as the Gothic Line, across Italy north of Pisa and Florence to Pesaro. But they could not be sure of holding it and Hitler now ordered the preparation of another line, the '*Voralpenstellung*', in the foothills of the Alps. The following series of teleprints was sent to the Commander-in-Chief South-west (Field Marshal Kesselring), the High Commissioners for operational areas in the Alpine Approaches and on the Adriatic Coast (Gauleiters Hofer and Rainer), and others concerned.

(a)

Teleprint.   26th July 1944.
High Command of the Armed Forces (Operations Staff).

Subject: *Alpine Approaches position.*

1. I order the construction of a system of rear positions in Northern Italy.
2. The following are to be constructed:

(a) The position in the Alpine Approaches, which is already laid down on broad lines.

(b) The adjacent Karst position (Tschitschen–Boden).*

(c) A cross-line extending from Ala to the Gulf of Venice.

(d) A cross-line extending from Belluno to the Gulf of Venice.

3. The following persons are responsible for constructing these positions:

(a) The High Commissioner for the Operation Area Alpine Approaches, for the Alpine Approaches position from the Swiss frontier to the Piave valley south of Longarone (inclusive).

(b) The High Commissioner for Operation Area Adriatic Coast, for the Alpine Approaches position from the Piave valley south of Longarone (exclusive), to Trieste (exclusive), and for the Karst position (Tschitschen–Boden) to the Gulf of Fiume.

Labour forces and materials will be recruited by a general call-up of the population, as in East Prussia.

(c) Commander-in-Chief South-west, for both cross positions between the Alpine Approaches position and the Gulf of Venice, with the help of the Todt Organization.

4. The purely military tasks for all positions are the responsibility of Commander-in-Chief South-west. With the help of tactical and engineering-technical staffs which will be formed for this purpose, he will determine:

(a) The operational and tactical siting of the positions.

(b) The priority for the completion of individual sectors.

(c) The form of the construction, in the light of the tactical situation, of tactical and technical battle experience, and the means available.

---

* The Karst is the part of the Julian Alps between Trieste and Fiume. The Tschitschen-Boden (now Čičarija) is the area formed by its southern slopes.

5. The intended organization for constructing these positions and the labour forces to be raised, will be reported to me as soon as possible. Progress reports will be submitted to me on the 1st, 10th, and 20th of each month after work has begun.

6. The High Command of the Armed Forces will issue detailed orders for carrying this out.

signed: ADOLF HITLER

(b)

29th July 1944.

Subject: *Führer's order of 26th July 1944* [*i.e. No. 60(a) above*].

The Führer has ordered paragraphs 2 and 3 of the above-mentioned order on the completion of a system of rear positions to be altered and supplemented as follows:

1. In addition to the two cross-lines which will be established in accordance with paragraph 2 of the order of 26th July, as many further cross-lines as possible will be constructed, taking advantage of the rivers, in order to render the enemy advance into the Udine Basin more difficult, to protect the air bases there, and to gain time for the completion of the Alpine Approaches position.

2. The High Commissioners for the two areas of operation will direct the construction of all the above-mentioned positions, as well as the cross-lines positions, on Italian territory.

Commander-in-Chief South-west retains responsibility for the construction in depth of the associated Apennine positions and the coastal fortification.

3. In building the two cross-lines, the High Commissioners will arrange directly, between themselves, the drawing up of boundaries between the two areas of operations.

In cases where positions are sited outside the areas of operations, and are therefore on Italian territory, the High

Commissioners there have the same powers in constructing
positions as they have in their own areas of operations. The
General Plenipotentiary for German Armed Forces in Italy,
and the authorities under his command, will support them
in this.

The Foreign Office is requested to explain to the Duce the
military necessity for the construction of these positions and
the measures required for them, which are of a purely military, and not a political, nature.

4. The following *construction units of the Todt Organization* and of the fortification construction staffs are available to
the High Commissioners:

(*a*) All resources already in their areas.
(*b*) The construction resources of the Air Force, which are
engaged in completing airfields north-east of the line
Verona–Po estuary. Commander-in-Chief Air Force
will apply for *exceptions* to this ruling (e.g. the quick
completion of work already begun and necessary for
the present operations of 2nd Air Fleet).
(*c*) Resources which will later be released from the Apennines position.

The Labour forces of the Todt Organization already
employed on coastal fortifications remain under command
of Commander-in-Chief South-west.

5. An order will follow concerning the support required
from the staffs and commands of all services in the Alpine
Approaches zone of operations, for ensuring the construc-
tional work.

signed: pp. JODL

(*c*)

3rd August 1944.

*Executive orders on the Führer's order for the construction of
a system of rear positions in Northern Italy*

1. *General Considerations.* The system of positions for the

defence of the Home theatre of war will be completed by a call-up of the civil population for total war. This is only possible by means of a political leadership conscious of its responsibilities. The great success which can be achieved by the employment of the masses in this way has already been shown in the East.

In addition, all authorities must rid themselves of the hitherto customary views about jurisdiction, form of co-operation, and other inhibitions, must imitate all successful improvisation, and must eliminate all superfluous organizational and administrative measures. The military authorities are in charge of the building. Their tasks, which are of a purely military nature, are clearly outlined in paragraph 4 of the Führer order.

In carrying out the construction the High Commissioners will be given a *free hand* in every respect, particularly in the employment of manpower and materials. All building workers employed on this project will be subordinate to them. *This also applies* to the *special construction units* (e.g. rock-drilling companies, and the construction troops trained in mine-laying), engaged on the Apennines and coastal positions, and now available for the Alpine Approaches.

2. *General operational instructions for planning and construction.* First, of special importance to the whole defensive system is the *front line,* namely a short connexion between the Swiss frontier and the Adriatic, which will take advantage of favourable terrain. This position will therefore be planned and built as a matter of *first priority.*

Then come the further positions in the system, whose most rearward will be the Alpine Approaches position itself, in so far as it does not coincide with the front line in its Western sector.

Strong-points will be incorporated in the construction where the enemy's main lines of thrust are probable – that is, on both sides of valleys and main thoroughfares, and in the sectors of the Adige and Piave rivers. The enemy is certain to attempt a thrust north-east, in the direction of the Udine basin.

3. *Military organization for this construction.* In accordance with paragraph 4 of the Führer's orders, General of Infantry von Zangen is appointed as permanent representative of Commander-in-Chief South-west in all *military* questions and tasks concerning the construction. The former Mountain Staff, Italy, will come under his command as a command staff.

The requisite planning staffs – together with sector staffs – will be set up under General von Zangen by Commander-in-Chief South-west, from personnel in his own area. These staffs will be composed of experienced officers of all arms and members of fortress-engineers staffs, and will be so equipped that they can undertake the necessary siting of the positions, and the civilian labour, with the least possible delay.

Any reinforcements required for von Zangen's staff, which will be kept as *mobile* as possible, should be requested through Commander-in-Chief South-west from the High Command of the Armed Forces (Operations Staff).

Requests from High Commissioners for the allocation of specialized construction troops, which may arise in the course of the construction, will be met by allocating labour no longer required in the Apennines. These Army construction troops will be subordinate to the High Commissioners in all matters concerning their actual work.

4. *General instructions from the General of Engineers and Fortifications* for the construction of fortifications in the Eastern theatre, and tactical and technical instructions on them drawn up by Special Engineer Staff 9, are enclosed in the appendix, as a basis for the construction of the key-defensive positions.

5. *Employment of the Todt Organization* on the construction: the Todt Organization will be employed, in accordance with agreement reached directly between the High Commissioners and the Todt Organization, so that the Todt Organization supplies the necessary building equipment and

assumes the *technical* supervision of the construction. The staffs of the High Commissioners concerned remain responsible for the construction. The respective local Todt Organization staffs will, however, be attached to them as their technical department.

6. *Mobilization of civilian manpower.* The mobilization of the civil population for work on the project is the responsibility of the High Commissioners, who may also use military authorities outside the areas of operations. The latter will, if necessary, have the final word in cases where the same labour forces are applied for several times.

7. *Procuring of materials.* The High Commissioners, with the assistance of the Todt Organization, are responsible for procuring all the normal building materials required for the project, and for their transport to the site (iron, cement, wood, etc.), including the necessary entrenching and other tools.

Mines, barbed-wire, and materials of all kinds for the construction of the whole defensive system will be allocated through Commander-in-Chief South-west by the High Command of the Armed Forces (Operations Staff) within the framework of the general allocation for Italy. Requisitions for mines, barbed-wire, and other materials will be made to Commander-in-Chief South-west through the High Commissioners.

8. The High Commissioners are responsible for *billeting and rations* for all civilian labour, including the Todt Organization. In special cases – e.g. for detached bodies of workers – the High Commissioners can apply for rations to be provided by the Armed Forces. Such requests will be made through Commander-in-Chief South-west.

9. The High Commissioners will assume responsibility for the *protection of building sites* against bandits, and for guarding working parties where necessary, with the forces available to them for this purpose. In order to provide additional forces for these tasks of *local* security and guards, Commander-in-Chief South-west may employ up to 40 per cent of the staff and officers of all branches of the Armed

Forces stationed in the operational zones of the Alpine Approaches and Adriatic Coast, in so far as they are not required for tactical reasons.

Active operations against bandits remain the task of Highest SS and Police Leader in Italy, in liaison with the local military authorities.

10. Commander-in-Chief South-west will report as soon as possible on the military organization which he proposes to place under General von Zangen's command (including command posts of his staffs), and on construction plans in accordance with paragraph 2.

signed: KEITEL

61

On all fronts similar defensive walls were being built, and the civilian population was being called up to build them. By mid-August it was the turn of the Western front. There, at the end of July, the Western Allies had been in a position to launch their offensive from their now well-established and enlarged bridgehead in Normandy, and by 20th August German resistance west of the Seine had been broken. On 25th August Paris fell. One day before this, Hitler issued his orders for building a new 'West Wall' for the defence of the Reich. On 29th August, orders followed for the defence of the North Sea coast (No. 62). Further orders for the West Wall followed on 1st September. All these orders were sent, primarily, to Martin Bormann and to the Gauleiters in the West. It was the Party, rather than the Army, on which Hitler relied to make the last stand.

Teleprint.
The Führer   24th August 1944.

Order for the construction of a German defensive position in the West

1. *I order the construction of a 'German defensive position in*

the West' by means of a call-up of the civil population *in the following sectors:*

(a) Gauleiter *Grohé*, Reich Commissioner in Belgium and Northern France, will be responsible for the lines Scheldt–Albert Canal to West of Aachen (where it will join the West Wall), as previously planned.*

(b) Gauleiter *Simon* will be responsible for the line of the Moselle from the West Wall south-west of Trier to the boundary between Gau Mosselland and Gau Westmark.

(c) Gauleiter *Bürkel* will be responsible for the line of the Moselle from the boundary of Gau Westmark via the arsenal of Metz–Diedenhofen–south of St Avold (part of the Maginot Line) to Saaralben.

(d) Gauleiter *Wagner* will be responsible for the Vosges position from Saaralben to Belfort, as previously planned, even if parts of the line are situated in the area of an *adjoining Gau*.

In addition, the Moselle line from south of Metz via Nancy–Epinal as far as St Maurice will be fortified later, through special orders, by the Military Commander in France.

2. The siting of the line proposed by Chief of Army Equipment and the Replacement Army in No. G105/44 (most secret) of 14th August is approved. The line between Maastricht and Aachen, via Valkenburg, will be completed first, the more southerly line planned via Eben–Emael receiving only secondary priority.

3. The Chief of Army Equipment and the Replacement Army is responsible for *the purely military tasks* relating to all positions, in accordance with directives from the High Command of the Armed Forces.

---

* An amendment sent on 7th September allocated responsibility for the sector running through Holland from Maastricht to the west of Aachen to Dr Seyss-Inquart, Reich Commissioner for Occupied Holland.

The following will be placed under his command, and will be responsible for carrying out the military tasks:

(a) Commander Armed Forces Belgium and Northern France.
(b) Deputy General XII Corps.
(c) Deputy General V Corps.

Their sectors will be adapted to those of the Gauleiters, even should parts of the positions come within the area of an adjoining military district.

The Chief of Army Equipment and, at his direction, the military commanders under him, with the help of the reconnaissance staffs already available and the specialist engineer staffs which will be allocated to them, will determine:

(a) The tactical *siting* of individual positions, based on reconnaissance already carried out.
(b) The priority of construction in the individual sectors.
(c) The form which construction will take, based on tactical and technical experience in battle, and the material available.

4. *The line* will be built so that the first construction is a continuous tank obstacle. Preparations will be made for creating a no-man's-land beyond our positions facing the enemy, and a continuous and tightly coordinated system of defences in depth will be achieved. This will be continually strengthened at strong-points by the adjacent line of permanent fortifications.

In the military arsenal of Metz–Diedenhofen, and in those parts of the Maginot Line which are to be incorporated, existing fortifications will be rebuilt, while *those which are not to be used will be put out of action*. General of Engineers and Fortifications at the High Command of the Armed Forces will issue special instructions for the construction.

5. All military authorities and troops employed in constructing these positions remain under command of their respective military superiors.

For the actual construction work they will be bound by Gauleiters.

6. *The mobilization of civilian labour*, and its employment, are the responsibility of the Gauleiters, as are its accommodation and rations, including those of the Todt Organization.

7. *Employment of the Todt Organization on the construction.* The Todt Organization will be employed in accordance with agreement reached directly between the Gauleiters and the Todt Organization, so that the latter supplies the necessary building equipment, and undertakes *technical* supervision of the execution of the work. The Gauleiter concerned remains responsible for the project as a whole. The local Todt Organization staff will be attached to him as his technical department.

8. *The procuring of all materials* (ordering, allocation, and transport) will be the subject of 'Special Instructions'.

9. The intended organization of the construction, and the manpower to be raised, will be reported to me as soon as possible by the Gauleiters through the Chief of the Party Chancery. Reports on progress and the state of construction will be submitted to me by the Chief of Army Equipment and the Replacement Army through the High Command of the Armed Forces (Operations Staff) on the 1st and 15th of each month.

signed: ADOLF HITLER

62

The Führer 29th August 1944.

Order for completion of defences in the German Bight

1. *I issue the following orders* for the strengthening of our defences in the German Bight.

   (a) *The fortification of the entire* coast from the Danish to the Dutch frontier, as well as those of the North and East Frisian Islands, which have not yet been fortified

(Programme A). The islands already fortified will be brought up to a full state of defence.

(b) *The planning* and preparation of all measures for the quick construction of a *second position*, which will run from the Danish frontier, in a depth of about 10 kilometres from the coast; a *cross-line* somewhere along the German–Danish frontier, *further cross-lines* in Schleswig-Holstein to the north of the Kaiser Wilhelm Canal. In addition, Commander Armed Forces Denmark will plan and construct further east-west cross-lines along the north of the German–Danish frontier.

2. Gauleiter Kaufmann will be responsible for this construction, for which all available means and the Todt Organization will be employed.*

3. Commander-in-Chief Naval Command North, as commander of forces for the defence of the German North Sea coast, will assume the direction of *purely military* tasks, according to the directives of the High Command of the Armed Forces (Operations Staff).

Deputy General X Army Corps will be responsible under him for carrying out military tasks.

Tasks:

(a) To plan the whole defensive system (including estimates of materials required), for the construction of a permanent system of field fortifications for which the estimate of forces necessary for an adequate garrison capable of full defence is the basic requirement.

(b) To settle the tactical siting of the line of defences in detail and

---

* On 31st August this paragraph was amended at the request of Martin Bormann. In the amended form, the Gauleiters of Schleswig-Holstein, East Hanover, and Weser–Ems were made responsible for construction in those parts of the position which fell within their areas, while Kaufmann, as Gauleiter of Hamburg, would supply them with resources available to him and act as spokesman in relation to X Corps.

(*c*) To establish priorities for the completion of the individual sectors.

(*d*) To decide upon the form which the construction should take, in the light of tactical and technical experience, and of the material available.

In addition, Deputy General X Corps will form three further *planning staffs*, in addition to those which already exist, composed of officers of all arms. These will be allocated to Deputy General X Corps by Army Personnel Office.

The Engineer Staffs required for construction will be formed by Deputy General X Corps.

In addition, the Naval Fortification Engineer Organization stationed in the German Bight will come under the command of Deputy General X Corps for these duties in this area.

Other personnel required in excess of this will be applied for by Deputy General X Corps to the High Command of the Armed Forces (General of Engineers).

4. *General Rules for the Construction.* The following will be fortified *as a first priority*: The North and East Frisian Islands, the coastal sector opposite Sylt (Hindenburg-damm); the Eiderstedt peninsula, the river defence of the Elbe–Weser estuary, and the coast from Brunsbüttel–Cux-haven–Wesermünde to Wilhelmshaven inclusive, the Ems estuary with Delfzijl. *Second priority:* The entire remainder of the coast. The construction will be executed so as to form first a continuous anti-tank obstacle, with an articulated defensive system in depth, which will *in addition* be continuously strengthened. Special general instructions for the construction will be issued by the High Command of the Armed Forces (General of Engineers and Fortresses).

5. All military staffs and forces engaged in the construction of the fortifications remain under command of their military superiors. For the actual construction work they will be bound by the regulations of the Gauleiter.

6. The Gauleiter will be responsible for *procuring and*

employing civilian labour, and for its accommodation and rations, which will include the accommodation and rations of the Todt Organization units employed.

7. *Employment of Todt Organization in the construction area*. The Todt Organization will be employed on the basis of direct agreement between the Gauleiter and the Todt Organization, so that the latter provides the necessary building equipment and assumes the *technical* supervision of the execution of the construction. Gauleiter Kaufmann or the authorities appointed by him remain responsible for the construction. The local Todt Organization staff will be attached to him as a technical department.

8. *The method of procuring all materials* (ordering, allocation, and transport) will be settled by 'Special Instructions'.

9. Gauleiter Kaufmann* will report to me through the Head of the Reich Chancery as soon as possible on his plans for organizing the work, and for the labour forces to be raised. *Naval High Command North Sea* will report on the 1st and 15th of each month through the High Command of the Armed Forces (Operations Staff) on the state and progress of the construction.

signed: ADOLF HITLER

63

Teleprint
The Führer   1st September 1944.

Order placing the West Wall in a state of defence

1. *I issue the following orders for placing the West Wall in a state of defence:*

(*a*) The position (including those portions of the Maginot Line which are to be incorporated) will be strengthened by the construction of field works.

---

* In the amended form (see footnote to paragraph 2), 'the Gauleiters'.

(*b*) The extension of the West Wall, already announced, will be strengthened by field works and, where possible, by permanent constructions extending as far as the Ijsselmeer.

2. The whole construction will be carried out by a call-up of the civil population, and the following will be charged with responsibility for it:

(*a*) The Reich Commissioner for occupied Netherlands territory, Reich Minister Dr Seyss-Inquart, with the assistance of the Chief of the Labour Department of the National Socialist Party, Oberdienstleiter Ritterbusch, for the sector from Ijsselmeer to Nijmegen.
(*b*) Acting Gauleiter Schlessmann (Gau Essen), for the sector Nijmegen–Venlo.
(*c*) Gauleiter Florian (Gau Düsseldorf), for the sector Venlo–German-Dutch frontier south-east of Roermond.
(*d*) Gauleiter Grohé (Gau Cologne–Aachen).
(*e*) Gauleiter Simon (Gau Moselland).
(*f*) Gauleiter Bürkel (Gau Westmark).
(*g*) Gauleiter Wagner (Gau Baden–Alsace).

Additional labour will be supplied where necessary from *neighbouring Gaus*. The following will be instructed to co-operate: Gau Essen with Gau Westphalia North; Gau Düsseldorf with Gau Westphalia North and South; Gau Cologne–Aachen with Gau Westphalia South; Gau Moselland with Gau Kurhessen and Hessen–Nassau; Gau Westmark with Gau Main–Franconia; Gau Baden–Alsace with Gau Württemberg. The necessary measures, including the number of workers required, will be decided directly among the Gauleiters.

3. The purely military tasks for the whole construction are the responsibility of the Chief of Army Equipment and the Replacement Army, in accordance with the directives from the High Command of the Armed Forces (Operations

Staff), and with the assistance of the Military Operations Staff, Western Defences. He is likewise charged with the military tasks connected with the construction and protection of the Western defences forward of the West Wall, from Trier to the Swiss frontier.

The following will be responsible under him for carrying out the military tasks:

(*a*) Commander Armed Forces Netherlands in the sector from the Ijsselmeer to Nijmegen.

(*b*) Deputy General VI Army Corps.

(*c*) Deputy General XII Army Corps.

(*d*) Deputy General V Army Corps, within their military districts.

Deputy General VI Army Corps will have in addition the sector Nijmegen to Roermond. Commander Armed Forces Netherlands comes under command of the Chief of Army Equipment and the Replacement Army for this operation.

4. General instructions for construction of the line will follow separately.

5. *The Reich Labour Leader* will place at the disposal of the Gauleiters the Reich Labour Service detachments employed in the Gaus charged with the construction. Calling-up dates for the Armed Forces will be adhered to.

6. The procurement of civilian labour is the task of the Reich Commissioner for Occupied Netherlands Territory, Reich Minister Dr Seyss-Inquart, and of the Gauleiters. *Its employment* is a matter for the Reich Commissioner for Occupied Netherlands Territory, Reich Minister Dr Seyss-Inquart, in his sector, and for the Gauleiters responsible for construction. The latter are also responsible for the accommodation and rations of these workers, including members of the Todt Organization employed on the work.

7. *Employment of Todt Organization in the construction.* The Todt Organization will be employed on the basis of direct agreement between the Reich Commissioner for

Occupied Netherlands Territory, Reich Minister Dr Seyss-Inquart, and the Gauleiters on the one hand, and the Todt Organization on the other, so that they provide the necessary building equipment and assume *technical* supervision of the execution of the construction. The Gauleiter concerned is responsible for the construction. The local Todt Organization staff will be attached to him as a technical department.

8. The procuring of all materials required, including ordering, allocation, and transport, will be carried out in accordance with the order for the construction of the German western positions issued by the High Command of the Armed Forces (General of Engineers).

9. *Local* anti-aircraft defence of the construction will be undertaken by the Air Force.

10. The Reich Commissioner for Occupied Netherlands Territory, Reich Minister Dr Seyss-Inquart, and the Gauleiters, will report to me as soon as possible through the Chief of the Reich Chancery on their plans for organizing the work and labour forces. The Chief of Army Equipment and the Replacement Army will report through the High Command of the Armed Forces (Operations Staff) on the state and progress of the construction on the 1st and 15th of each month.

signed: ADOLF HITLER

64

Hitler's orders on 1st September were accompanied by detailed orders signed by Keitel, for the imminent defence of the West Wall; but the advance of the Western Allies, already in Belgium and on the Meuse, had now deprived the Germans of the initiative, as Hitler's next order, of 3rd September (No. 64), shows. The very next day, September 4th, British forces entered Antwerp, thus cutting off the Channel ports and the Pas de Calais, with the launching-sites for the flying bombs. Hitler at once gave orders for the 'fortresses' of Boulogne and

Dunkirk to be reinforced and held at all costs and for the Albert Canal from Antwerp to Maastricht to be defended. Three days later, on 7th September, Hitler reversed his recent decision to entrust the defence of the Western frontier of the Reich to the Chief of the Replacement Army and restored full power to Field Marshal von Rundstedt, the Commander-in-Chief in the West (Nos. 64a and 64b).

Teleprint.

High Command of Armed Forces   3rd September 1944.
(Operations Staff).

Directive for further operations by Commander-in-Chief West

1. Our own heavily tried forces, and the impossibility of bringing up adequate reinforcements quickly, do not allow us at the present moment to determine a line which must be held, and which certainly can be held.

Therefore it is important to gain as much time as possible for raising and bringing up new formations, and for the development of the Western defences, and to destroy enemy forces by local attacks.

2. I therefore issue the following orders for the conduct of operations: *The right flank and centre of the Army in the West* (including 1st Army) will dispute every inch of ground with the enemy by stubborn delaying action. The likelihood of local penetrations must be accepted, but these must not lead to the encirclement of large German formations.

The protection of the Western position and of the West Wall from Roermond to the Swiss frontier is the immediate responsibility of the Chief of Army Equipment and the Replacement Army, with the forces at his disposal.

In the area forward of the Western position north of the Rhine–Marne Canal, command is transferred to 1st Army. The employment of forces and order of battle of this Army will be drawn up accordingly. Commander-in-Chief West will propose the time at which 1st Army will assume com-

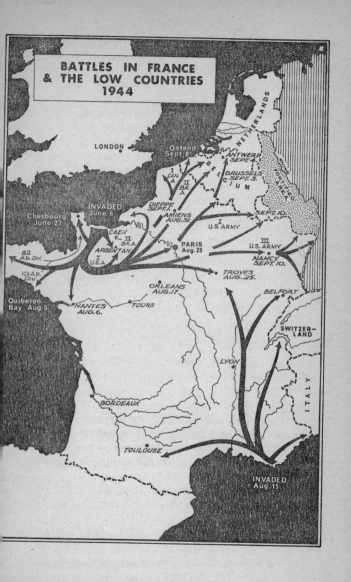

BATTLES IN FRANCE
& THE LOW COUNTRIES
1944

LONDON

Ostend
Sept. 8.

NETHERLANDS

ANTWERP
SEPT. 4.

BRUSSELS
SEPT. 3.

BELGIUM

GERMANY

SEPT. 10.

INVADED
June 6

Cherbourg
June 27

DIEPPE
SEPT. 1.

I
CAN.
A
II
BR.

AMIENS
AUG. 31.

I
U.S. ARMY

CAEN
II
BR. A

III
U.S. ARMY

82
Ab. Div.

ARGENTAN

I
U.S.A

PARIS
Aug. 25

NANCY
SEPT. 10.

101 Ab.
Div.

TROYES
AUG. 25.

Quiberon
Bay Aug. 5.

NANTES
AUG. 6.

ORLEANS
AUG. 17

TOURS

BELFORT

SWITZER-
LAND

LYON

ITALY

BORDEAUX

TOULOUSE

INVADED
Aug. 15

mand of the Western position. *On the left flank*, Army Group G will assemble a mobile force forward of the Vosges, to attack the deep eastern flank of the enemy. The *first* task of this force will be to protect the withdrawal of 19th Army and LXIV Army Corps, as well as the construction work in progress on the Western defences, by mobile operations against the southern flank of XII American Army Corps. Later, its *main* task will be to deliver a concentrated attack against the deep eastern flank and rear positions of the Americans. For the present XLVII Armoured Corps will take over command of this mobile force. After 7th Army again becomes capable of undertaking operations 5th Armoured Army will be withdrawn and employed in this task.

The following will be assembled under command of XLVII Armoured Corps, and later of 5th Armoured Army:

> 3rd and 15th Armoured Grenadier Divisions.
> 17th SS Armoured Grenadier Division and, if possible, Armoured Training Divisions.
> 106th, 107th, and 108th Armoured Brigades, and 11th and 21st Armoured Divisions.

In addition, three further armoured brigades will be moved from the Home theatre of war, beginning 5th September.

To relieve the Armoured Division of 1st Army, 19th Infantry Division, which will start arriving in Trier on 4th September, will be available. In forming the group, care must be taken to ensure that newly arrived formations, and those resting and reforming, are not prematurely committed and used up.

In order to render the battle group available for its main task at the earliest possible moment, I require Army Group G to move with the utmost speed.

3. The fortress troops allocated to Commander-in-Chief West, by order dated 26th August 1944, will be employed first in the Western defences, in order to free 559th and 36th

Grenadier Divisions, which are temporarily stationed there for employment in front of the Western defences. Sufficient fortress troops for this purpose should have arrived by the middle of September.

Owing to delays in the raising of formations, only the following divisions of those promised for September will be ready for action:

564th Grenadier Division by 15th September.
565th Grenadier Division by 20th September.
566th Grenadier Division by 25th September.
570th Grenadier Division by 25th September.

These divisions will take up positions behind the right flank.

Commander-in-Chief West will notify their arrival-points in good time.

4. The urgent need for resting formations, particularly armoured forces and artillery, will be met as quickly as possible by withdrawing formations which have suffered heavy casualties behind the West Wall. This should be done on the largest possible scale. Plans and time-tables will be reported to me.

During the withdrawal and after it, Army Group G will bring its formations up to full establishment by drawing upon all human material capable of fighting, from every branch of the Armed Forces. Commander-in-Chief West will ascertain the weapons and equipment required to bring Army Group G up to full strength.

An organization staff, which will include representatives of the Navy and Air Force, will be set up by the Chief of Army Equipment and the Replacement Army, and posted to Army Group G. I will issue orders respecting its tasks.

signed: ADOLF HITLER

64a

The Führer.   7th September 1944.
Subject: *Military powers of Commander-in-Chief West.*

1. I confer plenary powers on Commander-in-Chief West, General Field Marshal von Rundstedt:

(a) To employ, in the execution of the tasks which I have entrusted to him, all available fighting forces and material of the Armed Forces and Waffen SS in his area of command, and of non-military organizations and formations. The following are excluded: crews of submarines and crews of motor torpedo boats, and nautical specialists as designated by Commander-in-Chief Navy; and operational flying personnel and specialists as designated by Commander-in-Chief Air Force.

(b) To take all steps necessary to restore and maintain order in his area of command. All Naval and Air Force Authorities, and non-military organizations and formations, come under his orders in this respect.

2. Commander-in-Chief West may – in so far as this has not already been done by the High Command of the Armed Forces – give to the Chief of Army Equipment and the Replacement Army instructions for the distribution of protective forces along the West Wall and the Western defences, which may be necessary for bringing these dispositions into conformity with the general situation in the West. The directives of Commander-in-Chief West are also valid for the Party and State authorities, when military tasks in the Western frontier areas are transferred to the latter.

3. Commander Armed Forces Belgium and Northern France, and Commander Armed Forces Netherlands, are fully subordinate to Commander-in-Chief West in all respects.

signed: ADOLF HITLER

64b

Teleprint.

High Command of the Armed Forces 9th September 1944.
(Operations Staff)

1. Commander-in-Chief West will assume *command of the German Western defences* (including the West Wall) and all protective forces there, from 11th September 1944, 00.00 hours.

He will thus take over all the tasks which I have transferred to the Chief of Army Equipment and the Replacement Army, for the fortification and defence of the German Western position.

2. *For this purpose the following are subordinate to Commander-in-Chief West:*

(a) The Command staff for construction of the Western defences (Commandant Fortified Area, West 2, General of Engineers Kuntze).

(b) Temporarily, Commanders of Military Districts VI, XII, and V, with regard to their tasks connected with completion, equipment, and defence of the Western position.

3. *The Chief of Army Equipment and the Replacement Army* will ensure that formations and fortress troops for garrisoning the German Western position come under the command of Commander-in-Chief West at the stipulated time.

4. As newly raised formations arrive, *Commander-in-Chief West* will relieve the troops from the Chief of Army Equipment and the Replacement Army, which have been employed in the German Western position (the Valkyrie Units), and place them again at the disposal of the Chief of Army Equipment and the Replacement Army.

Military District Headquarters VI, XII, and V will be shortly relieved of their tasks in the Western position by staffs of the Field Army.

5. Commander-in-Chief West will report when he takes over command, and submit his proposed time-table for the withdrawal of the Military District Headquarters and Valkyrie units from the German Western position.

signed: ADOLF HITLER

65

Meanwhile on other fronts too the blows were falling. In the East, Finland sued for an armistice on 25th August, and next day Rumania, where a *coup d'état* had overthrown the pro-German dictator Marshal Antonescu, changed sides and declared war on Germany. On the same day General Alexander launched his attack on the Gothic Line in Italy. By 1st September the Germans had evacuated Bucharest and in Italy the Eighth Army had made the first breach in the Gothic Line. Hitler had some reason to believe that the next blow would fall in the Balkans. (Winston Churchill and Marshal Tito had met in Naples on 12th August and discussed a landing in Yugoslavia.) On 2nd September Hitler issued new orders for the defence of 'Fortress Crete'. On 12th September he ordered fortifications to be built in Southern Austria, against a possible attack from the Adriatic coast, in conjunction with Yugoslav partisans (No. 65). Six days later, similar orders (not printed here) were issued for the fortification of Slovakia against the impending Russian advance in the East.

Teleprint.

High Command of the Armed Forces   12th September 1944.
(Operations Staff)

Orders for defences in the South-east

1. I order the construction of a frontier defensive position

in the Gaus Carinthia and Styria, on the territory of the German Reich, along the following approximate line:

> Tolmein (joining the Blue Line here) – north of Laibach* – course of Save river to north-west of Gurkfeld – thence north-east to west of Varazdin.

2. Construction will be carried out by a call-up of civilian labour, and responsibility will be delegated as follows:

(*a*) To the High Commissioner of the Operation Area, Adriatic Coast, and to the Gauleiter of Gau Carinthia, Gauleiter Dr Rainer.

(*b*) To the Gauleiter of Gau Styria, Gauleiter Uberreither, each in their respective Gaus.

3. The purely military tasks involved in this construction are the responsibility of the Chief of Army Equipment and the Replacement Army, acting in accordance with directives from the High Command of the Armed Forces (Operations Staff). Under him, Deputy General XVIII Corps will cooperate with Gaus Carinthia and Styria, and will be responsible for the execution of military tasks.

4. Military tasks:

(*a*) Protection against bandits of personnel involved in planning and construction, as well as of the fortifications themselves, by means of security forces drawn from each area of command.

(*b*) Tactical siting of positions, based on current reconnaissance. For this, Deputy General XVIII Corps, in direct agreement with Commander-in-Chief Southwest, will define the points at which the positions link up with one another.

(*c*) Establishment of priorities for construction in individual sectors.

(*d*) Decision on the form of construction, based on tactical and technical operational experience, and the means available. The reconnaissance and engineering staffs

---

* The German name of Ljubljana.

required to carry out tasks (*b*) to (*d*) will be formed by Deputy General XVIII Corps in his own area. Any necessary additional requests will be submitted, to a limited extent, through the Chief of Army Equipment and the Replacement Army to the High Command of the Armed Forces (Operation Staff).

5. The construction itself will be carried out so that, wherever strong tank attacks can be made, a continuous anti-tank obstacle will be presented, as well as an articulated continuous defensive position in depth. Preparations will also be made for a no-man's-land on the enemy side of the position.

6. All military authorities and forces employed in constructing the position remain under the orders of their military superiors. For the actual construction work they will be bound by the instructions of the Gauleiters.

7. The procurement and employment of civilian labour is the responsibility of the Gauleiters. They will also undertake the accommodation and provisioning of this labour, including that of the Todt Organization detachments engaged.

8. Employment of the Todt Organization in the area of construction:

So far as detachments of the Todt Organization are available for construction, they will be employed on the basis of agreements reached directly between the Gauleiters and the Todt Organization, so that the Todt Organization supplies the necessary building equipment and undertakes the technical supervision of the construction. The Gauleiters will remain responsible for the construction, but the respective local authorities of the Todt Organization will be attached to them as a technical department.

9. Supplies and building materials of all kinds will be provided in accordance with orders from the High Command of the Armed Forces (General of Engineers and Fortifications).

10. The Gauleiters will report to me as soon as possible, through the Head of the Reich Chancery, their plans for

organizing the construction, and for the labour to be raised. The Chief of Army Equipment and the Replacement Army will report to me on the 1st and 15th of each month on the progress and state of the work.

signed: ADOLF HITLER

66

On 12th September American forces reached the German frontier and pierced it south of Aachen. Four days later Hitler issued an order demanding 'fanatical determination' from 'every able-bodied man in the combat zone'. 'There can no longer be any large-scale operations on our part. All we can do is to hold our positions or die. Officers of all ranks are responsible for kindling this fanaticism in the troops and in the general population, increasing it constantly, and using it as a weapon against the trespassers on German soil.' Next day General Montgomery attempted to seize the bridges over the Meuse, the Waal, and the Rhine at Grave, Nijmegen, and Arnhem, by a bold airborne operation, which would have opened the way into North Germany. The situation which Hitler had envisaged when he issued his two decrees of 13th July 1944 (above, No. 57) had now arisen, and on 19th and 20th September Hitler signed two new decrees replacing them. These two new decrees, (*a*) and (*b*) below, were issued on 22nd September, accompanied by a circular letter from Dr Lammers, the head of the Reich Chancery, dated 22nd September, which is here printed before them. They were distributed – one hundred copies as before – on 26th September.

The Reich Minister and Head of the Reich Chancery

Berlin, W.8, 22nd September 1944.

Subject: *Second Decree of the Führer on powers of command in an area of operations within the Reich.*

With reference to my circular letter of 16th July 1944 – Rk 901 E gRS.

The Führer has deemed it necessary that the decree forwarded to you with my circular letter of 16th July 1944 should in certain respects be amended. He has drawn up a second decree on the powers of command in an area of operations within the Reich, in the form which can be seen from the document enclosed. I am to ask you to take the necessary action. These regulations also apply to areas under control of a Head of Civil Administration.

In drawing up the decree, the Führer has expressed the opinion that it is self-evident that all civilian authorities, particularly those enumerated in paragraph IV sub-paragraph 2 of the decree, should maintain the closest contact with the military authorities concerned. I am to request you to instruct the authorities concerned in your sphere of action on these lines.

The decree will not be published.

A corresponding new regulation deals with the domain of the Party.

signed: DR LAMMERS

(a)

Second decree of the Führer on cooperation between the Party and the Armed Forces in an area of operations within the Reich, dated 19th September 1944

My decree on cooperation between the Party and the Armed Forces in an area of operations within the Reich is hereby cancelled. Should enemy forces advance into the territory of the Reich, I order as follows:

I. The offices of the National Socialist Party, their branches and associated organizations, will continue their activities in the area of operations.

II. 1. The military Commander-in-Chief will address his demands arising from the needs of the military situation in the domain of the National Socialist Party, and its branches and associated organizations, to the Gauleiter in the area of operations.

2. In immediate battle areas, whose boundaries will be determined by the military Commander-in-Chief in agreement with the Reich Commissioner for Defence in the area of operations, senior military commanders are empowered to issue direct to the authorities of the National Socialist Party, its branches and associated organizations, such directives as may from time to time be necessary for the execution of their operational duties.

3. I shall appoint the Gauleiter for the area of operations.

III. It is the task of the Gauleiter for the area of operations to advise the military Commander-in-Chief in questions affecting the National Socialist Party, its branches and associated organizations.

IV. Gauleiters whose Gaus lie wholly or in part within the area of operations will appoint a liaison officer, who will be attached as adviser to the Gauleiter for the area of operations.

V. The Gauleiter for the area of operations will carry out his tasks with all available forces of the National Socialist Party, its branches and associated organizations.

VI. The Gauleiter for the area of operations may delegate the execution of his duties in an area under a subordinate commander to the competent Gauleiter in that area.

VII. This decree also applies to Eastern territories incorporated into the Reich. It applies to the Protectorate of Bohemia and Moravia, to the General Government,* as well as to territories controlled by a Chief of Civil Administration.

---

* of Poland.

VIII. The Head of the Party Chancery will issue the instructions necessary for the execution of this decree.

Führer Headquarters. 19th September 1944.
The Führer.

signed: ADOLF HITLER

The Head of the Party Chancery.
signed: M. BORMANN

The Chief of the High Command of the Armed Forces.
signed: KEITEL

Second decree of the Führer on powers of command in an area of operations within the Reich, dated 20th September 1944

My decree on powers of command in an area of operations within the Reich of 13th July 1944 is hereby cancelled. Should enemy forces advance on to the territory of the Reich I order as follows:

I. The civil administration will continue to operate fully in the area of operations. State and local authorities will continue to carry out their duties.

II. I shall appoint the Reich Commissioner for Defence for the area of operations.

III. 1. The Reich Commissioner for Defence in the area of operations has plenary powers. The uniform execution throughout the Reich of all the measures to be taken by the Reich Commissioner for Defence in accordance with this decree will be the responsibility, subject to my general instructions, of the Reichsführer SS Heinrich Himmler.

2. The military Commander-in-Chief will address his demands, arising from the needs of the military situation, in the civil sphere, to the Reich Commissioner for Defence in the area of operations.

3. In the immediate battle areas, where boundaries will be determined by the military Commander-in-Chief in agreement with the Reich Commissioner for Defence in the area of operations, senior military commanders are empowered to issue direct to civilian authorities of the State and the municipalities such directives as from time to time may be necessary for the execution of their operational duties.

IV. 1. In the exercise of his plenary powers, the Reich Commissioner for Defence in the area of operations may –

(*a*) Take all measures rendered necessary by threatened action of the enemy.
(*b*) Give instructions to all state and local authorities.
(*c*) Issue regulations having the force of law.

2. The Reich Commissioner for Defence in the area of operations will avail himself of the following authorities:

In Police matters – of the competent Higher SS and Police Leader.

In matters concerning the state railways and inland shipping – of the Plenipotentiary of the Reich Minister of Transport.

In matters concerning maritime shipping – of the deputy of the Reich Commissioner for Shipping.

In matters concerning armaments and war production – of the chairman of the competent Armaments Committee or sub-Committee.

V. The Reich Commissioners for Defence whose districts come wholly or partially within the area of operations will appoint a liaison officer, who will be attached to the Reich Commissioner for Defence in the area of operations in an advisory capacity.

VI. The Reich Commissioner for Defence in the area of operations may delegate the execution of his duties to those

Reich Commissioners for Defence whose defence districts are a part of the area of operations.

VII. This decree also applies to the incorporated Eastern territory. It applies to territories under a Head of Civil Administration, and to the General Government.*

VIII. Instructions which run counter to this decree are hereby cancelled.

IX. The Reich Minister of the Interior will issue the legal and administrative instructions required for the implementation of this decree.

Führer Headquarters, 20th September 1944.
The Führer.
signed: ADOLF HITLER

The Reich Minister and Chief of the Reich Chancery.
signed: DR LAMMERS

The Chief of the High Command of the Combined Services.
signed: KEITEL

67

In the last months of 1944 the Germans fought back fiercely on all fronts. The Allied airborne attack on the river bridges in South Holland was checked at Arnhem, although the Allies cleared the Scheldt and were soon able to use the port of Antwerp in order to supply their northern armies. In Italy, the German position was reinforced and when winter came the Allies were still held in Tuscany. But on the Eastern front the Russians, having occupied Rumania, advanced into Hungary and Yugoslavia, forcing the Germans to evacuate Greece, which was occupied by the British. On 14th October the

---

* of Poland.

British entered Athens, and six days later the Russians took Belgrade. All this time, the Germans were continuing to build fortifications on both Eastern and Western frontiers. On 18th September the first orders had been sent out to fortify Slovakia. On 22nd October further measures were undertaken: Slovakia, like the Western and Alpine fronts, was to be guarded by a deep system of forts built by forced labour under the direction of the Chief of Army Equipment and the Replacement Army, Heinrich Himmler. On 23rd November new positions in Slovakia were fortified, and on 5th December, when the Russians had crossed the Danube and were besieging Budapest, Bratislava itself, the capital of Slovakia, was declared a fortress. Meanwhile new fortifications were being built in the West too and orders were given, on 5th December, that the West Wall was to be held at all costs. Within Germany, the Party asserted its control over the organization of resistance. On 13th November Keitel gave orders to adjust the Western military districts to the frontiers of the Party districts (Gaus) on the grounds that total war necessitated the closest cooperation between Army and Party, and ten days later Himmler, as Commander of the Replacement Army, issued orders from the Führer Headquarters defining the relations between the *Volkssturm*, the resistance movement of the Party which Hitler had raised by decree on 25th September, and the Army. On 25th November Hitler addressed himself to those units of the Army which, being surrounded by the enemy outside the German frontiers, could not feel the direct coercion of the Party. It is printed here as issued by Keitel on 28th November.

Führer Order on the exercise of command in units which are left to their own resources

The Chief of the High Command of the Armed Forces (Operations Staff).

Führer Headquarters, 28th November 1944.

Subject: *Exercise of command in units which have been isolated.*

The following Führer order on the exercise of command in units which are left to their own resources will be made known to troops forthwith.

It will be ensured forthwith that the contents of this order become the common property of every individual soldier.

Operation orders providing a summary of the hitherto published orders concerning fortifications, fortified areas, local strong-points, etc. will follow.

Enclosure

The Führer   Headquarters,
                                         25th November 1944.

The war will decide whether the German people shall continue to exist or perish. It demands selfless exertion from every individual. Situations which have seemed hopeless have been redeemed by the courage of soldiers contemptuous of death, by the steadfast perseverance of all ranks, and by inflexible, exalted leadership.

A commander is only fit to lead German troops if he daily shares, with all the powers of his mind, body, and soul, the demands which he must make upon his men. Energy, willingness to take decisions, firmness of character, unshakable faith, and hard, unconditional readiness for service, are the indispensable requirements for the struggle. He who does not possess them, or who no longer possesses them, cannot be a leader, and he must withdraw.

Therefore I order:

Should a commander, left to his own resources, think that he must give up the struggle, he will first ask his officers, then his non-commissioned officers, and finally his troops, if one of them is ready to carry on the task and continue the fight. If one of them will, he will hand over command to that man – regardless of his rank – and himself fall in. The new leader will then assume the command, with all its rights and duties.

signed: ADOLF HITLER

68

But Hitler did not intend merely to resist: he still had plans of counter-attack. On 16th December Field Marshal von Rundstedt launched a powerful surprise attack against the centre of the Western front, where the Allies were weakest, and broke through in the Ardennes sector. But the attack, after initial success, was squeezed out within a month. By 21st January 1945 the Germans were back on the defensive and Hitler, who had personally insisted on the Ardennes attack, was on the defensive too, seeking to maintain his personal control over strategy.

Teleprint.

High Command of the Armed Forces   21st January 1945. (Operations Staff)

I order as follows:

1. Commanders-in-Chief, Commanding Generals, and Divisional Commanders are personally responsible to me for reporting in good time:

(*a*) Every decision to carry out an operational movement.

(*b*) Every attack planned in Divisional strength and up-wards which does not conform with the general directives laid down by the High Command.

(*c*) Every offensive action in quiet sectors of the front, over and above normal shock-troop activities, which is calculated to draw the enemy's attention to the sector.

(*d*) Every plan for disengaging or withdrawing forces.

(*e*) Every plan for surrendering a position, a local strong-point, or a fortress.

They must ensure that I have time to intervene in this decision if I think fit, and that my counter-orders can reach the front-line troops in time.

T—K

2. Commanders-in-Chief, Commanding Generals, and Divisional Commanders, the Chiefs of the General Staffs, and each individual officer of the General Staff, or officers employed on General Staffs, are responsible to me that every report made to me either directly, or through the normal channels, should contain nothing but the unvarnished truth. In future, I shall impose draconian punishment on any attempt at concealment, whether deliberate or arising from carelessness or oversight.

3. I must point out that the maintenance of signals communications, particularly in heavy fighting and critical situations, is a prerequisite for the conduct of the battle. All officers commanding troops are responsible to me for ensuring that these communications both to higher headquarters, and to subordinate commanders, are not broken and for seeing that, by exhausting *every* means and engaging themselves personally, permanent communications in every case are ensured with the commanders above and below.

signed: ADOLF HITLER

69

By the end of January 1945 the Russians were already in Germany. In the North, they had overrun East Prussia, except for Königsberg. In the Centre, they had entered Silesia. The time had therefore come for the Volkssturm to act. Its inefficacy in the East led to the following order.

Teleprint.

High Command of the Armed Forces   28th January 1945.
(Operations Staff)

Subject: *Employment of the Volkssturm.*

Experience in the East has shown that Volkssturm, emergency, and reserve units have little fighting value when left to themselves, and can be quickly destroyed. The fighting value of these units, which are for the most part strong in numbers but weak in the armaments required for modern battle, is immeasurably higher when they go into action with troops of the regular army in the field.

I therefore order: where Volkssturm, emergency, and reserve units are available, together with regular units, in any battle sector, mixed battle-groups (brigades) will be formed under unified command, so as to give the Volkssturm, emergency, and reserve units stiffening and support.

signed: ADOLF HITLER

70

The invasion, first of German occupied territory, then of Germany itself, created a problem of evacuation. On 25th August 1944 Hitler had issued a 'Führer Order' to prepare for the evacuation from allied, friendly, or occupied countries, in certain circumstances, of all Germans not essential to the conduct of operations. On 10th September this order was applied throughout Europe. Orderly evacuation was to be prepared by the military commanders 'so that, in case of a surprise attack, a panic and a disgraceful retreat of military and civilian personnel will be avoided'. But with the advance of the Russians into the Reich itself, a new and greater problem of evacuation was created. At first Hitler attempted to use Denmark as an evacuation area. The following order was addressed to the Naval High Command.

Teleprint.

High Command of the Armed Forces
(Operations Staff)
Qu.1 (Transport)   5th February 1945.

Subject: *Transport of refugees from the East to Denmark.*

The Führer issued the following orders on 4th February 1945:

In order to relieve the transport situation in the Reich immediately, I order as follows: Our compatriots temporarily moved back from the Eastern part of the Reich will be accommodated in Denmark as well as in the Reich. In particular, civilians will be evacuated to Denmark who:

1. Can be moved by the Navy by sea, without prejudice to the day-to-day movement of troops and supplies, or who:

2. Have been landed in Western Baltic ports, including Stettin and Swinemünde, and must be moved from there by rail.

The Reich Plenipotentiary will cooperate with the local Danish authorities in arranging suitable accommodation for evacuated civilians. The Armed Forces will afford all possible assistance in this respect.

signed: ADOLF HITLER

Comment by the High Command of the Armed Forces for the Armed Forces:

The Armed Forces will make special efforts to help by making use of all means of transport returning west, by sea, rail, or road; by assistance with rations, medical care, and arrangements for accommodation at intermediate points on the journey.

pp. signed WINTER, Lieutenant General and Acting Chief of the High Command of the Armed Forces, Operations Staff.*

71

Orderly evacuation was soon rendered impossible by events. On 21st February systematic evacuation from the West (as distinct from tactical evacuation, controlled by the Gauleiters) was stopped since 'such migrations expose those concerned to

---

* General Winter had replaced Warlimont, on the latter's illness, in September 1944.

great dangers and privations', and there were now no areas to which they could be evacuated. By 7th March the Western allies had reached the Rhine on almost all fronts and the Americans had captured a bridgehead at Remagen. Next day, on Hitler's orders, the High Command of the Armed Forces issued terrible threats against deserters, who were 'to be shot at once', and against soldiers surrendering 'without being wounded, or without proof that they have fought to the last', whose relatives were to be penalized. But all these threats availed nothing. By 20th March the last German stand in the West had been defeated and the Western allies were preparing to force the Rhine and occupy the country up to the demarcation line already agreed with the Russians, who, at this time, were still in East Prussia, Silesia, and Hungary. It was in these circumstances that Hitler issued the following Scorched Earth' directive.

Teleprint.

High Command of the Armed Forces
(Operations Staff)   20th March 1945.

The Führer issued the following order on 19th March 1945.

Subject: *Demolitions on Reich territory*.

The struggle for the existence of our people compels us, even within the territory of the Reich, to exploit every means of weakening the fighting strength of our enemy, and impeding his further advance. Every opportunity must be taken of inflicting, directly or indirectly, the utmost lasting damage on the striking power of the enemy. It is a mistake to think that transport and communication facilities, industrial establishments and supply depots, which have not been destroyed, or have only been temporarily put out of action, can be used again for our own ends when the lost territory has been recovered. The enemy will leave us nothing but scorched earth when he withdraws, without paying the slightest regard to the population. I therefore order:

1. All military transport, and communication facilities, industrial establishments and supply depots, as well as anything else of value within Reich territory, which could in any way be used by the enemy immediately or within the foreseeable future for the prosecution of the war, will be *destroyed*.

2. The following are responsible for carrying out these demolitions:

The military commanders, for all military establishments, including the transport and communications network; the Gauleiters and Reich Commissioners for Defence, for all industrial establishments and supply depots, and anything else of value. The troops are to give to Gauleiters and Reich Commissioners for Defence such help as they require to carry out their tasks.

3. This order will be made known to all officers commanding troops as quickly as possible. Directives to the contrary are invalid.

signed: ADOLF HITLER

72

Hitler's 'scorched earth' order raised several doubts which later orders sought to resolve. The duty to destroy had to be reconciled with the duty to use until the last minute. Demolition required fuel, but so did resistance. Which had priority? Such questions were to be referred 'in each individual case' to the Chief of the High Command of the Armed Forces who, however, was to comply with the Führer's decision when circumstances demanded it. On 30th March new instructions regulated destruction in the sphere of armaments and war-production. On 4th April a further document laid down the responsibility for all this destruction: military material and installations were to be destroyed by the Armed Forces, civil

establishments by Gauleiters and Reich Commissioners for
Defence, acting under the direction of the Reich Minister for
Armaments and War Production, Albert Speer. But these
orders had by now lost meaning, and in fact Speer refused to
cooperate. The Armed Forces also had other preoccupations.
In the West their unity was being destroyed, and Hitler's next
order was, once again, an attempt to reorganize their command.

Teleprint.

High Command of the Armed Forces
(Operational Staff)   7th April 1945.

The development of the position in the West, and the loss
of many operational communication links, make it necessary
to adjust the organization of command in the Western
theatre of war to conform with changed conditions. I therefore order the following reorganization of command in the
West.

1. The following are immediately subordinate to *the High
Command of the Armed Forces:*

> Commander-in-Chief North-west (High Command
>   Army Group H).
> High Command Army Group B.
> Commander-in-Chief West.
> Naval High Command West.

2. The following come under command of *Commander-
in-Chief North-west (High Command Army Group H):*

(*a*) The present command area of *Command Staff, North
     Coast*. Commander, High Command North Coast
     Staff, is available to Commander-in-Chief North-west,
     to assume command in this area.
(*b*) *Commander-in-Chief Netherlands.*
     The following come under his command: 25th Army;
     Commander Armed Forces Netherlands; Admiral

Netherlands; and Air Force units stationed in the Netherlands. Commander-in-Chief Netherlands is personally responsible to me for the defence of Fortress Holland, for the exhaustive use of all necessary and available means for this task. Commander-in-Chief Netherlands will make use of Commander 25th Army in the execution of his duties.

As soon as land communications with the Reich are interrupted, the instructions issued in my comprehensive order on fortresses will apply to the cooperation between Commander-in-Chief Netherlands and the Reich Commissioner for Occupied Territories in the Netherlands.

(*c*) Colonel General Student's Army Group, Parachute Army.

(*d*) Military District XI.

3. The following remain under command of *High Command Army Group B*, as hitherto: 5th Armoured Army; 15th Army; von Lüttwitz Army department, and all units and soldiers of all arms in the Army Group area.

4. The following remain under command of *Commander-in-Chief West*: High Command Army Group G, with 1st Army and 7th Army; 11th and 19th Armies direct; also Military Districts V, VII, IX, and XIII.

5. *The boundary* between Commander-in-Chief Northwest and Commander-in-Chief West runs as follows: Paderborn–Holzminden–Salzgitter–Oschersleben–Schönebeck (these towns belonging to North-west).

6. The organization of *air forces* stationed in the West will conform with Army organization. In addition, an appropriate Command Staff will be attached to Commander-in-Chief North-west and Commander-in-Chief West, and the support of Army Group B is particularly important. My order of 3rd April for the subordination of air and anti-aircraft formations supporting the Army in the West applies also to the new system of command. These formations will con-

sequently come under operational command of Commanders-in-Chief North-west and West. Commander-in-Chief
Air Force will notify me of the new disposition of forces.
The assumption of command in the new areas will be notified.

7. Details of *territorial chain of command* (subordination
of Military Districts) are contained in the order of 7th April.

8. I am to be notified when command of the new areas has
been assumed.

Signed: ADOLF HITLER

73

By mid-April all prospects of effective German resistance had
gone. In the East the Russians held Vienna and stood on the
Oder, only fifty miles from Berlin. In the West, the Allied
advance was reaching the Elbe. It seemed that Germany would
be cut in two. The death of President Roosevelt on 12th April
encouraged Hitler to believe that a political miracle might yet
save him, but even he could no longer hope for a military
miracle. On 15th April he issued two orders, one reorganizing
the command organization yet again in case Germany was cut
in two (73); the other (74), an order of the day sent to the
Army Groups in the East with instructions to pass it down at
once to company level. It was to be published in the Army
newspaper but not in public newspapers.

*Führer's Order on the organization of command in the
separated areas of Northern and Southern Germany*

On 15th April the Führer issued the following fundamental order:

'In case land communications in Central Germany are
broken, I order as follows:

1. In the separated area in which I am not present myself,

a Commander-in-Chief appointed by me will conduct all military operations, and will take command of all forces of the three branches of the Armed Forces in the area concerned, of all fronts, of the Reserve Army, the Waffen-SS, the Police, and other organizations attached to them.

2. If I myself should be south of the interrupted communications, *Admiral Doenitz* will be appointed Commander-in-Chief in the Northern area. An Army General Staff (Commander, Lieutenant General Kinzel), which will be kept as small as possible, will be attached to him as Operations Staff. The following will come under his command:

    (*a*) Commander-in-Chief Army Group Vistula, who will command the Eastern Front.

    (*b*) Commander-in-Chief North-west, who will command the Western front.

    (*c*) Commander Armed Forces Denmark.

    (*d*) Commander Armed Forces Norway.

    (*e*) Commander-in-Chief Air Fleet, Reich, for the air forces engaged.

3. If I myself should be north of the interrupted communications, *General Field Marshal Kesselring* will be appointed Commander-in-Chief in the Southern area. The following will come under his command:

    (*a*) Commanders-in-Chief of Army Groups South and Centre, for the Eastern front.

    (*b*) Commander-in-Chief Army Group G, for the whole of the Western front.

    (*c*) Commander-in-Chief South-east.

    (*d*) Commander-in-Chief South-west.

    (*e*) Commander-in-Chief 6th Air Fleet, for the air forces engaged.

4. The Commanders-in-Chief appointed for separated areas in paragraphs 2 and 3 will conduct the overall defence of the Reich in their areas, if necessary independently, should

my orders and decisions, even by wireless, not reach them in time, in view of the communications position. They are personally responsible to me for exhaustive employment of their entire war potential, in the closest cooperation with the Reich Commissioner for Defence of the separated area. Apart from this, as far as communications allow, the unified control of operations by myself personally, as hitherto, will not be altered. In particular, the duty of supplying day-to-day reports is not affected.

The High Command of the Air Force, and the Reichsführer SS, as the superior officer responsible for the military duties of the Waffen-SS, will be kept informed of decisions as quickly as the technical possibilities of communications allow.

5. The Commander-in-Chief in an area which is temporarily cut off will also avail himself of the services of the local representatives of the supply, transport, communications, and armaments organizations laid down in the order issued on 11th April 1945.

6. The headquarters of the proposed Commander-in-Chief of a separated area will be sited and prepared forthwith, in agreement with the Chief of Armed Forces Signals, General of Signals Praun, and in accordance with the order by the Chief of the High Command of the Armed Forces dated 12th April 1945, 'Establishment of subsidiary headquarters'.

7. The activity of the Commander-in-Chief of a separated area will be initiated only on special orders from me. These will also define the Army Groups under whose command each Army will come.

8. Similarly, I shall appoint a Supreme Reich Commissioner for Defence for a separated area, under whom all authorities of the Party and the State will be coordinated, and who must cooperate closely with the Commander-in-Chief of the separated area.

9. The Chief of the High Command of the Armed Forces will issue operation orders.

The following supplementary order is for Commander-in-Chief Navy:

I entrust Commander-in-Chief Navy with immediate preparations for the exhaustive use of all possible sources of manpower and material, for defending the Northern area, should land communications in Central Germany be interrupted. I delegate to him plenary powers to issue the orders necessary for this purpose to all authorities of the State, the Party, and the Armed Forces in this area.

74

Führer Order

Order of the Day   15th April 1945.

Soldiers of the German Eastern front!

For the last time our deadly enemies the Jewish Bolsheviks have launched their massive forces to the attack. Their aim is to reduce Germany to ruins and to exterminate our people. Many of you soldiers in the East already know the fate which threatens, above all, German women, girls, and children. While the old men and children will be murdered, the women and girls will be reduced to barrack-room whores. The remainder will be marched off to Siberia.

We have foreseen this thrust, and since last January have done everything possible to construct a strong front. The enemy will be greeted by massive artillery fire. Gaps in our infantry have been made good by countless new units. Our front is being strengthened by emergency units, newly raised units, and by the Volkssturm. This time the Bolshevik will meet the ancient fate of Asia – he must and shall bleed to death before the capital of the German Reich. Whoever fails in his duty at this moment behaves as a traitor to our people. The regiment or division which abandons its position acts so disgracefully that it must be ashamed before the women and children who are withstanding the terror of bombing in our cities. Above all, be on your guard against the few treacherous officers and soldiers who, in order to preserve their pitiful lives, fight against us in Russian pay, perhaps even wearing German uniform.* Anyone ordering you to retreat will, unless you know him well personally, be immediately arrested and, if necessary, killed on the spot, no matter what rank he may hold. If every soldier on the Eastern front does his duty in the days and weeks which lie ahead, the last assault of Asia will crumple, just as the invasion by our enemies in the West will finally fail, in spite of everything.

Berlin remains German, Vienna will be German again, and Europe will never be Russian.

Form yourselves into a sworn brotherhood, to defend, not the empty conception of a Fatherland, but your homes, your wives, your children, and, with them, our future. In these hours, the whole German people looks to you, my fighters in the East, and only hopes that, thanks to your resolution and fanaticism, thanks to your weapons, and under your leadership, the Bolshevik assault will be choked in a bath of blood. At this moment, when Fate has removed from the earth the greatest war criminal of all time,† the turning-point of this war will be decided.

signed: ADOLF HITLER

In spite of the temporary euphoria induced by the death of Roosevelt, Hitler had really, by 15th April, recognized his defeat. His last convulsions were rather a gesture of defiance, directed to posterity, than an immediate struggle for survival. Already, on 2nd April, he had admitted that National Socialism had been overthrown; but it was the duty of his followers,

---

* A reference to the German officers who, as Russian prisoners, were formed into an anti-Nazi propagandist group and had broadcast from Russia to Germany. The leaders of this group were Field Marshal Paulus and General von Seydlitz.

† i.e. President Roosevelt.

he added, 'to go on fighting, even without hope, to the very end', although 'I personally would not endure to live in the Germany of transition which would succeed our conquered Third Reich'. In fact, within a week of Hitler's last Order of the Day, Germany was cut in two. Soon afterwards Berlin itself was surrounded by the Russians. Hitler could no longer direct his war, and indeed, on 22nd April, he appeared to resign the direction of it. It did not much matter now who directed it. On 30th April Hitler committed suicide in Berlin. On 2nd May the German armies in Italy surrendered to General Alexander. On the 4th the armies in the North-west surrendered to General Montgomery. On the 7th the general capitulation was signed at General Eisenhower's Headquarters at Reims, and the war, on all fronts, was over.

LIST OF CODE-NAMES

Achse (Axis): Occupation of Italy 1943. 215

Alarich (Alaric): Earlier version of *Achse*. 215

Alpenveilchen (Alpine Violet): Intervention in Albania 1941. 101

Anton = Attila 1942. 184

Attila: Occupation of Unoccupied France 1940–42. 88–90, 98, 169, 184, 203

Augsburg: Delay of offensive in the West, November 1939. 53

Barbarossa: Attack on Russia 1941. 93–8, 101, 104, 106, 129–30

Blücher: Attack from Crimea on the Caucasus by Army Group South 1942. 188–91

Braunschweig (Brunswick): Attack on Caucasus by Army Group South 1942. 193

Danzig: Proceed with offensive in the West November 1939. 53

Edelweiss: Attack on Baku 1942. 195

Elbe: Earlier version of *Augsburg*. 53*n*.

Felix: Attack on Gibraltar 1940–41. 82, 83, 87, 98, 101, 130*n*., 133

Feuerzauber (Fire Magic): Earlier version of *Nordlicht*. 197.

Fischzeiher (Heron): Attack on Stalingrad 1942. 195

Gelb (Yellow): Attack in the West 1939. 49, 56

Grün (Green): Attack on Czechoslovakia 1938. 25

Ilona: Attack on Spain 1942. 184–6

Isabella: Earlier version of *Ilona* 1941. 130*n*., 184

Lachsfang (Salmon-trap): Seizure of Murmansk railway 1942. 192

Marita: Attack on Greece 1941. 90–2, 98, 107, 109

Merkur (Mercury): Seizure of Crete 1941. 117–19

Nordlicht (Northern Light): Capture of Leningrad 1942. 197

Rhein (Rhine): Earlier version of *Danzig*. 53*n*.

Schamil: Parachute attack on Maykop 1942. 190

Seelöwe (Sea Lion): Invasion of England 1940. 76, 80, 86, 98

Sonnenblume (Sunflower): Expedition to Tripoli 1941. 101

Taifun (Typhoon): Attack on Moscow 1941. 152

Weiss (White): Attack on Poland 1939. 37, 38

Weserübung (Weser Exercise): Invasion of Denmark and Norway 1940. 61–4

Wiesengrund (Meadowland): Seizure of Fisherman's Peninsula in Arctic Ocean. 192

GLOSSARY

Glossary of Offices

The principal military, naval and air-force offices or posts held by persons mentioned in this book, in the various theatres of war, are listed here (for further details refer to list of PERSONS).

CHIEF OF THE HIGH COMMAND OF THE ARMED FORCES (Chef. Oberkommando der Wehrmacht, or Chef. OKW), for duration of war – Keitel.

CHIEF OF THE ARMED FORCES OPERATIONAL STAFF (Chef. Wehrmachtführungamt, later Wehrmachtführungstab; or Chef. WFA, later Chef. Wfst), for duration of war – Jodl.

HOME DEFENCE DEPT. OF WFA (Wfst) (Abteilung Landesverteidigung, or WFA (Wfst)/L) – from 10 Nov 38 to 31 Dec 41, Warlimont; from 1 Jan 42 to 6 Sep 44 (under its new title Wfst/L), Warlimont; from 6 Sep 44 to 7 Nov 44, von Buttlar; from 8 Nov 44 to 21 April 45, Winter.

Subordinate to the OKW – the three services, Army, Navy, and Air Force (Heer, Marine, und Luftwaffe), whose heads were C-in-Cs (Oberbefehlshaber des Heers, der Marine, und der Luftwaffe):

C-IN-C ARMY (Oberbefehls. Heer) – from 4 Feb 38 to 19 Dec 41, von Brauchitsch; from 19 Dec 41 to 30 April 45, Hitler.

C-IN-C NAVY (Oberbefehls. Marine) – from 1 June 35 to 30 Jan 43, Raeder; from 30 Jan 43 to 1 May 45, Dönitz; from 2 May 45 to 23 May 45, von Friedeberg.

C-IN-C AIR FORCE (Oberbefehls. Luftwaffe) – from 1 March 35 to 23 April 45, Göring; from 25 April 45 to 8 May 45, von Greim.

CHIEFS OF ARMY GENERAL STAFF (Chef. Generalstab des Heers) – from 31 Aug 38 to 24 Sep 42, Halder; from 24 Sep 42 to 20 July 44, Zeitzler; from 10 June 44 to 21 July 44, Heusinger; from 21 July 44 to 28 March 45, Guderian; from 29 March 45 to 30 April 45, Krebs.

Commanders in various theatres of war:

West

25 Oct 39 to 15 March 41, von Rundstedt; from 15 March 41 to 28 Feb 42, von Witzleben; from 1 March 42 to 6 July 44, von Rundstedt; from 7 July 44 to 17 Aug 44, von Kluge; from 18 Aug 44 to 5 Sep 44, Model; from 5 Sep 44 to 10 March 45, von Rundstedt; from 11 March 45 to 25 March 45, Kesselring.

Italy

From 1 Dec 41 to 24 Oct 44, Kesselring; from 24 Oct 44 to 14 Jan 45, von Vietinghoff; from 14 Jan 45 to 10 March 45, Kesselring; from 10 March 45 to 2 May 45, von Vietinghoff.

Africa

From 23 Feb 41 to 9 March 43, Rommel; from 10 March 43 to 13 May 43, von Arnim.

Balkans

From 9 June 41 to 15 Oct 41, List; from 25 Oct 41 to 31 July 42, Kuntze; from 1 Aug 42 to 26 Aug 43, Löhr; from 26 Aug 43 to 25 March 45, von Weichs; from 25 March 45 to 8 May 45, Löhr.

Eastern Front

It would serve no purpose here to list all the Army commands in the Russian campaign. There were in all, under changing titles, some 20 Army groups, whose commanders were also continually changing. It may be noted, however, that from the 19 Dec 41, when Brauchitsch was relieved of the post, Hitler became the C-in-C of all the armies operating in the east (Chef. OKH).

A full list of these commanders is given in *Die Höheren Dienststellen der Deutschen Wehrmacht*, by Siegler, published '53, Munich, by the Institut für Zeitgeschichte (p. 18 *et seq.*).

Replacement Army (*Ersatzheer*)

From 1 Sep 39 to 21 July 44, Fromm; from 21 July 44 to 27 April 45, Himmler.

A note on the Valkyrie units (mentioned p. 277)

The code name Valkyrie was given to emergency measures to be taken in the event of internal unrest, mutiny or sudden attack. According to the extent of the danger, Wehrkreise (military districts) were ordered to mobilize the requisite number of emergency units drawn from home establishments, such as schools and courses of various kinds, training units and depot troops of the replacement army. These units were referred to as Valkyrie units.

A note on the Volkssturm (mentioned p. 290)

The Volkssturm was the name given to units of a local defence 'militia', which was brought into being by a Hitler decree of 25 Sep 44. The basic unit was the battalion, composed of men varying from 16 to 60 years of age, including men invalided out of the services, or otherwise medically unfit for service in the Armed Forces. When called upon to fight, these units came under the orders of the local army commander. They were armed, in theory at least, with basic infantry weapons, and were only intended for use in their own locality. Volkssturm units saw action on both East and West fronts.

Glossary of Named Personnel

BOCK, FEDOR VON. Field Marshal, 19 July 40. Commanding Army group North (Poland), 1 Sep 39 to 3 Oct 39; Commanding Army group B (West), 5 Oct 39 to 12 Sep 40; Commanding Army group Centre (Russia), 1 April 41 to 18 Dec 41; Commanding Army group South (Russia), 18 Jan 41 to 15 July 42. Killed in air-raid 4 May 45.

BORMANN, MARTIN. Head of Party Chancellery (succeeding Rudolf Hess). One of Hitler's closest advisers. Condemned to death *in absentia*, Nürnberg 46. Now presumed killed in battle of Berlin at end of war.

BRAUCHITSCH, WALTHER VON. Field Marshal. C-in-C Army (Oberbefehlshaber des Heers) from 4 Feb 38 to 19 Dec 41. Died in British captivity 18 Oct 48.

CANARIS, WILHELM. Admiral, Chief of Amtsgruppe Ausland/Abwehr (Intelligence in OKW) 38–44, when dismissed owing to frequent quarrels with the SS. Involved indirectly in plot of 20 July 44. Hanged in Flossenburg concentration camp April 1945.

DÖNITZ, KARL. Grand Admiral 43. Commander of submarines 1 Jan 36 to 1 May 45; C-in-C Navy 30 Jan 43 to 1 May 45;

C-in-C Operations staff (North) 17 April 45 to 23 May 45; Supreme Commander of Armed Forces 1 May 45 to 23 May 45. Condemned at Nürnberg to 10 years' imprisonment in 47.

FALKENHORST, NICOLAUS VON. General. C-in-C Armed Forces Norway 24 April 40 to 18 Dec 44. Condemned to death by British court Aug 46 for his part in execution of captured British commandos. Commuted to life imprisonment; then 10 years' imprisonment. Freed 23 July 53.

FELMY, HELLMUTH. General of Air Force. C-in-C Armed Forces Southern Greece June 41 to Oct 43. Condemned at Nürnberg to 15 years' imprisonment; commuted to 10 years. Freed Dec 51.

GÖRING, HERMANN, Reichsminister for Air. Reichsminister for the Five year plan. C-in-C Air Force throughout the war. Relieved of all posts and commands 23 April 45. Condemned to death Nürnberg, and committed suicide, 15 Oct 46.

HALDER, FRANZ. General 19 July 40. Chief of Army General Staff 1 Nov 38 to 24 Sep 42.

JODL, ALFRED. General. Head of Armed Forces Operational staff [Wehrmachtführüngamt (stab)] throughout war. Condemned to death Nürnberg 46, and hanged 16 Oct 46.

KAUFMANN, KARL. Reich Commissioner for overseas shipping 1942.

KEITEL, WILHELM. Field Marshal. Chief of High Command of Armed Forces (Oberkommando der Wehrmacht) throughout the war. Condemned to death Nürnberg, and hanged 16 Oct 46.

KESSELRING, ALBERT. Field Marshal (Air Force) 19 July 40. C-in-C. Armed Forces South (Mediterranean) 2 Dec 41 to 10 March 45; C-in-C Armed Forces West 11 March 45 to 25 March 45; C-in-C Armed Forces South 25 March to 6 May 45. Condemned to death by British court 6 May 47; commuted to life imprisonment Oct 47; pardoned and freed 23 Oct 52.

LAMMERS, HANS HEINRICH. Lawyer. Reichsminister and head of Reich Chancellery. Close collaborator of Hitler. Sentenced April 49 to 20 years' imprisonment.

LIST, WILHELM. Field Marshal. C-in-C Armed Forces SE

(Balkans) 10 June 41 to 15 Oct 41; Commander Army Group A (Russia) 15 July 42 to 10 Sep 42. Condemned to life imprisonment Nürnberg Feb 48. Pardoned and released Christmas 52.

MANSTEIN, ERICH VON. Field Marshal. Principal commands: Commander Army group II (Russia) 18 Sep 41 to 21 Nov 42; Commander Army group Don 28 Nov 42 to 14 Feb 43; Commander Army group South 14 Feb 43 to 30 March 44. Sentenced by British court 24 Feb 50 to 18 years' imprisonment; commuted to 12 years; freed 6 May 53.

NEUBACHER, HERMANN. Austrian engineer. Special envoy to Rumania for economic question 40; special envoy to Greece 41 to 42.

PAULUS, FRIEDRICH. Field Marshal. Commanding 6th Army (Russia) 30 Dec 41 to 1 Feb 43. Captured by Russians at Stalingrad 1 Feb 43.

RAEDER, ERICH. Admiral. C-in-C Navy 35 to 43, when replaced by Dönitz. Sentenced to life imprisonment at Nürnberg 46. Released 55.

RUNDSTEDT, ERICH VON. Field Marshal. C-in-C Armies in west May-June 40. Commander Army group South (Russia) 41. C-in-C West, with two short intermissions, from March 42 to March 45. Died 24 Feb 53.

SCHÖRNER, FERDINAND. Field Marshal. Commander various army groups in Russia from 15 Nov 43 to July 44. After the assassination plot '44, made C-in-C West, being one of the few generals who were Nazis and whom Hitler felt he could trust.

SCHRÖDER, LUDWIG VON. General of AA Artillery. C-in-C Armed Forces Serbia June 41 to Aug 41. Died in aeroplane accident Aug 41.

SEYSS-INQUART, ARTUR. Austrian leader of Nazi party before the Anschluss. Austrian Minister of Interior and Security 40. Reich Commissioner for Occupied Netherlands 41 to 45. Condemned to death Nürnberg and hanged 16 Oct 46.

SPEER, ALBERT. Professor of Architecture. Succeeded Todt as Reichsminister for Armaments after the latter's death in 1942. Also became head of Todt Organization. Condemned to 20 years' imprisonment Nürnberg Oct 47.

STUDENT, KURT. General. Commander of various air corps and parachute groups – the most notable being 7 air division in the west May and June 40; and Crete May 41.

TODT, FRITZ. Engineer. Creator of public works system which bears his name; also of Siegfried line 38–40. Reichsminister for Armaments during war, until death in aeroplane accident 42.

WARLIMONT, WALTER. General. Head of Home Defence dept of WFA (Abteiling Landesverteidigung) from Nov 38 to Sept 44 (WFA having become Wfst, as previously explained). Condemned Nürnberg to life imprisonment 48. Released 54.

WINTER, AUGUST. Deputy chief of Armed Forces Operational staff (Wehrmachtführungstab, or Wfst) Sep 44 to 21 April 45. Chief Operations staff South 24 April 45 to 8 May 45.

ZANGEN, GUSTAV VON. General. Commanded Army department Zangen (Abt Xangen) North Italy 23 Nov 43 to 20 Aug 44. Commander 15th Army West 22 Aug 44 to 17 April 45.

INDEX

Notes

1. References are to page numbers. Italic figures in brackets, e.g. *(5)*, are those of the Directives, Orders, etc., as given in the book.
2. All 'Operations' and 'Undertakings' are indexed under the word 'Operations', followed by their code names.
3. Hitler usually refers to the United Kingdom as 'England'; the Editor uses the name 'Britain'.

311

The July Plot 5/-

ROGER MANVELL and
HEINRICH FRAENKEL

The attempt to assassinate Hitler in July 1944

'A book which ought to be read, because it
is high time that people in this country
knew what risks with their consciences, as
well as with their lives, were taken by the
men and women who stepped deliberately
into the path of the Nazi juggernaut.'
THE GUARDIAN

'A book of fascinating interest, and
compulsively readable.'
PUNCH

The Last Days of Hitler 3/6

H. R. TREVOR-ROPER

'An incomparable book, by far the best
written about any aspect of the second
German war. A book sound in its
scholarship, brilliant in presentation,
a delight for historian and layman alike.
No words of praise are too strong for it.'
A. J. P. TAYLOR, NEW STATESMAN

'A masterpiece of its kind.'
THE TIMES